D0153498

Not Quite White

Not Quite White

WHITE TRASH *and the*

BOUNDARIES *of* WHITENESS

Matt Wray

Duke University Press Durham and London 2006

© 2006 Duke University Press
All rights reserved
Printed in the United States of America
on acid-free paper ∞
Designed by C. H. Westmoreland
Typeset in Minion with ITC Stone display
by Tseng Information Systems, Inc.
Library of Congress Cataloging-in-
Publication Data appear on the last
printed page of this book.

for

Jill, Zachary, *and* Maxine,

and in loving memory of

Eric Rofes

CENTRAL ARKANSAS LIBRARY SYSTEM
LITTLE ROCK PUBLIC LIBRARY
100 ROCK STREET
LITTLE ROCK, ARKANSAS 72201

Contents

Preface and Acknowledgments

This idea for this book grew out of a place where nothing much happened and no one really gave a damn. The people there were mostly white, and mostly poor. There wasn't much of a middle class, except for a few well-educated folk trying hard not to be snotty so their kids wouldn't get beat up at school. There wasn't a real upper crust either — the only rich people were summer folk at the lake and the weekend skiers up from their urban and suburban homes.

It could have been in New Hampshire, or West Virginia, or California, or one of thousands of places across America. A place full of weeds and broken glass, worn-out buildings and faded paint. Here the crumbling walls of an old mill, there the iron tracks of the old railroad, everywhere piles of busted tires laying toppled in stagnant heaps. Broken-down steel machines, rusted in place, are harsh reminders of jobs that came and went. In pickup trucks and trailer parks, A M stations play songs of failure and loss, the twang of bad endings and hard regrets cutting into the air like spikes of old barbed wire.

In church on Sundays and Wednesday nights, preachers preach sermons on hard work, coping with sin, and coming to Christ. Tuesday is league night at the bowling alley: big men, their bellies gone flabby with beer, roll balls at the pins, while their girlfriends and wives smoke menthol cigarettes and drink gin and tonics in the lounge. Thursday is ladies' night and the women bowl for free. Friday and Saturday nights the kids pack into muscle cars and pickups and cruise the town, looking for something — anything — to do. Party at the gravel pit: drink cheap beer around an oily fire, smoke some sticky ditch weed, get hammered, and drive home. I grew up in this kind of place. For a time, my father was the minister of a small local church where members lived in trailers and, in winter, rode their snowmobiles to Sunday service. Compared to so many in our community, my family had a degree of middle-class stability and respectable status. That is, until my parents divorced. Then, quite suddenly, we were on welfare. I took to hiding in the car when my mother bought groceries with food stamps. Just eleven years old, I knew there was shame in being too poor to pay for your own food. I knew the common names given to the people like us who inhabited these broken-down worlds, and so do you: *cracker, redneck, hillbilly*, and *poor white trash*.[1]

As I began the research for this book, I found myself drawn toward trying to understand more about how these places and peoples have come over time to be imagined and perceived. Why, for instance, does the above description of small-town life seem stereotypical and hackneyed to some readers, even as it rings true for me, one who lived it? Where do stigmatizing stereotypes—as I call them, *stigmatypes*—of poor rural whites come from? What gives them their power? How and why do they enter the culture and what purposes do they serve? What role do they play in bringing about human misery? How and what kind of power do they really have? Asking these questions set me on a rather strange intellectual path.

I opted early on for an interdisciplinary approach, primarily because that is what the topic seemed to demand. So many different forms of disciplinary knowledge had been called upon to construct the image of poor white trash that relying on a single disciplinary approach seemed to me to be a sure way to fail. Interdisciplinarity is fraught with many conceptual and methodological difficulties and dilemmas and, at times, I felt like every single one of them dogged my research. One thing, however, is clear: truly interdisciplinary work satisfies almost no one. Historians may find that this work does not rely enough on primary sources, or treats its historical periods too breezily; sociologists may fault it for relying too much on primary sources or for not being methodologically sound or rigorous; literary critics may dismiss it as lacking an adequate theory of representation or for being indiscriminate in the way it handles texts; anthropologists may find the discussions of ethnic groups and culture to be poorly grounded in observation; and so on. The problem is, all are more or less right in their critiques. At times, therefore, I have felt compelled to engage arguments from history, sociology, anthropology, and half a dozen other subfields. In order to improve readability and in order not to distract general readers with these border skirmishes, I have placed most of these arguments in the notes. Interested readers can find them there and, while important, they do not represent the main ideas in this book. It is with no small degree of irony that I confess that immersing myself in an interdisciplinary project has warmed me to the seductions of disciplinary perspectives. However, this work does not wish to be, nor does it pretend to be, disciplined. My hope is that whatever may have been lost by sacrificing disciplinary depth has been offset by gains in interdisciplinary breadth.

I consider myself very fortunate to have met many wonderful guides and fellow travelers in interdisciplinarity, beginning with my first undergraduate mentor, Susan Harding. Warm thanks to my dissertation committee: José David Saldívar, for impressing upon me the importance of cultural boundaries, border crossings, and hybrid identities; Michael Omi, for pushing me to think sociologically and for his calm patience with me as I repeatedly mangled his theories of racial formation to suit my own perverse intellectual needs; and to the late Michael Rogin for, among many other things, requiring me to think beyond the narrow confines of class analysis. Howard Winant, as the unofficial fourth member of my committee, generously offered his intellectual insights and his enthusiasm for this project from its earliest stages.

Many of the ideas in this book were generated during the long discussions and arguments I had with those with whom I organized the 1997 Berkeley conference "The Making and Unmaking of Whiteness." That three-day conference, funded by the University of California Humanities Research Institute, garnered international attention and drew over 1,000 participants. That experience established for me the significance and seriousness of the topic of whiteness studies and inspired me to move forward with a research project that at times had seemed frivolous. "White trash? Are you kidding?" was often the response I got from anyone who asked about my research. The Department of Ethnic Studies at Berkeley not only generously cosponsored that conference, they also provided the following year a dissertation fellowship that proved decisive in helping me deepen my research. A university travel grant allowed me to conduct research at the Rockefeller Archive Center, where I was graciously assisted by Thomas Rosenbaum, and at Cold Spring Harbor Laboratories, where

Clare Bunce of the Carnegie Library proved informative and knowledge-able about the Eugenics Record Office. At Humboldt State University, Marianne Ahokas, Michael Eldridge, and the late Eric Rofes proved to be outstanding colleagues and provided good food and constant cheer as I finished my dissertation.

My postdoctoral research at the Smithsonian Institution's National Museum of American History was guided by Pete Daniel, whose knowl-edge about all manner of things southern and historical is simply un-matched. Other Smithsonian fellows, particularly Cindy Ott, Elena Raz-logova, Lauren Sklaroff, John Troutman, and Todd Uhlman, read several chapters, offered patient criticisms, and helped create a productive atmo-sphere for interdisciplinary intellectual exchange. Warm thanks also to Tony Kaye for showing me by example how to bring social theory and historical analysis into new and productive relationships.

At the University of Nevada, three consecutive years of course reduc-tions granted me time to rethink and reorient my project in ways that were, for me, extraordinarily fruitful and productive. In addition, a 2002 summer fellowship permitted me to conduct archival research I had been unable to finish during my stay at the Smithsonian. Jane Nichols, Mike Rentko, and George O'Connell graciously assisted in helping me search for the still buried mysteries of the Carroll-Caton estates, and Mary Jeske of the Maryland Historical Society helped interpret historical census data. At Lied Library, UNLV, Susie Skarl located the source of obscure images when no one else could.

I learned a great deal from those who participated in the forum discus-sions where I presented different stages of this research: faculty colloquia in the Departments of History and Sociology at UNLV; the sociology col-loquium at Northwestern University; and the Center for Cultural Studies at the University of California, Santa Cruz. In addition, my deep appre-ciation goes out to all the members of the Las Vegas Huntridge Writers Group for reading parts of the manuscript and giving valuable sugges-tions and encouragement. Graduate students in my cultural sociology seminar, especially Dana Maher, Katy Gilpatric, and Megan Hartzell, provided useful comments and criticisms as did many nameless inter-locutors who commented on my presentations at meetings of the Ameri-can Sociological Association, Southern Historical Association, American

Historical Association Pacific Coast Branch, the American Studies Association, and the Modern Language Association.

I am especially grateful to Eric Klinenberg, Eric Porter, Catherine Ramirez, and Vron Ware, for encouraging me on my haphazard journey from rural idiot to cosmopolitan intellectual, a journey they will all assure you is far from complete. I owe a special intellectual debt to John Hartigan Jr., from whose work I have learned more than I can say. Ken Wissoker, editor-in-chief of Duke University Press, saw the potential for this topic very early on and has proven himself to be one of the most patient and able editors on earth. Thank you, Ken! The four anonymous readers Duke provided made excellent suggestions that helped improve the manuscript, and assistant editor Courtney Berger gave generously of her time and energy to enhance some of the illustrations. My friend Sara Miles provided extraordinary editorial assistance. Needless to say, any and all errors in thought and execution are entirely mine.

In the years that I have worked on this book, I have been sustained by the companionship and affection of family members and loved ones: H. Donley Wray and his partner Carol Delle kept me supplied with free books and good cheer, and Janette Wray was my number-one fan. My deepest thanks go to Jill Gurvey. She has accompanied me in my wayward academic progress from one coast to the other and most of the way back and she never failed to supply emotional support and intellectual enthusiasm for my work. In my life, this gift has been exceeded by only one other: the arrival of our children, Zachary Lang and Maxine Ava. It is with love and affection that I dedicate this book to them.

introduction

White Trash as Social Difference

Groups, Boundaries, and Inequalities

Let us hope that we never grow so sanctimonious that we cannot
listen to the mean things people say. They are our data.
—EVERETT C. HUGHES AND HELEN MACGILL HUGHES
(1952: 132), quoted in Lewis 1983: 1

Can there be any people who confound sacredness with uncleanness?
—MARY DOUGLAS (1966/1984: 159)

White trash is a curious phrase. At first, its meanings and reasons for being
seem easy enough to understand: it's an insult, or the punch line to a joke,
or maybe just a way to name those people down the road with the wash-
ing machine and the broken-down truck in the front yard. It conjures
images of poor, ignorant, racist whites: trailer parks and wife beaters, too
many kids and not enough government cheese. It's hard to care about
such people. It's even harder to take them seriously. Maybe that's why, for
so many, *white trash* rolls off the tongue with such condescending ease.

This book is an attempt to move beyond simplicities and condescen-
sion and to take *white trash* seriously, to come to grips with it as name,
label, stigma, and stereotype. Far from having clear meanings and purposes, *white trash* is, like *nigger*, a very troublesome word.[1] For much of
its long history, *white trash* has been used by Americans of all colors to
humiliate and shame, to insult and dishonor, to demean and stigmatize.
Yet beneath that general usage lies a long-concealed history of shifting
representations and meanings in American lexical culture. This book argues that understanding the story of *white trash* and other terms of abuse

can help us better understand social difference and inequality and how they are produced.

Treating *white trash* as a serious case study of how social difference and inequality are produced requires a multidisciplinary perspective. It involves hacking through thickets of theoretical brush and wading through methodological quagmires. To grasp general social dynamics without losing sight of specific historical dynamics — all the while remaining focused on a single stigmatizing stereotype — presents a number of challenges. It's like trying to see the social world through a single grain of culture. Perhaps for this reason, there are precious few examples of this kind of research.[2] While we have volumes of sociological studies that chart stratifying structures of social inequality, shelves of historical research delving into the rich details of social structures and lived experiences of them, and, increasingly, studies of culture that illuminate the ways that people assign meaning and significance to those structures and experiences, we are in need of research that can draw such work together into a common analytical project. This book attempts to do just that, bringing approaches to historical sociology (drawn from interactionism) and ideas in cultural theory (drawn from boundary theory) into dialogue with recent writing on whiteness as a way of demonstrating the utility and explanatory power of a combined perspective.

But why *white trash*? Split the phrase in two and read the meanings against each other: *white* and *trash*. Slowly, the term reveals itself as an expression of fundamental tensions and deep structural antinomies: between the sacred and the profane, purity and impurity, morality and immorality, cleanliness and dirt. In conjoining such primal opposites into a single category, *white trash* names a kind of disturbing liminality: a monstrous, transgressive identity of mutually violating boundary terms, a dangerous threshold state of being neither one nor the other. It brings together into a single ontological category that which must be kept apart in order to establish a meaningful and stable symbolic order. Symbolic orders are those shared representations of reality and collective systems of classification that are key elements in bringing about social solidarity. *White trash* names a people whose very existence seems to threaten the symbolic and social order. As such, the term can evoke strong emotions of contempt, anger, and disgust. This is no ordinary slur.[3]

White trash also speaks to another tension, that between what have for too long been competing categories of social analysis: race and class. Indeed, split *white trash* in two again and read the meanings of each: *white* now appears as an ethnoracial signifier, and *trash*, a signifier of abject class status. The term conflates these two aspects of social identity into an inseparable state of being, suggesting that if we are to understand *white trash* and the condition it names, we must confront the multithreaded nature of social inequality. However one looks at it, *white trash* is a puzzle with two pieces. Which word is the modifier and which the modified? Does *white* modify *trash* or is it the other way around? Is this a story about a residual, disposable class, or one about a despised ethnoracial group? Between these two choices, meaning is suspended.

Until quite recently, when stories of poor rural white people have been told by social scientists, they have been told mostly as stories about class. These studies have been inadequate in part because the lens of class analysis has always had trouble focusing on the lowest status groups. Like Marx's ill-defined *lumpenproletariat*, the "poor white trash" in these class-based accounts seems to be only a residual category, a theoretical afterthought. As those that opted out of or were left behind in the wake of capitalist modernization, poor whites appear more like a caste than a class, and as such are thought to have no social worth and only regressive political tendencies.

If the lens of class proves distorting, what about race? Why not view *white trash* as primarily a racial slur? There are perhaps good reasons for doing so, especially since the history of the term coincides with periods of intense ethnoracial conflict.[4] The recent rise of whiteness studies, an interdisciplinary field of research that takes as its subject the historical development and contemporary nature of white skin privilege, would seem to offer a promising alternative to class-based perspectives. However, as with class analysis, racial analysis in the form of whiteness studies has failed to bring the term *white trash* into focus. Scholars of whiteness have become extraordinarily sure-footed and nimble when the word that follows *white* is *supremacy, power, privilege,* or *pride,* but they tend to stumble badly when it is followed by *trash.*

Inventing Whiteness

Whiteness studies began to take shape as an interdisciplinary field of research in the 1990s. Early influential works by Roediger (1991, 1994) and Morrison (1992) set the agenda of much of the research that followed: whiteness studies would focus on the historical development of race-based social domination in the United States and would explore what the legacies of white supremacy had meant not just for people of color, but for whites as well. What does it mean to be part of the racial majority, and how have different social groups achieved that? Whiteness studies wanted to know. This was a significant shift of the theoretical and empirical gaze, from the subordinate to the dominant, from the minority to the majority, and it shared a family resemblance to the contemporaneous shift in women's studies from studying women to studying men and masculinities. With whiteness studies, the analytical tools and perspectives employed to study processes and effects of subordination and minoritization could now be adapted and applied to processes and effects of superordination and majoritization (and if those terms sound odd, perhaps it is because we have not paid much attention to them before).

Within academia, the consequences of the shift in gaze could potentially be significant: No longer need the scholarly study of race be confined to small, poorly funded departments or institutionally weak programs organized around minority groups. The study of ethnoracial domination need not be ghettoized, for some of its most important lessons were for ethnoracial majorities. While not uncontroversial — would this move not entail a recentering of white experts in discussions of race? — whiteness studies exerted broad appeal across the disciplines and by the end of the 1990s, historians and literary critics were joined by anthropologists, art historians, educational theorists, film and theater critics, geographers, philosophers, political scientists, psychologists, sociologists, and interdisciplinary scholars in cultural studies, ethnic studies, and women's studies.[5]

In retrospect, I believe that the major contribution of whiteness studies lay with its novel ways of conceptualizing and talking about two of the most general and yet consequential problems in society: privilege and inequality. In whiteness, many scholars believe they have found a general concept that synthesizes decades of research into various forms of inequality based on race, class, gender, and sexuality. Whiteness as a privileged category of identity, they say, has been a key aspect of social domination, not only in the United States, but around the globe, too.[6]

As a contribution to whiteness studies, this book has two main goals, one conceptual and one methodological. First, I argue that conceiving of whiteness primarily in terms of racial domination unnecessarily limits the scope of our analyses. *Whiteness* is most often used as analytical shorthand to refer to the psychological and cultural advantages and the economic and political privileges of having white or light colored skin, where skin color is conceptualized as a marker of racial identity. When one thinks about it, it seems apt and true: those whose racial identity appears to be white generally fare better when it comes to social opportunities and rewards. We whites get special privileges and advantages without even having to ask. When it is stated in this rather straightforward, commonsensical way, there are few who would argue against this formulation of the concept.

Yet we know that the power of dominant groups is secured not just by ethnoracial systems and practices, but also by systems and practices related to other axial processes that differentiate along lines of class, gender, and sexuality. Decades of research into these specific areas of social difference and inequality have provided unequivocal evidence of this social fact. Scholars of whiteness have joined interdisciplinary efforts to integrate these different areas of scholarship on inequality. It is now common parlance in whiteness studies to speak about the racialization of sex and class, the gendering of race, or the sexualization of race and class, all of which can often be confusing for lay audiences and academics alike.[7] One thing, it is clear from this new, awkward way of talking makes clear is that the modal categories of race, class, gender, and sexuality—the Big Four—are more interrelated and interdependent than current theoretical models allow. Instead of trying to account for domination and inequality by focusing on the Big Four as distinct, relatively autonomous processes, might not we better see them as four deeply related subprocesses of a single, larger process of social differentiation? It is this theoretical possibility that I explore in this book.

We need ways to rethink our core theoretical concepts and our research questions so that we can better coordinate our collective research efforts.

However, some critics of whiteness studies have suggested that we should reject the term *whiteness* as analytically useless (Arneson 2001) and others have argued for refining and historicizing its meanings (Foner 2001). I take a more pragmatic stance, as I am skeptical that calls for abandoning the term or for restricting its meanings are going to be well heeded, if at all. As an analytical category, whiteness shares some problems with the term *culture*. Even though its meanings are contested, flawed, and generally fuzzy, for those of us who study social differentiation and inequality in the United States and elsewhere, it has become a concept that we cannot do without. Given this situation, my proposal is simple and uncomplicated: we should reconceptualize whiteness as a flexible set of social and symbolic boundaries that give shape, meaning, and power to the social category *white*. I say more about what this means in the final chapter, as well as outlining what I think we gain from such a move.

The second contribution I want to make is directed toward methodological focus and approach. Having reconceptualized whiteness as boundaries, where do we look for them? What do we do when we find them? How do we capture their formation and their effects? The short answer to these questions is that we need to study social interactions of many different kinds. I explain my approach more fully below, but as before, my proposal is simple: let our methodological focus be on documenting and analyzing interactions and processes common to all modes of social differentiation. We need not decide in advance of our study which, if any, of the Big Four categories will prove most salient or offer the most explanatory power. To resolve tired and tiring debates about how much analytical weight to give to race versus class, or gender versus race, and so on, or about whether we are conceiving of such terms in essentialist or antiessentialist ways, or about what exactly it means for something to be socially constructed, we should allow our methodological focus to resolve to a level of greater abstraction — social difference — and a larger domain of social practices — social differentiation. It is at this most fundamental level that new knowledge will be found (Washington 2006). We are seeking a unifying theory of social difference and inequality.

After fifteen years, whiteness studies has left childhood and is now enduring adolescence. It's having its identity crisis right on time. Given the proliferation of claims and counterclaims about what whiteness studies is and is not, should or should not be, we need to assess what is analytically and conceptually useful here. This critical reevaluation is already well under way.[8] In this book I suggest that we all have much to learn from debates over the status of whiteness as an analytical object, but I also insist that much of the debate misses an important point: we lack a consensus about how social differentiation occurs and how social differentiation leads to social inequality. My hope is that this book will familiarize readers with tools for analyzing historical and contemporary mechanisms of social differentiation, ethnoracial division, and symbolic and structural inequality. My belief is that boundary theory offers the very best tool kit for this kind of work.[9]

Culture and the Boundaries of Difference

In taking boundary theory as its major theoretical orientation, this book is a response to developments in cultural sociology and an effort to push those developments in new directions.[10] In particular, this book advocates for a critical encounter between boundary theory and the race-class-gender-sexuality approach that has become a leading idiom in normal social science and of which whiteness studies is itself an expression. As growing numbers of researchers grow increasingly frustrated with the tangled webs of identity analysis spun out by recent analysts, boundary theorists are granted an opportunity to show how and why these theories and methods present a theoretically coherent and viable alternative, one that can move us beyond the limits and aporias of our present conceptions of group identity and social inequality.[11]

Boundary theory begins by asking how categories shape our perceptions of the world. Categories are classes or types that result from the processes of dividing and selection. In philosophical terms, to state that two things belong to different categories is to assert that they have nothing in common. To state that two things belong to the same category is to assert that they share a common identity. In everyday life, categories tend to be much messier and more fuzzily defined than they are in the tidy logic of philosophy. Nonetheless, even in everyday life, we recognize things as belonging to a category when they share (or are perceived as sharing) common properties, qualities, and characteristics. When, as the child's game goes, one of these things is not like the other, we rightly refuse it membership. Having made the determination that something belongs or does not belong in a given category, we can then cognitively mark off the boundary that separates and divides that which belongs from that which does not. Then and only then can we give that boundary marker a name.

Establishing categories, taking note of properties, qualities, and characteristics, and drawing boundaries are difficult, complicated, and time-consuming processes. Yet without such cognitive processes, we would be unable to comprehend the rushing stream of information our senses present to us every moment of every day. We manage this amazing feat of information processing in part by relying on what cultural sociologists sometimes call collective or shared representations. These representations, made up of categories, properties, and boundary markers, offer us cognitive shortcuts, a kind of automatic cognition that offers us quick understanding without having to expend much thought.[12]

So it is with the social categories that we use in everyday life. We tend to learn the shared representations and the cognitive schemas relevant to our social worlds and to assimilate our own perceptions of reality to them. In this way, stereotypes occur and recur without much thought. For instance, when it comes to interpreting the meaning of categories of gender, race, class, and sexuality, we tend to rely quite heavily on stereotypes because to do otherwise requires a significant amount of cognitive work. Instead, relying on our shared representations, we treat the category as if it were a fixed, naturally given thing and then assume the person we are fitting to the category shared some or all of the traits and characteristics of the category. In short, we reify the categories into identities. When those identities are organized into social hierarchies that rely on invidious comparisons and stigmatyping, then domination, injustice, and human suffering result. What's more, we can end up with various forms of political solidarity based on identity—which, because social groups attain solidarity at the expense of other groups, through, for instance, their stigmatization, can also result in exclusions and inequalities. Social distinctions are not just ways of orienting ourselves in the world, they are major agents of social power.

Boundary theory is extremely useful for gaining an understanding of how people attempt to classify and organize themselves and others into distinct groups—and how those same groups are then ranked and ordered into scales of relative human worth and achievement. Boundary theory can, for instance, direct our attention to asking how and why *white trash* became an active part of the "publicly available categorization systems" (Lamont 2000: 243) in U.S. culture.[13] As social power operates through boundaries, it creates different kinds of social stratification and inequality corresponding to those boundaries. In the broadest sense, then, boundary theory offers exceptionally coherent ways of thinking about identity, differentiation, and inequality at multiple levels of social organization.[14]

Symbolic and Social Boundaries

Distinctions, problematic as they sometimes are, remain an inescapable aspect of human experience. Distinctions and boundaries enable and structure our cognition and perception of our worlds. Moreover, representing a world without distinctions would be humanly impossible, since the very tools of representation — language, art, music — are themselves systems of differences and distinctions. The boundaries that enable social organization are primarily of two kinds: symbolic and social. Symbolic boundaries are part of our mental, collective representations, part of the cognitive schemas that we use to differentiate things that might otherwise appear similar and to render discontinuous what would otherwise be continuous (DiMaggio 1997). They may be thought of as the sense-making mechanisms embedded in every culture, with language and speech as the crucial resources in their production, maintenance, and transformation. Symbolic boundaries introduce difference into what might otherwise be experienced as similarity. For instance, the symbolic boundaries of race and ethnicity have been used to divide a single biological species — *Homo sapiens* — into different categories of identity. As learned cognitive schemas, race and ethnicity make salient and visible a series of arbitrary distinctions of phenotype, nationality, ethnicity, and so on. In so doing, they produce perceptions of human difference where there would otherwise be perceptions of human similarity.[15]

Once popularized or imposed, a symbolic boundary can help establish social distinctions and justify taboos. If it gains enough social power, such a boundary may result in laws and prohibitions, such as bans against interracial sex and other forms of racial propinquity. When this occurs,

SCHEMES OF RACES OF MANKIND.

RACE.	BRANCH.	STOCK.	GROUP.	Peoples (extinct peoples in italics).
Eur-af'ric-an (Caucasian).	South Mediterranean.	Hamitic.	Libyan.	*Amorites*, Berbers, *Etruscans*, *Getulians*, Kabyles, *Libyans*, *Mauritanians*, *Numidians*, Riffians, Tuareks.
			Egyptian.	Copts, Fellahs.
			East-African.	Afars, Bedjas, Bilins, Danakils, Gallas, Khamirs, Somalis.
			Arabian.	Arabs, Bedouins, Ehkilis, *Himyarites*, *Nabotheans*, *Sabeans*.
		Semitic.	Abyssinian.[6]	Amharis, Ethiopians, Gheez, Harraras, Tigrinas, Tigris.
			Chaldean.	Arameans, *Assyrians*, *Carthaginians*, Israelites, *Phenicians*, Samaritans, Syrians.
	North Mediterranean.	Euskaric.	Euskaric.	*Aquitanians*, Basques, *Cantabrians*, Euscaldonac, *Ligurians*(?), *Picts*(?), *Sards*, *Siculi*.
		Aryac (Aryan).	Celtic.	Bretons, *Celtiberians*, Cymri, *Gauls*, Irish, Manx, Scotch Highlanders, Welsh.
			Italic.	French, Italians, *Latins*, *Oscans*, Portuguese, Rumanians, *Sabines*, Spanish, *Umbrians*, Wallachians.
			Illyric.	Albanians, *Illyrians*, *Macedonians*, *Pelasgi*, *Japyges*(?), *Thracians*.
			Hellenic.	Greeks, *Lydians*, *Macedonians*, *Pelasgi*, *Phrygians*.
			Teutonic.	East-Teutonic — Danes, *Goths*, Scandinavians, *Suevi*, *Vandals*. West-Teutonic — *Angles*, Anglo-Americans, Dutch, English, *Franks*, Germans, *Saxons*.
			Slavonic.	Bulgarians, Croatians, Czechs, Montenegrins, Poles, Russians, Servians, Wends.
			Indo-Iranic.	Iranic (Eranic) — Armenians, *Bactrians*, Baluchis, Persians. Indic — Gipsies, Hindus, Hunzas.
		Caucasic.	Lesghic.	Avars, Kurins, Laks, Udes.
			Circassic.	Abkhasians, Circassians.
			Kistic.	Karabonlaks, Tush.
			Georgic.	Georgians, Lazs, Mingrelians.
Aust-af'ri-can (Negroid).[2]	Negrillo (Dwarf Negroid).		Equatorial (Pygmy).	Akkas, Dokos, *Kimos* (of Madagascar), Obongos, Tikkitikkis, Vouataous.
			South-African.	Bushmen, Hottentots, Namaquas, Quaquas.
	Negro.[1]		Nilotic.	Baris, Bongos, Dinkas, Kiks, Nuers, Shillaks.
			Sudanese.	Akras, Battas, Bornus, Haussas, Kanoris, Ngurus.
			Senegambian.	Banyums, Foys, Serrerus, Wolofs.
			Guinean.	Ashantis, Dahomis, Fantis, Krus, Mandingoes, Veis, Yorubas.
	Negroid.		Nubian (Lametan).	Barabras, Dongolowis, Monbuttus, Nubas, Nyam-Nyams, Poüls, Tumalis.
			Bantu.	Barolongs, Bassutos, Bechuanas, Bengas, Congoese, Dainas, Duallas, Herreros, Kafirs, Ovambos, Sakalavas, Suahelis, Wagandas, Zulus
A'sian.[8]	Sinitic (Sinian).		Chinese.	Chinese.
			Tibetan.	Bhotanese, Ladakis, Nepauiese, Tibetans.
			Indo-Chinese.	Anamese, Burmese, Cambodians, Cochin-Chinese, Siamese, Tonkinese.
	Sibiric.[4]		Mongolic.	Manchus, Tunguses.
			Tataric.	Kalmuks, Mongols.
			Finnic.	Cossacks, Huns, Kirghiz, Turcomans, Turks, Uzbeg, Yakouts. Esthonians, Finns, Karelians, Lapps, Livonians, Magyars, Mordvins, Ostiaks, Samoyeds, Ugrians, Voguls.
			Arctic.	Ainos, Chukchis, Ghiliaks, Kamchatkaus, Koraks, Nannollos.
			Japanese.	Coreans, Japanese.
In-su-lar and Lit'to-ral (Interoceanic).[3]	Negritic.[2]		Negrito.	Aetas, Mantras, Mincopies, Sakales, Schobaengs, Semangs.
			Papuan.	Papuans, New-Guineans.
	Malayic.[8]		Melanesian.	Fijians, Loyalty-Islanders, New-Caledonians, etc.
			Malayan.	Battaks, Dyaks, Hovas (of Madagascar), Javanese, Macassars, Malays, Sumatrese, Tagalas.
			Polynesian.[2]	Maoris, Micronesians, Polynesians.
	Australic.[4]		Australian.[2]	Australians, Tasmanians.
			Dravidian.[7]	Dravidas — Canarese, Khonds, Malayalas, Tamuls, Telugus, Todas. Mundas — Bhillas, Hos, Kohis, Mitas, Santals.
A-mer'i-can.[5, 8]			Arctic.	Aleutians, Eskimos.
			North-Atlantic.	Allsapascans, Algonkins, Caddoes, Dakotas, Iroquois, Muskokis, Shoshonees, Jinneh, etc.
			North-Pacific.	Californians, Haidahs, Pueblos, Tlinkits.
			Mexican.	Aztecs, Mixtecs, Zapotecs, etc. Mayas, etc.
			Inter-Isthmian.	Barbacoas, Chibchas, Chocos, Cunas, Mocoas.
			Columbian.	Aymaras, Kechuas, Puquithas, Yuncas.
			Peruvian.	Arawaks, Caribs, Carirts, Panos, Tapiyas, Tupis.
			Amazonian.	
			Pampean.	Abipones, Araucanians, Calchiquis, Patagonians, Yahgans.

1 Another classification divides these into (1) True Negroes, including Nubians (classified above with the Negroid), Nigritians (including generally the Nilotic and Sudanese), Senegambians, and Guineans, and (2) Mixed Negroes, including Fan, Fula, Tibbu, and Masai. 2 Another classification includes all the Negritic groups, with the Australian, in a variety of the Negroid race called Oceanic Negroid. 3 The Interoceanic race excludes those groups classified as Negroid. See previous reference. 4 Sometimes divided as Ural-Altaic, including the first four groups, Coreo-Japanese, the fifth. 5 See also table of linguistic stocks, under AMERICAN. 6 Sometimes classed as Hamitic or as Hamito-Semitic. 7 Sometimes classed as Asian or made a separate race. 8 The yellow Asian, the Malayic, and the American races are sometimes classed together as Mongoloid. 9 For linguistic classification, see LANGUAGE.

II. Classification Based on the Character of the Hair, as Prepared by the Smithsonian Institution.

Ulotriches (Woolly).	Lophocomi (In Tufts).	I. Papuans, *Homo Papua,* — 1. Negritos. 2. Papuans. 3. Melanese.
		II. Hottentots, *Homo Hottentotus,* — 4. Tasmanians. 5. Hottentots. 6. Bushmen. 7. Zulu Kafirs. 8. Bechuanas.
	Eriocomi (Fleecy).	III. Kafirs, *Homo Kafer.* — 9. Congo Kafirs.
		IV. Negroes, *Homo Niger.* — 10. Tibboo Negroes. 11. Sudan Negroes. 12. Senegambians. 13. Nigritians.
Lissotriches (Smooth)	Euthycomi (Straight).	V. Australians, *Homo Australis,* — 14. North-Australians. 15. South-Australians.
		VI. Malayans, *Homo Malayus.* — 16. Sundanese. 17. Polynesians. 18. Madagascans. 19. Indo-Chinese.
		VII. Mongolians, *Homo Mongolus.* — 20. Coreo-Japanese. 21. Altaians. 22. Uralians. 23. Hyperboreans.
		VIII. Arctics, *Homo Arcticus.* — 24. Eskimos.
	Euplocomi (Curly).	IX. Americans, *Homo Americanus.* — 25. North-Americans. 26. Central-Americans. 27. South-Americans. 28. Patagonians.
		X. Dravidas, *Homo Dravida.* — 29. Deccanese. 30. Singalese. 31. Shangallas.
		XI. Nubians, *Homo Nuba.* — 32. Dongolese. 33. Foolahs.
		XII. Mediterraneans, *Homo Mediterraneus.* — 34. Caucasians. 35. Basques. 36. Semites. 37. Indo-Europeans.
		Half-breeds.

The Classifying Impulse. A late-nineteenth-century racial schema devised by D. G. Brinton, a prominent American anthropologist. From *Funk and Wagnall's Standard Dictionary of the English Language* (1895).

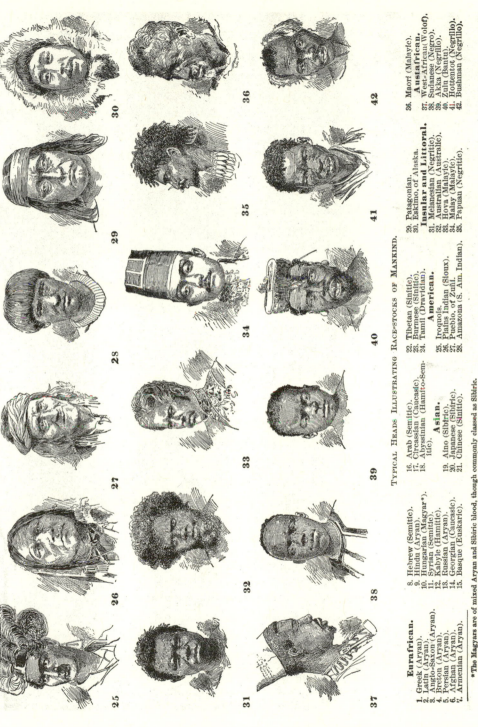

TYPICAL HEADS ILLUSTRATING RACE-STOCKS OF MANKIND.

Eurafrican.

1. Greek (Aryan).
2. Latin (Aryan).
3. Anglo-Saxon (Aryan).
4. Breton (Aryan).
5. Persian (Aryan).
6. Afghan (Aryan).
7. Armenian (Aryan).

8. Hebrew (Semitic).
9. Hindu (Aryan).
10. Hungarian (Magyar*).
11. Syrian (Semitic).
12. Kabyle (Hamitic).
13. Russian (Aryan).
14. Georgian (Caucasic).
15. Basque (Euskaric).

16. Arab (Semitic).
17. Circassian (Caucasic).
18. Abyssinian (Hamito-Semitic).

Asian.

19. Aino (Sibiric).
20. Japanese (Sibiric).
21. Chinese (Sinitic).

22. Tibetan (Sinitic).
23. Burmese (Sinitic).
24. Tamil (Dravidian).

American.

25. Iroquois.
26. Plains Indian (Sioux).
27. Pueblo, of Zuñi.
28. Amazona (S. Am. Indian).

29. Patagonian.
30. Eskimo, of Alaska.

Insular and Littoral.

31. Melanesian (Negritic).
32. Australian (Australic).
33. Hova (Malayic).
34. Malay (Malayic).
35. Papuan (Negritic).

36. Maori (Malayic).

Austafrican.

37. West-African (Wolof).
38. Sudanese (Negro).
39. Akka (Negrillo).
40. Zulu (Bantu).
41. Hottentot (Negrillo).
42. Bushman (Negrillo).

*The Magyars are of mixed Aryan and Sibiric blood, though commonly classed as Sibiric.

Race as a way of seeing. From *Funk and Wagnall's Standard Dictionary of the English Language* (1895).

the symbolic boundary has become a social boundary. Like symbolic boundaries, social boundaries vary across societies and culture and across time and place. However, social boundaries are not primarily symbolic or cognitive. They are embodied and materialized in our collective practices, our shared activities, and our social institutions. Such practices, activities, and institutions give social boundaries extraordinary administrative power, authority, and legitimacy. They also make social boundaries seem natural and unremarkable. For instance, turning again to the examples of race and ethnicity, they are not only symbolic boundaries, they also operate to organize and constrain the ways that humans interact with one another. They are artificial structures that exert structuring forces in everyday life, but they seem to be part of the natural order of things.[16]

Symbolic and social boundaries can be rigid or flexible, static or fluid, stable or unstable, permeable or impermeable, weak or strong. The same boundary may exhibit these different qualities at different historical moments, or it may present itself as a weak boundary to one social group and as a strong boundary to other groups. For instance, as a racial category, *white* has, in the United States, historically been more open and porous to European and Latino immigrants than it has been to African Americans.

This unstable and inconstant quality of boundaries directs our attention to the social interactions among those on either side of the boundary and to the social interactions across the boundary. For if the boundary changes or moves, who or what, we must ask, is responsible for that? How does it happen? How might we capture and observe those actions?[17] *Boundary work* is a shorthand term for any of the activities that go into the formation, maintenance, or transformation of boundaries. The various social and cultural mechanisms that do this work are just now being inventoried and catalogued by sociologists.[18] One of the common, everyday ways that boundary work is performed is through the use of words and concepts that serve as sociocultural dividing lines, or *boundary terms*.[19] Boundary terms typically arise when groups with differing values, ideas, and practices come into contact and when such encounters involve conflict of any kind — over economic and social resources, for instance. Under these circumstances, boundary terms can become symbolic weapons in the struggle for domination and control. The invention, repetition, circulation, and ongoing exchange of these terms can, if social conditions are favorable, effect an institutionalization of the term and its meanings in language and speech.

Focusing on the institutionalization of boundary terms and their meanings raises some important methodological questions for social scientists. One aim of this book, for example, is to compare different occurrences of white trash as they appear in various social and cultural sites. The primary domains I consider are literature, journalism, historical writings, scientific and medical writing, and social science. While these different arenas of institutionalized knowledge production appear to be relatively autonomous, governed by different aims and goals and using different methods, they also influence each other. Throughout the book, I carefully observe how meanings that arise in one area of knowledge are transposed and recur in other domains. The effects of this transposition are twofold and appear somewhat contradictory: first, a powerful convergence of meanings from different domains can and often does occur, giving the appearance that objective commentators and observers from disparate perspectives and disciplines have, independently of one another, arrived at the same conclusions about the nature and characteristics of, for example, poor white people. A second effect is that, over time, new interpretations produce newly transformed meanings that diverge from previous ones, allowing for new and different conclusions about the group in question. The twofold and contradictory nature of this process is important. It suggests that boundaries and the collectives they delineate are built through historical layering and sedimentation, through apparently natural accumulations and overlays of popular notions and intellectual concepts, through the invention and imposition of scientific descriptions and legal proscriptions, and through various encounters of discourses high and low. Because such constructions are heteroglossic and polyglot, linguistic interactions and semantic exchanges of all kinds become important sources of sociological data.[20]

Learning from *White Trash*

Regarding the explanatory frameworks I drew upon in this study—boundary studies and whiteness studies—neither was entirely adequate to the task I had set for myself. Some of the ideas central to whiteness

studies have been rejected as conceptually inadequate to the task of ac-
counting for the historical situations of poor whites. In the field of boundary studies, we have yet to clearly conceptualize different processes and
aspects of boundary making and, as a result, our methods may not be
adequate to produce the knowledge we seek. Given that these two areas
of research are still in the relatively early stages of development, none of
this is particularly surprising. I hope this study will serve in some small
way to advance both fields.

With regard to the array of cultural representations of poor whites examined here, the study shares many conclusions with the findings of historians and anthropologists who have studied poor whites in different
historical periods and geographic regions.[21] However, while many other
studies have tended to deploy class analysis as a general framework, or
to engage in various forms of community study, I have opted for a historical interactionist approach, one that is shared by few researchers of
this topic.

The book provides significant evidence for the argument that making
and marking group boundaries are processes deeply rooted in both our
individual and our collective consciousness alike. Group boundaries are
revealed to be inevitable consequences of both our cognitive processes
and recurring conflicts over material and social resources. Social differentiation is thus a permanent aspect of human existence, even if social
domination based on social differentiation may not be.

The research also strongly supports the theory that symbolic boundaries have a distinctly moral dimension. This is not a novel finding.
Boundaries are normative in that they are routinely used to establish basic
distinctions between good and bad people—distinctions used to determine who belongs where in social space.[22] In every period I examined,
in every stigmatypical representation I analyzed, and in virtually every
historical document I read, strong claims were made about the moral un-
worthiness of poor whites. This finding is so consistent, so significant,
and so prevalent in all the cases I examined that it is tempting to jump to
the conclusion that the basis of all social organization and social differentiation is morality.[23] The study also supports the theory that emotions
such as moral outrage, disgust, anger, contempt, and fear have served
as dynamic resources in mobilizing social movements for reform and
change. Over the roughly two-hundred-year period I examine, the pas-

sions evoked by disturbing images of "crackers" and poor white trash sparked dramatic social action in the form of moral panics and symbolic crusades that led to changes in policies, laws, and institutional practices.[24] At times, these changes harmed some poor whites; at other times, some of them benefited. This is, perhaps, befitting, for as we will see, the historical situation of poor whites has always been one of ambiguity and liminality, attributes shared by the identity — white trash — so frequently ascribed to them.

An Overview of the Book

In structuring this book, I sought to offer a rough chronology of the development of *white trash* and related boundary terms over the course of two centuries of American history, from the 1720s to the 1920s. This is a rather unwieldy chunk of time, and my strategy for managing it has been to focus on four different but overlapping periods — from the colonies of the 1720s to the early republic of the 1830s; from the 1830s to the Civil War; from Reconstruction to the late 1920s; and from the early 1900s to about 1915 — and to devote a chapter to each period. While I do not offer broad historical accounts of any of these time periods, what emerges is, in part, a kind of historical inventory of the collective representations of white trash in America.

This first chapter has been given over to introducing the theoretical underpinnings of the book. Chapter 1 focuses on the figurative precursors to white trash in British America. Throughout the seventeenth and eighteenth centuries, the colonial elite and yeomanry of the Chesapeake tidewater region sometimes characterized formerly indentured and escaped white servants as distinct social groups who shared a common antipathy toward the emerging colonial order. "Lubbers" and crackers, as they were called, either failed to achieve or resisted the cultural mold planters sought to establish and refused to respect the dominant moral boundaries regarding property, work, gender arrangements, and color lines. They sometimes transgressed colonial boundaries, forming border communities with Native Americans and escaped black slaves. For their refusals and resistance, these poor whites, not yet marked as poor white trash, were at times viewed as odd, backcountry curiosities. In moments of political and economic crisis, however, they were regarded as criminal savages, dangerous for the threat they posed as potential allies of rebellious slaves and inciters of Indian violence. As the American Revolution approached, these low-status, landless whites increasingly became the targets of violent colonial repression all along the frontier. In the aftermath of revolution, they continued to be perceived as a problem social group, one whose place in the newly independent republic was uncertain and tenuous. Chapter 1 ends with accounts of how poor white servants in 1830s Maryland were labeled *poor white trash* and reveals the different meanings and interpretations that circulated around this new boundary term.

The shifting status of southern poor whites during the antebellum era is considered in chapter 2. Against the historical backdrop of the expansion of black slavery, the sharpening of sectional differences, the rise of immigration in the North, and a corresponding reactionary nativism, two opposing perceptions of southern poor whites emerged. Beginning in the 1830s and 1840s, abolitionists put forth the notion that the poor white trash of the South were victims of the immoral slave economy: pushed to the margins, with no means of economic viability or social advancement, they suffered the ravages of poverty and want. According to abolitionists, the social and economic environment of the slave south was responsible for turning otherwise respectable whites into the degraded and dishonorable poor white trash. Predictably, southern secessionists and proslavery apologists had a markedly different take. Poor whites in the South were poor not because of slavery—they were poor because they were suffering from hereditary defects. It was, in southern secessionists' eyes, not bad environment but "bad blood" that tainted the poor white trash. Despite the intense disagreements between abolitionists and proslavery apologists, both groups agreed that the existence of poor white trash posed serious questions for the new democratic social order: where might such people who were nominally white, but whose morals, manners, and reputations were worse than those of black slaves, fit in the new republic? How could such disreputable and dishonorable whites be granted the democratic right of self-governance? These and other questions rose to the level of national significance in the years leading up to Civil War and Reconstruction, and the poor white trash were no longer seen as merely a regional problem, they soon became the focus of major efforts of Progressive era social reform.

The debate over poor whites begun by abolitionists and secessionists played out in the American eugenics movement, one of the first major social movements that followed Reconstruction. Chapter 3 examines how in the post-Reconstruction South, the disfranchisement of newly emancipated blacks and many poor whites and the emergence of coercive forms of agricultural labor signaled the beginning of a new era of social relations. This era of rapid social change also witnessed the rise of a group of middle-class professional scientists who were engaged in various forms of boundary work aimed at securing and defending their status and authority. Drawing upon the young science of eugenics, which sought to analyze the social and biological effects of heredity, social scientists and biologists conducted extensive fieldwork among poor whites in rural communities across the North, South, and Midwest. Eugenic field researchers found evidence to confirm the received wisdom that poor rural white families exhibited higher levels of criminality, feeblemindedness, sexual promiscuity, and alcoholism than did other populations of whites. The root of these problems, eugenicists believed, was cacogenics—kinds of sexual reproduction deemed deviant and unhealthy, most often in the form of incest (consanguinity), although the studies also documented cases where cross-class and interracial sex were thought to be the cause. As social movement leaders took their eugenics arguments to governmental agencies and sought state and federal intervention, they pushed for sharp restrictions on foreign immigration, but they also targeted poor whites—especially poor white women—through legislation that mandated involuntary institutionalization and sterilization of the poor and indigent. I conclude chapter 3 with a look at the controversial U.S. Supreme Court case of *Buck v. Bell*, a 1926 ruling that upheld the rights of states to eugenically sterilize, without consent, those it considered "unfit."

Eugenicists were extremely effective in portraying white trash as racially degenerate and biologically inferior and therefore incapable of making any positive contribution to a democratic society. However, not all middle-class professionals agreed with this damning assessment. Chapter 4 focuses on the place of white trash in yet another major social movement: the Rockefeller Foundation's crusade to eradicate hookworm disease, a public health effort carried out in eleven southern states between 1909 and 1915. Although hookworm disease affected many different social groups in the South, the hookworm reformers targeted poor whites as central to their campaign. In opposition to the racial degeneracy argument of eugenicists, hookworm campaigners updated the abolitionist claim that environment, not biology, was the cause of the deplorable condition of poor whites. Biology was still considered a crucial determining factor, but it was biological infection and disease, not bad genes, these doctors argued, that were the root problems facing the southern poor white; if they could only be cured, the poor white trash could and would become productive workers and citizens. Hookworm crusaders asserted that crackers, "dirt-eaters," and poor white trash were actually purely Anglo-Saxon in origin and so, like "better" white Americans, capable of the very highest modes of civilization and cultural achievement. Though short-lived, the hookworm crusade profoundly influenced national perspectives on southern poor whites, effectively opening the door for this group to lay claim to their "groupness," to insist on their identities as fully white Americans, to shed the taint and stigma of moral, racial, and sexual degeneracy, and to further distance themselves from black Americans and immigrants.

The final chapter of the book summarizes the historical argument and offers the main conclusions drawn from my research. I discuss ways in which sociologists and other researchers, rather than abandoning the concept of whiteness entirely, might usefully reconceptualize it. The chapter also ponders the question of how boundary theory, while presenting some definite advantages over the now-dominant analytical paradigm, can be pushed in different directions to develop a new approach to examining the complex processes of social differentiation, group formation, and persistent inequalities.

chapter one

Lubbers, Crackers, and Poor White Trash

Borders and Boundaries in the Colonies

and the Early Republic

They are devoured by musketas all summer and have agues every spring and fall, which corrupt all the juices of their bodies, give them a cadaverous complexion and besides a lazy, creeping habit, which they never get rid of.

—WILLIAM BYRD II (1728/1929: 54)

They delight in their present low, lazy, sluttish, heathenish, hellish life, and seem not desirous of changing it.

—REV. CHARLES WOODMASON (1766/1953: 52)

The fact is, that in America, a conflict is going on between opposite principles, and the consequences of the struggle show themselves chiefly in the relation between master and servant.

—HARRIET MARTINEAU (1838/1988: 198)

In 1728, William Byrd II, the scion of a vastly wealthy Virginian family and member of the governor's Council of Virginia, complained sardonically about the poor whites who inhabited the borderlands of the colonies of Virginia and North Carolina. "I am sorry to say it," he observed, "but Idleness is the general character of the men of the Southern parts of this Colony [Virginia] as well as in North Carolina. . . . Surely there is no place in the world where the inhabitants live with less labor than in N[orth] Carolina. It approaches nearer to the description of Lubberland than any other, by the great felicity of the climate, the easiness of raising provisions, and the slothfulness of the people. . . . To speak the truth, 'tis a thorough aversion to labor that makes people file off to N[orth] Carolina, where plenty and a warm sun confirm them in their disposition to laziness for their whole lives" (1728/1929: 91–92).

Byrd had set out with a team of surveyors in 1727 to settle a long-standing geographic boundary dispute between North Carolina and Virginia, faithfully keeping diaries (including secret diaries written in code) and later using them to write up a popular account of his explorations. That account, *The History of the Dividing Line*, and Byrd's accompanying secret diaries, contain some of the earliest stigmatizing depictions of poor, low-status whites in the North American colonies. As the passage above suggests, they comprise a particularly unflattering portrait. These depictions, although written in a comical tone, have had rather serious effects on the shared perceptions of poor whites that followed.[1]

Byrd was certainly not alone among his peers in viewing low-status whites as a distinct, inferior social group. By the 1760s, other elites had joined Byrd in deploring the habits and morals of socially outcast whites. In 1766, a colonial official reported to his superior that certain "lawless" colonists were harassing the neighboring Cherokee. These colonists, known locally as crackers, were apparently a significant problem for the British colonial authorities, who were at pains not to agitate the Cherokee to whom they had recently promised an end to British colonial expansion.[2] This Revolutionary-era portrait of the colonial poor white cracker differs in important respects from the earlier depiction of the "lubber," because of a new emphasis on the economic and political threat that such a group posed to the maintenance of social order in the British colonies.

In the wake of the American Revolution, as the young republic struggled to define its national character and to understand itself, social observers continued to focus on the peculiar status of marginal whites. Invariably, such whites were compared unfavorably to black servants and slaves and to American Indians. By the 1830s a new term had emerged for socially downcast whites: *poor white trash*. This new term, like *cracker* before it, altered popular conceptions of poor and outcast whites and offered new ways to make sense of their stigmatized identity and their low status.

From the seventeenth to the early nineteenth century, the language of race and the language of class were not nearly as distinct as we presume them to be today. To be sure, they were considered different categories, but between the lower classes and the lower races, there was considerable overlap in the symbolic properties, characteristics, and traits ascribed to each. Behaviors and attitudes regarding conventional morality and work were particularly salient here, with the lower classes and lower races typically characterized as holding deep aversions to both. Also highly salient in the minds of observers were behaviors regarding cleanliness — the lower sorts were consistently characterized as dirty, smelly, and unclean. What is striking about reading historical documents of the period then is the similar ways in which poor whites, Indians, and blacks are described — as immoral, lazy, and dirty.[3]

The terms *lubber, cracker,* and *poor white trash* offer us little reliable information about the objective social structures of the times. However, they are exemplary of a specific type of symbolic boundary. These labels are *stigmatypes* — stigmatizing boundary terms that simultaneously denote and enact cultural and cognitive divides between in-groups and out-groups, between acceptable and unacceptable identities, between proper and improper behaviors.[4] They create categories of status and prestige, explicitly, through labeling and naming, and implicitly, through invidious comparison. The classification *cracker* has meaning in part because there exists another, unnamed, unmarked class: non-*cracker*.[5]

Each of the stigmatyping boundary terms considered in this book raises questions: Where did it come from? To whom was it meant to refer? More significantly, what needs were served by its invention, and, if the term endured over time, what accounted for its popularity and staying power? In short, to whom was the stigmatype useful and why? This chapter is an effort to sort out some possible answers to these questions and to begin an investigation into some of the historical meanings the terms conveyed. It pays particular attention to analyzing the specific social and historical conditions that gave rise to the terms and to discussing the different social and symbolic operations the terms may have performed. The approach is first to attempt a reconstruction of some of the social circumstances that helped produce the terms and to try to recapture some of the meanings and interpretations that circulated around and through them. In some instances, I then focus on the various social effects of these efforts at naming and classification. My purpose in so doing is to draw attention to how boundary terms can illuminate the historical struggles over social and cultural identity and belonging that are key forces in the formation of social hierarchies and concomitant social inequalities.[6] The

histories of these stigmatypes—some of which have proven to be remarkably resilient and remain widely used today—also offer us genealogies of
some of the symbolic and cultural exclusions that persist in contemporary society.

Finally, the analysis I develop here demonstrates how a single boundary term can mark off multiple aspects of human identity. A single term
can and often does carry meanings about class, status, race, gender, and
sexuality; although one or more of these meanings often dominates, the
others can be and usually are simultaneously present, even if only in
muted or transmuted form. It is precisely this insight about connected
boundaries that motivates much of the recent work on intersectionality.
Yet scholars following that paradigm tend to begin by isolating different
identity categories for analysis before moving on to the difficult work of
reconstructing the connections their own analysis has severed. Boundary
theory suggests a better way. It offers the ability to capture the complicated intertwining effects of different categories of social difference and
inequality, and it provides a model for understanding how they are experienced, interpreted, and perceived as a whole identity.

Boundary Work on the Colonial Frontier

William Byrd II was heir to the Byrd colonial fortune amassed by his
father. Born in 1674 in Virginia, he was sent to England for safekeeping
when Bacon's Rebellion broke out two years later.[7] There, he lived with
this grandfather and received his education, graduated in 1696, and was
immediately admitted to the bar. Upon returning to his native land in
1708, he assumed all the rights, responsibilities, and status of a highly
educated, wealthy colonial planter. He raised tobacco, using slave and
indentured servant labor together, and, despite bad luck and a series of
financial missteps, amassed even greater wealth and property than had
his father before him.[8] Byrd was unquestionably a member of the transatlantic elite, a product of the colonial aristocracy with privilege, power,
and authority matched only by a few peers.

Byrd's 1728 survey of the disputed boundary line between Virginia and
North Carolina was, of course, boundary work of the most literal kind.

The geographic survey took him west from the shores of the Atlantic through the Great Dismal Swamp and beyond to the rising plateaus of Appalachia. All along this 240-mile route he encountered frontier settlers and squatters living in rude huts and cabins, eking out nomadic lifestyles with small herds of cattle or pigs or, more rarely, subsiding on modest plots of cultivated land. The entire region had long had a reputation as a haven for runaway servants and slaves, criminals, and ne'er-do-wells of all sorts. In his travel writings and diaries, Byrd, borrowing a term from English culture, dubbed these backcountry dwellers "lubbers."

To Byrd's transatlantic audience—English readers and fellow colonial elites who had been educated in England—Lubberland was known as an imaginary place of plenty without labor, a land of laziness where inhabitants lolled about without purpose. Through this association with Lubberland, Byrd was also imaginatively linking the colonial borderlands and its lazy denizens to a centuries-old peasant utopia that had existed in the cultural imagination of Western Europe since at least the Middle Ages, when it was known as the Land of Cockaigne.[9] Throughout that era, innumerable texts made reference to Cockaigne, a dream world where "work was forbidden . . . and food and drink appeared spontaneously in the form of grilled fish, roast geese, and rivers of wine. One only had to open one's mouth and all that delicious food practically jumped inside . . . there was the added bonus of a whole range of amenities: communal possessions, lots of holidays, no arguing or animosity, free-sex with ever willing partners, a fountain of youth, beautiful clothes for everyone, and the possibility of earning money while one slept" (Pleij 2000: 3). Cockaigne represented not just any sort of utopia, but one that resonated most vibrantly with the disenfranchised and the dispossessed, with the downtrodden and the marginalized—those for whom hunger and want were constant features of everyday life. Through these associations, Lubberland symbolized a place of relaxed, lusty ease, a place of unimpeded libidinal energies and uninterrupted flows of carnal desire that stood in sharp contrast to the disciplined, ordered, and morally upright culture of Byrd's world—the social and cultural universe of the eighteenth-century tidewater planter. Any place that even approximated Lubberland's social conditions would have been something of a symbolic and moral threat to a nascent, rather fragile colonial order (Greenblatt 1988: 129–63).

In comparing the colonial borderlands to Lubberland/Cockaigne, Byrd was authoring and authorizing the idea that the inhabitants of these out-of-the-way places were not just different from other colonial settlers, but also morally, culturally, and socially inferior.[10] For Byrd, the key moral quality in life was an eager disposition toward work. Byrd's attitudes on this matter reflected a dominant idea shared throughout the colonies — that idleness was a grave sin. To describe an individual or social group as "idle" or "lazy" was to simultaneously express moral condemnation and the highest degree of contempt.[11] Moral condemnation and contempt, it must be noted, are highly emotionally charged judgments, and they mobilize visceral feelings of disgust. Moral condemnation is directed against what people do, while contempt is directed against who they are. This perception, this structure of feeling, was deeply embedded in the core of British imperialism and it was made manifest throughout the empire. As Anne McClintock (1995) has noted, since at least the sixteenth century, the British had associated slothfulness with corruption and poverty. By the eighteenth century, Puritans had articulated an elaborate set of moral, political, and cultural traits based on sharply delineated conceptions of industriousness versus idleness. The boundaries separating those who worked hard from those who did not operated as important cultural resources in the colonial struggle to transform labor regimes and enforce labor discipline upon unruly natives and truculent colonists. Cultural inducements to labor — in the form of boundary terms that separated good colonists from bad — were propagated by colonial elites with missionary-like fervor. Indeed, the reputation of the colonies as places where the poor, the indigent, and the criminal could be redeemed through hard work served as a major ideological justification for the entire colonial enterprise.[12]

We can see this throughout Byrd's writings, where he strives to uphold the virtues of industriousness and hard work, religiosity and good Christian practice, and cleanliness and health as the hallmarks of an upright life. Indeed, it was largely the belief in the spiritually redeeming value of these habits of industry that led Byrd and his contemporaries to keep diaries in the first place — to record a daily account by which their industriousness and religious commitment might be judged. These cultural ideals and values are thrown into sharp relief by Byrd's depictions of lubbers as lazy, irreligious, filthy, and diseased. The moral distinctions drawn by Byrd communicated spiritual meanings, but they also served as crucial markers of social difference.

While it is perhaps straightforward enough to understand the utility of *lubber* as a way of marking off boundaries of morality, the term also carried significant meanings about gender, racial, and sexual difference in the colonies, as well as signaling distinctions of status and class.[13] Yet Byrd's representations amount to caricature: perhaps there were real, living human beings behind these distorted sketches? Who did Byrd think he was describing in inventing these lubbers, these useless inhabitants of the colonial borderlands? A brief description of the changing and dynamic social organization of the southern colonies provides intriguing clues.

Status and Social Collectives

The mid-seventeenth century saw the emergence of new and complex sets of social groups in the Chesapeake colonies. Social historians have typically described these collectives in terms of their relationships to land, labor, and capital, having identified as many as six different groups.[14] The first group, generally positioned outside the institutions of slavery and servitude, were dwindling numbers of American Indians, mostly confined to areas at the western frontiers and borderlands of the colonies. African slaves comprised a second group, held to the bottom of the hierarchy by their status as property. A third group, composed of white servants and slaves, were laboring under the various terms of their indentures. The fourth were freemen, former servants and slaves, white and black, who had been freed upon the completion of the terms of their bondage. Above them, in the fifth group, were the so-called yeomen, the smallholders with property consisting of small land holdings and few servants. At the top end of the structure were the elites, men who held large estates and lucrative public offices in the colonial government.[15]

It is the fourth group, the freemen without property, wedged between the servant class and the smallholders, that deserves our close attention here. Due to many factors, the number of indentured servants rose precipitously between 1650 and 1700. One key factor was the head right system, whereby planters received additional land for each servant they brought over from England. This system acted as a strong material incentive for planters to increase the number of indentured servants they sponsored, while making land less available to freemen in the colonies. In addition, by the middle of the seventeenth century, the colonies had become more securely established, and the heavy mortality rates that had plagued the earliest settlements declined. As a result, the entire population, including freemen, increased in size. Another factor was the intentional limiting by elites of the size of the smallholder class, which had begun to grow in economic and political influence. In some regions these smallholders, who, like the planters, grew tobacco for export, began to pose a threat to the oligopoly of the elites, reaping some of the tobacco profits for themselves. Beginning in 1658, the planter elite of Virginia began to take steps to minimize the size and influence of this group, imposing longer periods of indenture and servitude through a series of laws and doing what they could to limit access to land. Finally, and crucially, the increasing reliance on African slave labor rendered free white labor superfluous and produced a group of whites that was unable to find work or land and who therefore could not afford slaves for themselves. Taken together, these historical and social conditions created a situation where more and more freemen were chasing fewer and fewer plots of arable land. Theirs was the most rapidly growing group, but while they were legally entitled to set up households of their own, the freemen found it very hard to do so. As elites closed opportunities and hoarded land and other resources for themselves, fewer freemen were able to achieve the upward mobility they sought.[16]

When tobacco prices fell and, consequently, credit became more difficult to obtain, these recently freed men were simply unable to compete with established smallholders and elites. By the latter half of the seventeenth century, the social group of poor, landless freemen had vastly increased in size. Given these difficulties, many freemen apparently chose to settle the colonial frontiers and outlying zones where they led the lives of nomadic herdsmen, raising hogs and cattle and living off the land where boundaries of ownership and jurisdiction were largely undetermined and often in dispute.

Color Lines

While some historians have argued that the concept of race in the eighteenth-century British colonies did not draw upon scientific or theological notions of human difference and that *race* did not take on these meanings until the mid-nineteenth century (Gossett 1977; Stocking 1993), others have argued that by the mid-eighteenth century, the colonial experience had already produced a "racialization of savagery" that marked off Indians and slaves not just as culturally different, but as biologically distinct and thus immutably inferior (Takaki 1992). Byrd's narratives offer evidence for both sides of this debate; his observations about racial others are at best ambiguous, contradictory, and murky. His confusion reflects the fact that in the 1720s, English colonizers had yet to reach any intellectual consensus on the causes or even permanence of different complexions, skin colors, and racial difference.[17]

However, Byrd repeatedly noted similarities between lubbers and Indians. Among both, he wrote, the women were forced to do all the work; both appeared to prefer herding and nomadism over agricultural work and farm life; both, he wrote, were dirty and lived in filth; and both tended to have disregard for personal property. Moreover, Byrd observed in both a reversal of traditional gender roles and a deviation from sexual mores and norms.[18] Given that he drew these parallels between the two, it is possible that while Byrd saw lubbers as racially distinct from Indians—a social collective already treated as nonwhite by the laws and institutions of the colonies—he saw each as culturally akin to the other. Thus while social domination—based in part on loose notions of skin color and cultural hierarchy—was already well entrenched as a primary organizing principle for colonial life, Byrd's lubbers occupied an ambiguous place: their dirt-encrusted skin was white, but their behavior and attitudes were not.

In another passage that touches on racial meanings, Byrd offers a portrait of a runaway African or African American slave and his companion:

> We were told that on the south shore, not far from the inlet, dwelt a Marooner, that modestly called himself a hermit, tho' he forfeited that name by suffering a wanton female to cohabit with him. His habitation was a

bower, covered with bark after the Indian fashion. . . . Like the Ravens, he neither plowed nor sowed, but subsisted chiefly upon oysters. . . . Sometimes too, for a change of diet, he sent [the woman] to drive up the neighbor's cows, to moisten their mouths with a little milk. Thus did the wretches live in a dirty state of nature, and were mere Adamites, innocence only excepted. (1728/1929: 46)

It is quite likely that this unnamed character lived on the edges of one of the scores of maroon communities that dotted the colonial borderlands during this period.[19] These mixed-color communities—the subject of much speculation and contention among historians—were common throughout the Americas. Known as *palenques, quilombos, macombos, cumbes, ladeiras,* or *mambises*, these communities ranged in size from small groups to large states with thousands of citizens (Price 1973/1996: 1). In his survey of maroon societies in the southeastern United States from 1672 to 1864, Herbert Aptheker (1996) described the residents as "black Robin Hoods" who sometimes led settled existences, but who more often led migratory lives, carrying on illegal trade with white people living in the colonial borderlands. These communities were "seriously annoying . . . sources of insubordination" for the colonial government (151).[20]

We can infer from Byrd's passage that he believed the marooner was somehow distinct from the lubber—why else would he mention them separately? The two groups, lubbers and marooners, may have shared similar modes of subsistence, but they were not in Byrd's mind, identical. What exactly distinguished the one from the other, however, is left unclear. Yet Byrd's derisive tone and sarcasm suggest he believed lubbers had more in common culturally with Indians and blacks than they did with him and his fellow planters. For one thing, all three groups shared a willingness to trespass the color lines so carefully established by the colonial elite. Was this, then, part of the reason they were stigmatyped?

However the status and racial identity of lubbers was ultimately assessed by colonial elites, the prospect of armed alliances between recently freed bondsmen and Indians and escaped slaves engendered a great deal of anxiety and fear. Elites were few in number, and they knew their position at the top of the social hierarchy was precarious; open rebellion by a coalition of the much more numerous dispossessed—such as Bacon's

Rebellion in 1676 — was a constant worry, especially in times of economic downturn and social discontent.

Gender Borderlands and Sexual Frontiers

As some historians (K. Brown 1996; Fischer 2002) have suggestively argued, the colonial frontier was not just a geographic region but also a borderlands where different cultural systems of gender and sexuality collided. Gender relations, sexual regulation, and racial identity were, according to these scholars, more fluid and indeterminate in these peripheral regions than they were in the colonial cores.

In spite of his broad characterizations of Indians and lubbers as immoral, lazy, and dirty, Byrd often portrayed the Indian and lubber women he encountered as industrious and hardworking. This suggests he meant to reserve his scorn and dismissive humor for the men in each group. The following description is typical:

> The men, for their parts, just like the Indians, impose all the work upon the poor women. They make their wives rise out of their beds early in the morning, at the same time that they lye and snore, 'til the sun has run one third of his course, and dispersed all the unwholesome damps. Then, after stretching and yawning for half an hour, they light their pipes, and, under the protection of a cloud of smoke, venture out into the open air; tho', if it happens to be never so little cold, they quickly return shivering into the chimney corner. When the weather is mild, they stand leaning with both their arms upon the corn-field fence, and gravely consider whether they had best go and take a small heat at the hoe; but generally find reasons to put it off until another time. Thus they loiter away their lives, like Solomon's sluggard, with their arms across, and at the winding up of the year scarcely have bread to eat. (1728/1929: 92)

That the men would avoid work and instead impose it upon women, that they would shy away from the elements or from tending their crops, that they would procrastinate rather than provide for their families — these characteristics were no doubt for Byrd's audience explanation enough of why the lubbers deserved their low status and the poverty and social marginalization that accompanied it. The plantation ideal of womanhood was one where the lady of the house was protected from physical labor. Her domain was the house; her husband's, the field and market. White servants and black slaves did the work of the plantation. For men to stay at home by the hearth while women went out to work was a near perfect reversal of the gender codes of the plantation elite. In Byrd's eyes, the gender arrangements of lubbers, like those of Indians, were further evidence of their cultural backwardness and inferiority.

The boundaries of sex and sexuality were somewhat less fixed than those of gender. Byrd's various writings are richly supplied with details about his active sex life, and scholars are divided about how to interpret his sexual obsessions and adventures. One psychoanalytic line of interpretation (K. Brown 1996) reads Byrd's frequent sexual encounters with a wide array of partners—willing and unwilling—as evidence of basic insecurities about his virility, his sexual prowess, and his status as a colonial patriarch. A more sociological line of interpretation (Godbeer 1998) reads these same encounters as quite the opposite—evidence of Byrd's social power and his supreme comfort in his role as a member of the dominant elite. Whatever general conclusions one might reach about his sexual proclivities and appetites—that, in addition to conjugal relations with his different wives, included frequent visits with prostitutes, numerous liaisons with white servants, and the occasional interracial conquest of women he encountered on his travels and journeys—Byrd's writings about his survey expedition make it clear that he and his men regarded Lubberland as a kind of sexual frontier where boundaries regulating sexual behavior were more relaxed than those of the plantation.

In many examples, Byrd recounted the sexual predations of his survey crewmembers as they imposed sexual demands on various women they encountered on the frontier. During the course of the survey, crew members "offered several gross freedoms" to the daughters and sisters of their hosts, and sometimes they became "more boisterous and employ'd force" when their advances were rebuffed. In one instance, a woman "would certainly have been ravish't if her timely consent had not prevented the violence." Byrd typically portrayed himself as the gentleman who intervened in time to save the poor women from sexual assaults, but he too engaged in sexual "freedoms": he and a fellow commissioner visited with a free black family where "a Dark Angel supriz'd us with her charms."

When Byrd's partner grabbed hold of her, "she struggled just enough to make her Admirer more eager." Other examples abound in these texts, each one lending evidence to the reading that, for Byrd and his men, Lubberland was a sexual playground, its female inhabitants their erotic playthings.[21]

Lubbers operated as a stigmatyping boundary term that conveyed information not only about class and social status, but about social differences involving color, race, gender, and sexuality as well. As a group, lubbers defied easy categorization: they were of the lowest social rank, to be sure, as low as or lower than Indians and black slaves, but their pale skin color somehow set them apart from those groups. Lubber women worked, a fact that placed them at cultural odds with the planter ideal, but their very exploitability eroticized them as sexual objects. To Byrd's classifying mind, lubbers were ethnological oddities.

Looking back, it is tempting to envision Lubberland and its lazy lubbers as powerfully symbolic indictments of the overly repressive and regimented world of the English colonial elites. One could, following this logic, make the argument that the "laziness" of lubbers was not a moral failure, but a principled resistance to oppressive colonial labor regimes that enriched only wealthy planters and a few middling freemen. In the small realms of freedom carved out by these border-dwelling lubbers, planter cultural ideals were turned on their heads. Such an argument, largely speculative, is probably overly ideological and sentimental. For those excluded from the plantation system, as for the slaves who toiled within it, life in the borderlands was most likely desperate and difficult.

Despite its lasting influence as a literary icon, *lubber* is the least well-remembered epithet to be employed against low-status whites. As a stigmatype and boundary term, it was never widely adopted, and there is little evidence of its use after the mid-eighteenth century. Why did it not become popular as a figure of speech? Why did it pass so quickly into obsolescence and desuetude? Perhaps *lubber* was simply too English an idiom and, like many things English, did not survive the cultural tumult of revolution. However, it is also likely that, as the Revolution began to take hold, the poor white on the colonial frontiers began to appear to colonial authorities as a haunting specter of social disorder. Whatever the reasons, within half a century, the laughable lubber had been replaced by a different and much less amusing figure: the cracker.

Crackers, Regulators, and Rural Insurrections

The same historical and demographic pressures that had set the stage for the appearance of the lubber had, by the 1760s, caused widespread frustration throughout the British colonies. As in Byrd's era, planter elites continued to hoard land and to rely ever more heavily on slave labor, leaving the poor and landless white freemen with few options for social mobility. The conclusion of the French and Indian War in 1763 ended French colonialism in North America and consolidated British control, although this control, soon to be challenged, would prove remarkably short-lived.

Lacking access to the land required for upward social mobility, many poor white colonists opted for geographic mobility and, in defiance of colonial authorities, pushed aggressively and violently into the western trans-Appalachia frontier. There they encountered surviving tribes of American Indians. While these encounters often resulted in fierce skirmishes, they also resulted in the mutual trade and exchange of consumer and cultural goods. On this tenuous new frontier — the upper Ohio River Valley, the western reaches of Virginia, the Carolinas, and Georgia — poor white colonists carved out settlements and grew in number, but it was brutal and violent work. The image of the lazy lubber was hardly fitting to describe these outlaw frontiersmen. A new boundary term was needed.

According to Mitford Mathews, *cracker* was the first term to be widely and popularly applied to these poor whites in the western reaches of the British colonies. Mathews writes: "The term in the sense of 'a poor white'" was first used and defined in a 1766 administrative report to the Earl of Dartmouth. Gavin Cochrane, a colonial officer, wrote to inform the earl about the behavior of certain British subjects in the upper Ohio River Valley:

> Reported complaints came from the Cherokees that white people came into their hunting grounds and destroyed their beavers which they said was everything to them. . . . I [sent] orders to have those Beaverers made prisoners. . . . [I] thought it my duty to act for the public good; everything succeeded as I could have wished; the Officer at Fort Prince George told the Indians the orders he had received and bid them seize the Beaverers and

bring them to him without hurting them. They brought three of the lawless people called crackers, who behaved with the greatest insolence and
told the Officer they neither valued him nor the Lieutenant Gov[ernor].
(Mathews 1959: 126)

This is, in many respects, an odd report. What sorts of boundaries are
being drawn here? What characteristics, behaviors, and attitudes are
being attributed to the crackers? Segregation of Indians and whites appears to be a significant issue, with the Cherokee noting that it was "white
people" who had destroyed their primary economic resource. So too does
common morality appear as a line that has been crossed and must be redrawn, with Cochrane deciding to take action against the crackers in the
interest of "the public good." And clearly the crackers stand in violation
of not just the moral code, but the legal code too: Cochrane acted under
the authority granted him by the Proclamation of 1763, a law that forbade
British settlers and colonists from occupying any of the lands west of the
Appalachian ridge, that were set aside as "hunting grounds" for several
tribes of Indians, including the Cherokee. While the proclamation did
precious little to halt the expansionist drive of the frustrated colonists,
it did make provisions for colonial officers to seize, imprison, and bring
to trial any white settler found in violation of the law. The crackers had
run afoul of this law, and the Cherokee turned them in. Boundaries of
race, common morality, and law are all visibly at work in Cochrane's brief
account.

The crackers, captured by the Cherokee and brought to the fort for
imprisonment, defiantly scoffed at the officer and heaped scorn on his superiors, rather than bow their heads and plead leniency. Who *were* these
characters? Mathews asserts that the term *crackers* was used in the mid-
eighteenth century to refer to the white outlaws who flourished in the
wake of the French and Indian War. He draws his conclusions from a
section of Cochrane's report that offers an explanation and definition of
cracker:

I should explain to your Lordship what is meant by crackers; a name they
got from being great boasters; they are a lawless set of rascals on the frontiers of Virginia, Maryland, the Carolinas, and Georgia, who often change
their places of abode. They steal horses in the southern provinces and sell

them in the northern and those from the Northern they sell in the southern. They get merchants by degrees to trust them with more and more
goods to trade with the Indians and at first make returns till they have
established some credit, then leave those that trusted them in the lurch,
return no more but go to some other place to follow the same practice.
(Mathews 1959: 127)

These outlaws, Mathews infers, were groups of backwoodsmen who stole
goods and perhaps even operated organized crime syndicates on an inter-
colonial scale. As the Cochrane fragment attests, crackers had reputations for being ill-mannered, arrogant, treacherous, and cruel, stealing
from Indians and propertied white colonists alike. If the report is accurate in its description, they stole through outright thievery as well as
through elaborate confidence games that left merchants holding worthless paper. Clearly, crackers had no respect for the laws of the land and
feared little the powers of the colonial authorities. From Cochrane's description, Mathews concluded "these crackers were the thin outer fringe
of the first organized band of criminals that ever operated in this country"
(127). Their lawlessness made them enemies to the colonial government
and to the local Cherokees alike.

Whether or not the historical evidence bears out Mathew's claims,
Cochrane's report contains a very different view of frontier colonial
whites than the one put forward by Byrd forty years earlier. Cochrane's
report—a sanctioned document carrying the authority and bearing the
power of a government official—presented this group of outcast whites
as dangerous, cruel, and threatening rebels. Crackers appeared here, a
decade before the Boston Tea Party, as protorevolutionaries scattered
throughout the colonial frontiers of the eastern seaboard, rejecting British colonial law and governance and asserting their own authority and
autonomy.[22] In the eyes of British officials, the threats crackers posed
to the colonial structure of governance could not have been more clear.
They not only constituted a source of ongoing and serious open rebellions and resistance, they also represented the frightening possibility of
an Indian/poor white alliance: "Some of [the crackers] stay in the Indian
country and are perpetually endeavoring to stir up a war by propagating
idle stories that they may join them and share in the plunder. They delight
in cruelty which they often practice even to one another," Cochrane wrote

(Mathews 1959: 127). As with the lubbers before them, perhaps what made crackers such a despised and dishonored group was their close social relations—at times as allies, at times as enemies—with other stigmatized and outcast social groups.[23]

Historical dictionaries cite numerous references to *cracker* after 1766, and virtually all references are imbued with connotations of criminality and unlawfulness.[24] The new emphasis on the criminality of poor frontier whites marks a significant shift in meaning. *Lubber* connoted idleness, squalor, filth, and perversity—evoking pathos, bathos, scorn, and laughter, but not terror or alarm. *Cracker*, on the other hand, signified a dangerous and volatile social group, one to be feared and respected, posing a distinct threat to the stability of the colonial social order and the security of other colonists. *Cracker* was not so much a term of contempt as it was a term that spoke to the fears and anxieties and grudging respect that these poor whites evoked among other colonists.

As a boundary term, *cracker* symbolically marked out a crucial difference in identity between white colonists who were lawful and properly subordinate to colonial authority and those who were not. However, unlike Byrd's lubbers, who did nothing to directly provoke hostilities, the guerrilla rebellions of the crackers managed to incite the repressive violence of planters and smallholders.

In 1767, just one year after Cochrane wrote his report to the Earl of Dartmouth, a group of Piedmont farmers and yeomen smallholders, most of whom held less than 400 acres of land and owned no slaves, joined forces and declared themselves "the Regulators." The Regulators, described by one historian as the first organized group of vigilantes in American history (R. M. Brown 1963: vii), were situated between the fertile lowcountry and the backcountry frontier that bordered on Cherokee country. This geographic location meant they were subject to frequent Indian raids and also to attacks from crackers. Tiring of the nonresponsiveness of the colonial leaders, who were mainly concerned with protecting the interests of the wealthier planters in the lowcountry and honoring the terms of the Proclamation of 1763, and the ineffectiveness of a judicial system too weak to offer legal protections, the Regulators took matters into their own hands. Throughout the fall of 1767, Regulators rampaged throughout the backcountry, burning the cabins of known outlaws, capturing others and their families subjecting them to public whippings, and hunting down escaped slaves, sometimes executing them on the spot (Stock 1996: 93).

Elite planters in the South Carolina lowcountry were shocked and disturbed by the blatant vigilantism and demanded that the Regulators desist. However, having rid the backcountry of all the known outlaws through murder and intimidation, the Regulators, rather than putting down their weapons, chose a new set of victims. They turned their violence on other poor whites, the "Rogues and other Idle, worthless, vagrant People," who stole from gardens and orchards and subsisted "on the Stocks and Labors of the Industrious Planter." These poor frontier whites, who either failed or resisted the cultural requirements of morality and industry were, in the eyes of the Regulators, no more than "Indolent, unsettled, roving Wretches" (from the 1767 Regulator Manifesto, quoted in R. M. Brown 1963: 46–47). According to one source, the victims of Regulator violence

> were of diverse origins and varied circumstances. Some were "Crackers" —motley backcountry ruffians who lived on the fringes of settlements. Others were unfortunate small planters who had settled in the bleak, infertile Sand Hills. Still others were hunters and squatters, absconded debtors, idlers, gamblers, and unsavory refugees from the northern colonies, settlers who had never recovered from the trauma of the Cherokee War, deserters from the military forces, and often, mulattoes, Negroes, or people of mixed white, Indian, and Negro blood. To upstanding inhabitants all these people were a public nuisance and a menace. (1963: 28)[25]

Here we have a boundary term operating, in effect, as a legitimation of that most extreme form of social exclusion: extermination. The Regulators had responded with an extraordinary degree of violence to the perceived threat to social order posed by the crackers and other low-status and outcast whites. But how should we characterize this violence? Was it interclass warfare? Ethnic violence? Posed in either/or terms, the answer is not entirely clear.

The armed violence and the killing were relatively short-lived and were resolved only by institutionalizing a different strategy for domination. At the end of 1768, a newly established Congress of Regulators passed a vagrancy law that required landless whites to work six days a week or face public flogging and humiliation. The violence of the Regulators had resulted in real gains for the small landowners: they simultaneously rid the backcountry of troublesome crackers and created a new source of exploitable labor for themselves.[26]

Did the refusals and resistance of crackers inspire other colonists to refuse their masters? Did their persistence in pursuing their own ideas and practices of freedom—whatever freedoms large or small they gained by choosing to resist and defy the authorities and the law—serve as a model for American revolutionaries seeking to throw off the oppressive yoke of British rule? How did cracker notions of independence and liberty differ from those espoused by Regulators and elites? These lines of historical inquiry have yet to be fully explored, but recent scholarship suggests these questions are worth pursuing if we are to begin to understand the historical agency of poor whites in the pre-Revolutionary era.[27]

What we do know without doubt is that poor whites made up the majority of those who served—willingly and unwillingly—in the militias and armies that repelled British forces during the war. Yet despite their service to the new nation, in the wake of the revolution poor whites were again marked off as inferior and unworthy whites—as social outcasts whose possible roles in and contributions to the newly formed nation were deeply in question. *Cracker*, with its connotations of criminality and backwardness, continued to be used throughout the revolutionary era and into the early decades of the new republic. However, it was soon joined by new boundary terms that differentiated among whites.

Dirt-Eaters and Poor White Trash

Comic portrayals of poor whites, not seen since *crackers* eclipsed *lubbers* in the mid-eighteenth century, again became part of the set of collective representation in the early nineteenth century when Georgia lawyer, judge, and humorist Augustus Baldwin Longstreet first published his collection of stories *Georgia Scenes* in 1833. Longstreet's (1835) stories about "Ransy Sniffle"—"a sprout from Richmond who, in his earlier days, had fed copiously on red clay and blackberries" (54)—gained instant popularity and remained widely known well into the twentieth century. Through Sniffle, Longstreet introduced many readers, in both the North and South, as well as transatlantically, to the southern "clay eater." The

Ransy Sniffle, Augustus Baldwin Longstreet's (1835) dirt-eating cracker, the "sprout of Richmond, who in his earlier days, had fed copiously on red clay and blackberries." Note the distended limbs, the misshapen head, and the pugnacious attitude.

"dirt-eater" popularized by Longstreet was a grotesque comic character notable for his poor diet, his physical deformities, his laziness, apathy, and low intelligence, and his oddly colored skin, which was described as "tallow-colored." Of all of the different characteristics attributed here, it is difficult to gauge which might have been most salient. How are we to understand the attention paid to the color of the clay eater's skin? Under present-day regimes of perception, wouldn't this qualify as a racial observation? Perhaps, but in a historical context such as this, where the meanings of boundary lines and distinctions may be obscured by our present-day perceptions, what exactly constitutes a racial observation can be a matter of guesswork.

The clay eater was used by Longstreet and later by other humorists to amuse and disgust a growing audience of middle-class readers. The accounts were amusing because Longstreet wrote in the venerable satirical tradition of old southwest humorists (Blair 1953; Lynn 1959; and Inge and Piacentino 2001), and disgusting because, as a dietary habit, dirt eating was socially unacceptable and culturally offensive. The act of eating dirt—of incorporating what does not belong into the physical body—was for many a powerfully symbolic transgression of boundary lines, one that stigmatyped the entire region.[28] For this reason, according to one observer, "Southerners did not care to have the local perversion of dirt-eating noised abroad." Despite their wishes, however, through Ransy Sniffle, dirt eating became in the early nineteenth century "the mark of poor-white depravity most dwelt upon by Northern and foreign observers" (McIlwaine 1939: 57). The popularity of Longstreet's writings ensured that the clay eater served as a humorous and disgusting image of the southern poor white in the early republic.[29]

Coincident with the popularization of the clay eater was the arrival of a new boundary term: *poor white trash*. Frequently transcribed as *po' white trash* or simply shortened to *white trash*, the term must have been a compelling phrase: in just a few short decades, it rose from relative obscurity to become commonplace. The earliest recorded written use occurs in 1833, the same year that Longstreet published his Ransy Sniffle tales.

That year, English actress and vocalist Fanny Kemble toured the United States and, upon reaching the nation's capital, dined at the home of Richard and Mary Caton in nearby Baltimore. Mary Caton was the eldest daughter of Charles Carroll of Carrollton. Carroll—devout Irish Catholic, prominent statesman and slaveholder, last surviving signer of the Declaration of Independence—was at the time of his death, just a few weeks before, the wealthiest man in the United States. Over a lavish dinner in a large, Georgian townhouse, Mary Caton entertained Kemble "very much" with an account of "the slaves on their estates," whom, Caton said, "she found the best and most faithful servants in the world." "Being born upon the land," Caton explained, "there exists among them something of the old spirit of clanship, and 'our house,' 'our family,' are the terms by which they designate their owners. In the south, there are no servants but blacks; for the greater proportion of domestics being slaves, all species of servitude whatever is looked upon as a degradation; and the slaves themselves entertain the very highest contempt for white servants, whom they designate as 'poor white trash'" (Kemble 1835: 242; Clinton 2002: 62). At first glance, the passage appears somewhat inconsistent. Indeed, it appears to contradict itself, stating that in the South, all servants are black, but then going on in the same breath to speak of white servants in Maryland. However, when viewed as a social document that speaks to the everyday symbolic boundaries of the American elite, this passage yields several noteworthy insights. Such an interpretation requires exploring the social and historical conditions that surround this utterance.

In simple and literal terms, here is what the passage says: black slaves regarded with contempt the white domestic workers who labored in servitude.[30] This straightforward reading of the passage's manifest content, however, raises more questions than it answers. Given the time and place, it is rather unclear to whom the term *white servants* (and thus *poor white trash*) would have referred. Were these indentured white servants? It is unlikely. Indentured servitude, while once quite common in Maryland, would have been uncommon in the early 1800s, although not unheard of. It would also have been uncommon (although less so) for the term *white servants* to be applied to waged, "free laboring" whites. Even a successful determination of the exact nature of their labor—whether it was bonded or waged ("free")—still leaves unanswered the question of the status accorded to that group of laborers in early-nineteenth-century Maryland.

There is also the unanswered question of gender: were the white servants referred to male or female, or both? In the household economy of nineteenth-century Maryland plantations, the terms *domestics* and *servants*, when applied to whites, would have included men and women alike, and in a typical early-nineteenth-century elite household, there would have been about an equal number of each. In the early 1800s, domestic service was not just women's work.[31]

There is, moreover, the unresolved question of nationalism and citizenship. Given the time and place, the white servants were almost certainly Irish immigrants. Baltimore in the 1830s was home to one of the largest Irish immigrant populations in the United States. Was the status of these white servants as noncitizen "foreigners" part of what rendered them trash in the eyes of black slaves? Did the term originate as an early expression of black American xenophobia and nativism?

Furthermore, did the term originate with black slaves on the plantations and estates, or did it arise among the urban free blacks in Baltimore? What group of blacks was doing the naming and why? Was this a boundary being drawn within the master's house? In the fields? Did field and house slaves alike use the term? It is impossible to know, but it is clear that black slaves in northern Maryland were by no means the first to note that there were in the slave states poor whites whose means and standard of living was well below that of other whites. Blacks and whites of all classes used the earlier boundary terms *poor whites* and *crackers* to distinguish low-status whites from other whites.

However one might ultimately answer these questions about the origins and referents of the term, it is clear that upper-class whites found the term exceedingly useful and well worth repeating. Whites quickly appropriated the term and pushed it into a wider circulation than it would have otherwise had. Blacks may have invented and used the term *poor white trash* as an act of symbolic violence and micropolitical protest, but it was literate, middle-class and elite whites who invested its meaning with social power, granting it the powers of social stigma and prejudice and enforcing its discriminatory effects with regard to labor. In the larger social structure, black slaves were hardly in a position of power to directly diminish the quality of life for poor whites, but higher status whites certainly were. *Poor white trash* must have seemed to many of them an apt term for those whites who did not rise or live up to their ideals of industry, laboring not at all, or only in the most degrading jobs, toiling beneath or alongside the slaves.[32]

While the full meanings of historical status distinctions are now mostly lost, turning to the broader historical context can help reconstruct them. Kemble's passage relies for its sense upon a series of distinct categories of service laborers. The categories, however, remain hazily defined. "Black servants," "domestics," "servants," "slaves," and "white servants" are all mentioned in a somewhat confusing array, offering some suggestion of just how complex and finely articulated the social hierarchies of the antebellum plantation house were.

The confusion evident in the passage was likely a consequence of the fact that white servants were, at the time, ascribed a deeply ambiguous, liminal status. Catherine Sedgwick and other early American white middle-class feminists wrote extensively about "the servant problem" in the new republic, by which they meant not only a shortage of domestic laborers, but also the growing tendency of domestics to assert their feelings and ideas of independence. Sedgwick's 1835 description of white servants as "republican independent dependents" accurately captured the liminality and ambiguity of this group and spoke to its political mood. In the 1820s, the rise of Jacksonian democracy, with its elimination of property requirements for voting and the concomitant extension of the franchise to virtually all adult white males, had been accompanied by a rise in class pride and sensitivity among white servants. By the 1830s, white servants become famous for their touchiness on matters of status and class. As the social boundaries of class were widely perceived to be opening and becoming less rigid and aristocratic, white workers and domestics began to demand greater respect. To call a white person a servant or to require the use of the terms *master* or *mistress* was considered a grave insult by white domestics; scores of contemporary writers described the peevish reactions of white domestics who fiercely refused the demeaning labels, insisting instead upon being referred to as "help."[33] In short, the leveling of social distinctions among whites that was taking place during the early decades of the nineteenth century was widely perceived by contemporary elites to have as one of its primary consequences a rise in insubordination among the lower classes.

This historical situation suggests the likelihood that blacks, in labeling white servants *poor white trash*, were reacting with resentment and hostility to white domestics' claims to superiority. They were, after all, doing similar if not identical kinds of work, but the shifting political landscape meant that white servants, despite their immigrant status, could demand and reasonably expect to be granted limited privileges over blacks. In a world of scarce resources, where none of the minority groups had much power to enact social boundaries, such contests over status and privilege would have been especially fierce.[34] And 1830s Maryland was a place where these contests played out in very unusual ways.

Maryland was demographically unique among antebellum southern slave states: no other witnessed such a sharp and consequential rise in the numbers of free blacks and the numbers of free white laborers alike. Between 1820 and 1840, only Virginia had as many free blacks; by 1840, Virginia's free black people consisted of 10 percent of the total black population, while in Maryland, they constituted 41 percent. Such a large number of free blacks was a major source of anxiety for Maryland slaveholders, who feared the increasing visibility of free blacks would embolden slaves to open rebellion. By the eve of the Civil War in 1860, there were almost as many free blacks as slaves (Fields 1985: 1–6). This population growth and shift was particularly dramatic in the region surrounding Baltimore City and County—the area with which Mary Caton and her many slaves would have been most familiar. Between 1790 and 1850, the diversifying and increasingly industrial economy of Baltimore drew people into northern Maryland at a brisk pace, the regional population growing by an astounding 228 percent. Of all the demographic shifts that accompanied this ferocious growth, one of the most dramatic was the sharp increase in the number of free blacks. Maryland's rising free black population resulted in part from an increase in the manumission of slaves, but it also resulted from the increased abolitionist activities of slaves themselves. Baltimore was, after all, a major stop on the Underground Railroad.

Maryland's white population was unique among slave states as well. Between 1820 and 1830, the white population in Baltimore City and County grew from 72,399 to 92,329 — an increase of 28 percent. And there was an important third group, albeit very small in proportion to the whole population, who were counted separately in the census: immigrants. Here again, Maryland was unique. No other slave state in the antebellum period saw the high levels of immigration Maryland did. From 1820 to 1830, in the category "aliens—foreigners not naturalized" the numbers grew from 1,821 to 2,707, an increase of 49 percent.[35]

These three demographic trends—sharp increases in the number and proportion of free blacks and European immigrants, and a moderate rise in the number and proportion of free whites—are a crucial part of the background in the complicated story that *poor white trash* is trying to tell. Black domestics (the house servants who had a measure of status over other black slaves) and wage-laboring free blacks were now faced with a new status threat in the form of white domestics and immigrant laborers. In the realm of domestic service, the privileges of serving in the master's house would no longer be reserved for favored blacks, but would be shared with whites. In local industries, jobs typically done by blacks would now be open to competition by whites.[36] This newly created competition over scarce resources and over jobs would have inspired a range of responses, from jealousy and fear to greed and anger, animating prejudice and creating social distance between the groups.[37] In *poor white trash*, it also served to create a new boundary marker.

Why, one wonders, did Mary Caton trouble to share with Kemble her story about black contempt for certain whites? Perhaps she was prompted by a specific question or remark; perhaps she thought the anecdote would interest her English dinner guest, whose sensibilities, she knew, were sympathetic to abolitionism; perhaps the dinner conversation touched on a recently proposed British law, passed later that year, that would abolish slavery throughout the British Empire; perhaps it was even prompted by the recent reelection of Andrew Jackson, an event that deeply disturbed the aristocratic Catons. Whatever the occasion for its telling, the anecdote was surely intended to serve subtle but clear notice to Kemble that, in Mary Caton's opinion, if there was anything wrong with slavery it was not enmity and hostility between slaveholders and their human property. Instead, Caton suggested, it was the conflict between slaves and the lowest class of whites that constituted the more significant site of social friction and conflict. The group, not the social structure, was to blame for the strife. In her eyes, it was the poor white trash — not the slave system — that constituted the most pressing social problem.

In the rapidly changing environment of early-nineteenth-century northern Maryland, the problem of social order became acute. The influx of European immigrants and the sharp increase in the number of free blacks meant that once relatively well defined and fixed boundaries separating black and white, free and unfree, were now shifting and losing their definition. The arrival of new people occasioned new interactions and, inevitably, new conflicts over basic social and cultural resources. Out of these new contacts and conflicts, new identities were formed and forged through the development, elaboration, and extension of symbolic and social boundaries.

The terms considered above — *lubber, cracker, clay-eater,* and *poor white trash* — were not, before the 1840s, part of any national popular culture. While *lubber* passed quickly into obsolescence, the others remained common expressions only at the regional level. Yet by the end of the Civil War, there were likely very few Americans that had not heard the term *poor white trash* and fewer still that failed to grasp its pejorative meaning and stigmatyping effects. *Poor white trash,* in particular, morphed from a boundary term that had a specifically southern referent to one that became a more general, nonlocalized term for poor rural whites in every part of the nation. How do we explain this shift? The next chapter explores this question in detail.

chapter two

Imagining Poor Whites in the Antebellum South

Abolitionist and Pro-Slavery Fictions

In the colonial and early national eras, as we have seen, particular populations of colonists and citizens were stigmatyped and treated as immoral, lazy, and dirty and, alternatively, as dangerous, threatening, and dishonorable. The term that came to describe and collectively represent these people, *poor white trash*, may have derived much of its rhetorical power from its symbolic union of opposites. It suggested a paradoxical situation: if whiteness bespoke purity and godliness, then *poor white trash* implied an ungodly, desacralized, polluted whiteness. As a social category, it was laden with contradictory meanings.

The period from the 1840s to the end of Reconstruction in the late 1870s was a time when social observers began to actively debate the reasons for the impoverished condition and poor treatment of the people described by this term. During these years of intense political and cultural upheaval and violent sectional conflict, social observers both in the United States and abroad offered a variety of explanations for the deplorable conditions of poor white trash. The explanations drew upon preexisting folk concepts, literary creations, new scientific theories of human development, and the infant disciplines of sociology and anthropology. The aim of these explanations was to make sense of what was, given popular assumptions about the superiority of light-skinned peoples, otherwise difficult to explain: some people of northern European descent, particularly but not exclusively those in southern states, were clearly less than superior — were even inferior — to blacks and Indians.

Beginning in the 1850s, many different forms of print media became increasingly available to middle- and upper-class literate audiences. Travel writers, novelists, playwrights, and journalists offered sketches of the character and living conditions of poor white trash and crackers to hungry consumers of the printed word. Cartoonists and artists drew satirical and realist portraits as well. Northern readers consumed the vast majority of these popular novels, magazines, and journals, but educated and literate southerners also formed an important core audience.[1] Through these depictions, both fictional and nonfictional, audiences were offered expert and authoritative opinions on the many causes—biological, moral, social, political, economic, and cultural—of poor white degeneracy.

Not all the experts agreed with each other. In fact, as the sectional conflict over slavery sharpened and northerners and southerners regarded each other with increasing hostility, broad disagreement emerged over how to comprehend the existence of poor white trash and their assorted kin, called "crackers," "clay eaters," "poor whites," "low down" or "mean whites," "po' buckras," and other names too varied and obscure to mention here.[2]

Two major groups vied for interpretive authority: antislavery abolitionists, citing the narratives and testimonies of former slaves, criticized the evils of the slave system and deplored its degrading and dehumanizing effects on the nonslaveholding whites of the South. Poor whites, by this logic, were victims of a system that caused dishonorable behavior. Abolitionists argued, moreover, that southern poor whites had been fooled into helping perpetuate the very system that denied them any chance to be truly free—freedom, in this instance, understood in an economic sense as the ability to sell one's labor to the highest bidder. The poor white trash of the South were, according to abolitionists, redeemable through industrial capitalist labor and proper education. What was required was the abolition of the slave system and its replacement with an economic system of free labor for all workers, black and white.

Upholding the long line of interpretation established by William Byrd and other southern elites, a second group composed of proslavery secessionists and southern partisans saw no fault in the slave system that, they believed, reflected the natural order of things. Instead, they insisted that the poor white trash had only themselves to blame for their condition. If certain whites had sunk below the level of social respectability, it was due to their own physical and moral laziness, a laziness that, many would eventually argue, was less cultural than physical or biological in origin.

Furthermore, they argued that society required different levels of social distinction and achievement and that dependent and delinquent classes were an unavoidable — even desirable — outcome of human history and civilization. Yet, rather than viewing class inequalities as an impediment to democracy, southerner apologists tended to view them as important boundaries that gave order and discipline to what would otherwise be chaotic mob rule. Moreover, secessionists argued that a key piece of evidence exonerating the slave system was to be found in studies showing poor white trash could be found in free states as well. These southerners tended to view America's poor white trash as undeserving of democratic privileges and unable to bear the rights and responsibilities of other white American citizens. The root of this backwardness, they argued, was not the economic system, although they expressed the collective opinion that the ravages of capitalism would surely worsen the conditions of poor whites. The real cause of poor white degeneracy, they maintained, was "tainted blood" and was therefore not likely to be affected by a change of social or economic systems, or the abolition of the "peculiar institution." This was a powerful argument.

As abolitionists competed with secessionists for the authority to impose their particular interpretation and definition of the situation poor whites found themselves in, *poor white trash* became a symbol of national importance and recognition, but one whose meaning was hotly contested. Once a term of abuse confined to black vernacular speech, *poor white trash* entered the national lexicon and did so as a national problem. In order to explore how *poor white trash* was constructed and situated as a national problem, this chapter examines some of the era's shifting symbolic boundaries then surveys and analyzes some of the period's different representations of poor whites.[3]

City, Country, and Frontier

The rhetoric of both abolitionists and secessionists was conditioned, of course, by a preexisting set of intellectual commitments and cultural debates. Boundaries of geography, of class, and of race all shifted during this time, influencing the ways in which white trash would come to be understood and talked about. Long-held assumptions about the relationship between urban and rural cultures and emerging perspectives about metropolitan cores versus rural peripheries shaped the ways that northerners represented the South and its inhabitants, and the ways that southerners responded to those portrayals.[4]

When, in the *Communist Manifesto*, Marx and Engels (1848/1998) spoke of the redeeming role of the bourgeoisie in having "rescued a considerable part of the population from the idiocy of rural life" (40), they were giving voice to an idea with a complicated history. The conception of rural life and rural people as fundamentally different from urban life and urban people can be found in texts from classical antiquity. The comparisons were not always invidious. In the United States, however, a national preoccupation with rural people and rural life as backward and regressive, premodern and therefore unenlightened, began to take hold during the antebellum period. This view has persisted into our present historical era (Ching and Creed 1997).

Coming as it did in the historical context of political and social upheavals wrought by rapid industrialization and urbanization in Western and northern Europe, Marx and Engel's passing comment about idiocy is indicative of the complicated ways in which *rural life* has been invoked as a foil for stabilizing and bolstering inchoate, fragile, urban, and, above all, *modern* identities.[5] Again, rural/urban comparisons were not always unfavorable to rural areas. For instance, cities were frequently viewed as places of corruption and decay, and country life was often valued for its salutary effects and romanticized as a place of bucolic simplicity. In Europe, from the end of the eighteenth century until the middle of the nineteenth century, *the country* and *nature* were the idealized locales and revered objects of Romanticism, the broad, reactionary cultural movement that formed in response to the growing power of industrialism, technology, and science. Nevertheless, from the 1850s on, the countryside and its inhabitants were increasingly viewed as primitive, dirty, and hopelessly backward, left behind in the wake of progress and modernity. When it came to issues of culture and political life, the countryside was seen as the locus of tradition and conservatism.[6]

In the United States, the opposition between city and countryside was disrupted by a third term: *the frontier*.[7] Frederick Jackson Turner's concept of "the frontier," first articulated in 1893, challenged the elite, urban, institutional, and Eastern biases of U.S. historiography dominant at that time. Turner reasoned that "the frontier"—a space he described as empty and "free," functioned as a crucible of "Americanization," where "the wilderness masters the colonist." He attempted, with remarkable success, a revaluation of the frontier as a site of both heroic struggles against the forces of capitalism and agrarianism, and ironically, as a necessary staging era for the expansion of both. Turner's frontier hero was restless, constantly moving to stay ahead of the advancing forces of both farmers and businessmen, evading the "soft," feminizing traps of European influence and American domesticity and forging new pathways for "manly" democratic independence. Westward progress was seen by Turner as an essential element in constructing U.S. democracy, as it produced a primitive but healthy individualism, marked by suspicion toward centralized power and opposition to direct forms of social control (Turner 1894: 199).[8] Turner's irascible frontier character resembled Jefferson's yeoman republican, but with a loaded shotgun and a very bad attitude. This mythic character formed from the core image of Jacksonian democracy has established forms of white male self-fashioning that still persist strongly today.[9] Turner's image of the old frontiersman resonated symbolically with certain aspects of the cracker and poor white trash. In essence, Turner, rather than seeing poor frontier whites as marginal actors in American history, positions them as central elements in the development of our national character and political ideology.

Class, Status, and Region

In the mid-nineteenth-century United States, class boundaries, along with geographic boundaries, underwent significant shifts. The accelerated development of industrial capitalism and the market revolution; the rapid urbanization that accompanied both of these; the sharp rise in immigration, particularly from Ireland, and the continuing ideological influence of Jacksonian impulses marked this period as one of major economic, social, and political instability. Such instabilities are often accompanied by significant shifts in identity and community.[10] In addition to these transformations, the mid-nineteenth century also witnessed the rise of a distinct middle class on the eastern seaboard and in the Midwest. This group self-consciously nurtured its identity in a nascent culture of professionalism and, as an embattled buffer class, strongly valued group cohesion, order, and solidarity. Entrepreneurial, oriented toward progress through education, science, and technology, but deeply religious and moralistic, the mid-nineteenth-century American middle class of the East and Midwest exhibited both progressive and conservative tendencies. Its members differentiated themselves from upper and lower social classes in many different ways. They symbolized their class identities in part through their carefully chosen habits of consumption, habits made possible by the rapid expansion of markets. They eschewed, for example, both the opulent ornamentation they could not afford and the bare floors and cheap furnishings they could. Instead, their clean, modest, whitewashed and carpeted homes cultivated a sense of balance and moral propriety they believed was lacking in both the upper and lower social extremes.[11]

Boundaries of class varied sharply from place to place, with regional variation in class relations following the variation in economic systems. As a result, things were different in the American South and the frontier West.[12] While by the 1850s the shifting class boundaries and conflicts of early industrial capitalism predominated in the North, boundaries in the slave South had developed according to an entirely different historical dynamic and logic. The South was overwhelmingly agrarian and rural, with few immigrants and lacking any substantial middle class.

Nonslaveholding whites comprised the vast numerical majority of antebellum southerners. Population figures are imprecise, but a number of sources offer the following distribution: Of a total of 12 million people in the southern states in the 1840s, 4 million were classified as black and 8 million as white. Of the whites, less than 50,000 were slave owners with twenty or more slaves; more than 75 percent of whites owned no slaves at all. In this highly stratified society, black slaves were, for the most part, formally excluded from owning property or selling their labor (see Linden 1946; Den Hollander 1934; and Hahn 1983).

In most areas of the South, poor whites, although formally included in property rights, found it difficult to acquire property or to sell their labor: they had little capital to accomplish the former and, faced with an economic system that exploited the coerced labor of slaves, they had few opportunities to realize the latter. Under slavery, poor whites occupied a very unusual position: formally included in the system, they were in practical terms redundant labor. While slaveholders would sometimes hire white workers to perform tasks considered too dangerous or risky for slaves, in general, poor, nonslaveholding whites were left to fend for themselves, a situation that, as we have seen, earned them pity and contempt from black slaves.

Yet in the mid-nineteenth-century South, conflicts between slaveholding and nonslaveholding whites were less openly antagonistic and less prolonged than were conflicts between white urban workers and their bosses in the North. The reasons for this relative lack of class antagonism, which has been frequently noted, are still debated by southern historians. Some have argued that the divides of class and status in the South were bridged by a common "cracker culture" that united whites, both rich and poor, through a sense of shared belonging and common purpose. Others argue that the existence of a color line granted poor whites a sense of racial privilege that compensated them for class disadvantages and that this "psychological wage" bought their quiescence and solidarity. Still others have noted that southern poor whites, because they were separated into small rural communities, did not have opportunities to join in forging an aggrieved identity, a necessary precondition for most group-based collective action. Whatever the reasons—and these are all plausible—the antebellum political system succeeded for as long as it did in large part because it managed to successfully contain and repress the conflicts and social discontent that arose among whites. As a consequence, nonslaveholding whites of this era did not establish a strong, durable sense of group identity in opposition to slaveholding whites. Or if they did, they seldom acted on it.[13]

Racial Schemas

Racial boundary lines during this period were redrawn in ways that reflected new social and historical dynamics. The so-called Indian Question and slavery were primary historical impulses behind the mid-nineteenth-century development of racial science in the United States, a development that found expression in what is now known as the American school of ethnology, an important intellectual precursor to modern-day anthropology (Bieder 1986; Rogin 1975; Gossett 1977: 32–83; Horsman 1981; Otter 1999).

In the 1850s, ethnology was structured by three major debates. Before the 1859 publication of Charles Darwin's *Origin of Species*, there was an extensive debate regarding human origins. Monogenists took the view that all humans descended from the line of Adam and Eve and that observable racial differences were entirely due to environmental factors, particularly climate. Polygenists argued that observable differences were due in fact to differences in biological inheritance and natural hierarchies. In the early nineteenth century, polygenesis fit well the prevailing classificatory ideal suffusing natural history, ethnology, and biology and was widely accepted in scientific circles, eventually giving rise in the late nineteenth century to the evolutionary idea of human subspecies (Gossett 1977: 44–51, 58–60; Goldberg 1993: 63–66). Most crucially, for most of the nineteenth century, polygenesis formed the basis for scientific defenses of and justifications for slavery and Native American genocide, since polygenists viewed both Africans and Indians as separate, inferior species.

Darwin's *Origins* eventually quieted the polygenists, but it helped give rise to a second debate within ethnology about whether or not as a species humans were evolving to a higher stage of development. So-called degenerationists argued that some humanoid species were in decline due to poor breeding practices—specifically, miscegenation—and poor environmental conditions. Others took instead a progressive, Whiggish view, finding evidence for human ascendancy in the technological and social advancement of peoples all over the globe. A third ethnological debate took shape over the question of whether heredity or environment was the more decisive factor in determining racial characteristics. Here, for the first time, the age-old question of nature versus nurture was now being carried out in explicitly scientific and evolutionary terms.

From these key debates arose racial schemas that gave new shape and definition to the ideology and practice of white supremacy, the crucial philosophical justification for extending citizenship rights and political freedoms to those of European descent, while denying them to "non-whites."[14] *Race* operated as the legitimation for white dominance and social inequality along lines of color. As many historians have shown, the antebellum years saw crucial contests over the meaning and significance of white supremacy, and those contests focused to a great extent on the status and place of Indians, blacks, and, in the West and Southwest, those of Mexican and Asian descent (Almaguer 1994; N. Foley 1997). As we will see, the image of the southern poor white also played an important if ambiguous role in establishing the ideology of white supremacy, a role that has too often been overlooked. As new racial schemas began to emerge, scientists, intellectuals, and educated observers remained deeply puzzled about how and where to place poor whites.

Southern Literary Fictions

Writers of southern fiction in the antebellum era focused a good deal of attention on the conundrum of the southern poor white. Under the logic of white supremacy, wherein all whites are imagined to be superior to all people of color, the low social status, impoverishment, and immoral and lazy behavior of *poor whites* were damning evidence to the contrary. *Poor white trash* required explanation — how could a free white person sink so low as to be beneath a black slave?

Beginning in the 1820s, the literary fictions of antebellum southern writers like William Gilmore Simms and John Pendleton Kennedy presented the *poor white* to literate audiences in both the North and the South.[15] Although these and other southern antebellum authors varied in their views on slavery, they were united by a shared sense of conservative paternalism, one typical of antebellum planter elites. In their view, "natural inferiors," by whom they primarily meant women, blacks, and poor whites, should defer to their "natural superiors," the white men who could protect and lead them. Given its historical timing, antebellum southern fiction was, in political terms, a largely conservative reaction against what its authors considered the excesses of Jacksonian democracy.

Simms, Kennedy, and other well-known writers forged a genre of fiction, "the plantation novel," that took the form of the historical romance. The typical plantation novel featured heroic male protagonists from the planter class, who defended planter class women from the violent, sexual predations of poor whites and upstart, middle-class white men. While these authors had mixed things to say about the few middle-class white men that populated their narratives, they reserved their full contempt for the poorest whites. Throughout the genre, planter men were characterized as manly, courageous, honorable, and physically strong, while poor whites were consistently portrayed as rude, brutal, and criminal. Kennedy (1835/1866) offered a typical description: "The person of this individual might be said, from its want of symmetry and from a certain slovenly and ungraceful stoop in the head and shoulders, to have been protracted rather than tall. It better deserved the description of sinewy rather than muscular, and communicated the idea of toughness in a greater degree than strength" (cited in Tracy 1995: 186). Kennedy and other authors used to great literary effect fictive descriptions that focused attention on the corporeal stigma marks—sinewy, distorted, asymmetrical bodies, for example—that suggested that lineal degeneracy and biological inferiority were the root of the poor white trash problem. As was the case with Longstreet's (1835/1992) Ransy Sniffle, the dirt-eater, the outer deformities of the flesh were supposed to mirror the inner moral depravity of the poor white.

Beginning in 1856, William Gilmore Simms offered even more invidious portraits of poor whites. In two novels set during the American Revolution, Simms depicted outlaw gangs of poor whites, descriptions that bore close resemblance to those proffered by Cochrane. However, in Simms's novels, these criminal gangs, rather than defying British authorities as Cochrane's crackers did, allied with them, aiding the British troops by attacking planters loyal to the American bid for independence. "Rude, irregular, untrained and lawless," Simms (1856/1882) wrote, "the swarthy outlaws . . . [were] a fearless gang of blackguards. They could fight better than pray; could more easily strike than serve; their laws readily yielded to their moods" (cited in Tracy 1995: 189).

Simms had equal contempt for law-abiding poor white frontiersmen, whom he collectively described in 1840 as "squatters chiefly without means, tastes, education, or sensibility; rough, rude people; a people particularly fitted for the conquest of savages and savage lands, but utterly incapable of appreciating an art so exquisite and intellectual as that of the legitimate drama" (cited in Tracy 1995: 189), Simms's debasing depictions of frontier whites were deeply at odds with the heroic images crafted by other American writers and storytellers—the Natty Bumppos, Davey Crocketts, and Huck Finns celebrated in dime novels and the penny press. The images offered by Simms, Kennedy, and others aggressively countered the popular Jacksonian narrative about the frontiersman as the authentic source and true embodiment of the pioneering American spirit of independence and democracy. This departure from the prevailing symbolism may have been one reason southern novels did not attract larger followings than they did. Nevertheless, the shared representations of poor white trash offered by southern antebellum writers did enter into the emergent national popular culture in a significant way during this period.[16] American readers now had a dual image to contend with: poor frontier white as hero or poor white trash as villain. As this complex stigmatype proved ideologically useful to both northerners and southerners, it appeared with greater frequency in the national popular culture. No longer merely a regional portrayal of a stigmatized social people, the *poor white* began to emerge as a nationally recognizable character, even as its meaning was subject to debate and differing interpretations.[17]

Abolitionist Fictions

Many of the perceptions about poor white trash that were popularized through southern antebellum fiction were shared by northern and southern abolitionist writers — including the most famous among them, Harriet Beecher Stowe. Stowe arguably does more to popularize, nationalize, and internationalize the phrase *poor white trash* than anyone in antebellum history. While the term did not appear in her famous *Uncle Tom's Cabin* (1852), it occupied a prominent place in her subsequent *Key to Uncle Tom's Cabin* (1854), where an entire chapter was devoted to the subject. The term is also a key figure in her second novel *Dred: A Tale of the Great Dismal Swamp* (1856), which while not a runaway bestseller like *Uncle Tom's Cabin*, nonetheless sold thousands of copies in the United States and England, where it was favorably reviewed in the *London Times*. Like Simms, Kennedy, and other novelists, Stowe regarded the South's poor white trash as violent and criminal, as a "miserable class of whites [that] form, in all the Southern States, a material for the most horrible and ferocious of mobs. Utterly ignorant, and inconceivably brutal, they are like some blind, savage monster, that, when aroused, tramples heedlessly over everything in its way" (1854: 368). In Stowe's estimation, the South was home to "a poor white population as degraded and brutal as ever existed in any of the most crowded districts of Europe" (365).

Where Stowe differed from southern antebellum fiction writers — and it was for her a crucial difference — was in analyzing the *cause* of poor white depravity. The cause was not, as Kennedy and others had suggested, to be found in the degenerate body of the poor white, but in the economic and political system of the slave South: "The institution of slavery has produced not only heathenish, degraded, miserable slaves, but it produces a class of white people who are, by universal admission, more heathenish, degraded, and miserable," she wrote. The slave system, Stowe argued, established three important conditions for the ongoing degradation of southern poor whites: "1. The distribution of the land into large plantations, and the consequent sparseness of settlement, make any system of common school education impracticable. 2. The same cause operates with regard to the preaching of the Gospel. 3. The degradation of the idea of labor, which results inevitably from enslaving the working class, operates to a great extent in preventing respectable working men of the middling classes from settling or remaining in slave States" (1854: 365). For Stowe, the South's poor white trash suffered primarily from a lack of education and religious training, a situation brought about by the plantation system. Furthermore, the entire South suffered from the absence of dignified free white labor.

After Stowe, the idea that the southern poor white was an unfortunate victim of the slave system informed nearly every abolitionist account.[18] In 1856, George Weston, a northern abolitionist and Republican, echoed Stowe's sentiments when he testified before Congress that

> the whites of the South not connected with the ownership or management of slaves, constituting not far from three-fourths of the whole number of whites, confined at least to the low wages of agricultural labor, and partly cut off even from this by the degradation of a companionship with black slaves, retire to the outskirts of civilization, where they lead a semi-savage life, sinking deeper and more hopelessly into barbarism with each succeeding generation. The slave owner takes at first all the best lands, and finally all the lands susceptible of regular cultivation; and the poor whites, thrown back upon the hills and upon the sterile soils — mere squatters without

energy enough to acquire the title even to the cheap lands they occupy, without roads, and at length, without even a desire for education, become the miserable beings described to us. (1856: 5)

When it came to explaining the poor white, abolitionist rhetoric focused on causal explanations that emphasized not hereditary but social, economic, and political (i.e., environmental) factors. Yet the abolitionist writers maintained a complicated and ambivalent set of ideas that reflected the shifting boundaries of group identity in the mid-nineteenth century. It was not that abolitionists believed that blacks were equal to whites, intellectually or otherwise. Many, perhaps most, believed they were not. Instead, abolitionists argued that race had no place in a free and democratic society as a dividing line. Economic and social policies and practices, they argued, should be race-neutral and egalitarian. Yet despite these racially egalitarian values, much abolitionist rhetoric exhibited a strong residual commitment to racialist thinking and a palpable devotion to white supremacy.[19]

Northern writers with abolitionist sympathies extended their arguments to include all the stigmatizing labels attached to poor whites that were prevalent in the popular national culture, viewing them collectively as degraded specimens of the proud white race. J. S. Bradford (1870: 457), writing in *Lippincott's Magazine*, noted that

in Virginia, he is known as the "mean white" or "poor white" and among the negroes as "poor white trash." In North Carolina he flourishes under the title of "conch." In South Carolina, he is called "low-downer." In Georgia and Florida, we salute him with the crisp and significant appellation of "Cracker." But in all these localities, and under all these names, he is, with slight differences, the same being . . . [of] the genus Homo, though from the effects of long generations of ignorance, neglect, degradation, and poverty, it has developed few of the higher qualities of the race to which it belongs.[20]

Perhaps the most famous public speaker of this era, Bayard Taylor, who as a youth embraced Quaker precepts and attended abolitionist meetings, wrote in his 1861 lecture "The American People" that "the white trash of the South represented the most depraved class of whites I have ever seen. Idle, shiftless, filthy in their habits, aggressive, with no regard for the rights of others, these barbarians seem to have united all the vices of the negro with those of their own race, and they almost shake our faith in the progressive instinct of the Anglo-Saxon."[21] Here as in countless other examples what is most striking in these abolitionist representations, besides the sweeping generalizations about poor whites, is the heightened sense of moral repugnance and disgust that energizes and animates the descriptions. Talk of *poor white trash* consistently provoked strong emotions of loathing and contempt, mitigated only by the occasional expression of sympathy. This disgust, one that was shared by virtually every commentator, became a durable feature of the image and one that enabled those who used the term to unite in a shared experience of moral superiority and moral outrage and simultaneously to absolve themselves of responsibility for what was a deplorable state of affairs.[22]

Gradually, as abolitionists succeeded in melding antislavery rhetoric with the emergent white republicanism that emphasized free labor and free soil, their interpretation of the causes of poor white trash gained wide currency and acceptance in the North. However, this new interpretation did not so much supplant or overwrite previous meanings of *poor white, cracker*, and *dirt-eater* as it did assume its place alongside them. When it came to thinking about poor whites, Americans now had a variety of different stigmatypical images to choose from, as well as an appealing and intriguing set of opposing explanations. It is doubtful that many Americans took the time to sort out what they believed and disbelieved about the social realities of poor white Americans. Instead, as the excerpt from Bradford's article suggests, they tended to use the terms indiscriminately and interchangeably, resulting in an emotionally resonant, polysemous image, one that shared some features with the images of other despised social groups. Under these conditions, the phrase *poor white trash* further proved its ideological utility for abolitionists: just as it demonstrated the immorality of the slave system, it also helped explain how the frontier was settled and added moral weight to the claim that the West must be won for freedom, not slavery.

Secessionist Fictions

Ironically, the only works of nonfiction that offered a serious intellectual challenge to the abolitionist line regarding poor whites were written by sociologists. George Fitzhugh's book, *Sociology for the South, or The Failure of Free Society* (1854), was the first book with the word *sociology* in its title to be published in America. Fitzhugh followed this work with a spirited and highly polemic defense of slavery titled *Cannibals All! Or, Slaves without Masters* (1856/1960). In this latter work, Fitzhugh does not make mention of poor white trash, nor does he devote much discussion to nonslaveholding whites of the antebellum South, but his general argument suggests that he regarded the poor white problem in hereditary terms: "The order and subordination observable in the physical, animal, and human world," he wrote, "show that some are formed for higher, others for lower stations — the few to command, the many to obey. We conclude that about nineteen out of twenty individuals have 'a natural and inalienable' right to be . . . slaves" (69). Fitzhugh's research and scholarship, which was relatively careful and rigorous for his time, was sometimes obscured by his vituperative rhetoric and extremist conclusions. But his work was nonetheless considered a strong argument for secession and was taken seriously by commentators in the abolitionist *Liberator*, the southern partisan *De Bow's Review*, and several other highly regarded magazines of the day.[23]

A second sociological study, Daniel Hundley's *Social Relations in our Southern States* (1860/1979), followed Fitzhugh's.[24] Hundley, a lawyer turned sociologist turned Confederate officer, was an unabashed white supremacist and staunch supporter of slavery. He was also an astute observer and purveyor of social distinctions among whites. Where abolitionist observers tended to see two classes of southern whites, Hundley saw no less than seven. He devoted a chapter to each of these seven "social types," dispensing with blacks in a single and final chapter, "The Negro Slaves." Hundley divided white society into "Southern Gentlemen," "The Middle Classes," "Southern Yankees," "Cotton Snobs," "Southern Yeoman," "Southern Bullies," and "Poor White Trash." He arranged his chapters hierarchically and dealt with his social types in descending order, making his chapter on poor white trash the penultimate one, just before the "Negro Slaves."

For Hundley, abolitionists and critics of the South's peculiar institution were simply wrong to pity the degraded social condition of the southern poor white and to blame the slave system for their plight. In his view, the "natural [cause] of the existence in the south of a class of lazy vagabonds known as Poor Whites" was clear: it was bad blood. Hundley argued passionately and, at times, with humor, that poor whites were direct descendants of "those paupers and convicts whom Great Britain sent over to her faithful Colony of Virginia . . . those indentured servants . . . or [those] who followed their masters, the Cavaliers" (1860: 225). To strengthen his case, he noted that environment or climate were insufficient to explain the widespread presence of this particular type, since they are so variable. It must, therefore, be something more constant than the mercurial environment:

> Every where they are just alike, possess pretty much the same characteristics, the same vernacular, the same boorishness, and the same habits; although in different localities, they are known by different names. Thus, in the extreme South and South-west, they are usually called Squatters; in the Carolinas and Georgia Crackers or Sandhillers; in the Old Dominion, Rag Tag and Bob-tail; in Tennessee and some other States, People in the Barrens—but every where, Poor White Trash, a name said to have originated with the slaves, who look upon themselves as much better off than all "po' white folks" wherever. To form any proper conception of the condition of the Poor White Trash, one should see them as they are. . . . if what a citizen of Maine has told us be true, in portions of that State the Poor Whites are to be found in large numbers. In the State of New-York, however, in the rural districts, we will venture to assert that more of this class of paupers are to be met with than you will find in any single Southern State. . . . They are also found in Ohio, Pennsylvania, Indiana, and all the States of the North-west, though in most of these last they came originally from the South. But every where, North and South, in Maine or Texas, in Virginia or New-York, they are one and the same; and have undoubtedly had one and the same origin, namely, the poor-houses and prison-cells of Great Britain. Hence we again affirm, what we asserted only a moment ago, that there is

a great deal more in *blood* than people in the United States are generally inclined to believe. (257–58)[25]

Hundley's emphasis on blood surely reflects then novel Darwinian ideas about evolution. While Hundley's work did not circulate widely, it does offer some of the earliest and most prescient articulations of what would soon become the dominant social and political philosophy in the United States: Social Darwinism. As a social philosophy, Social Darwinism would not fully flower until the early decades of the twentieth century, but southerners like Hundley, reflecting on southern poor whites, embraced its core values *avant la lettre*.

Despite their radically different conclusions, proslavery apologists, abolitionists, and secessionists agreed on three key assumptions: first, that poor, nonslaveholding whites of the South constituted a group or class of individuals that was socially and culturally distinct; second, that what was most distinctive about the group was its degeneracy (although there was profound disagreement about the cause); finally, that poor whites were a social problem that must in some way be addressed in order to spare the nation and the white race from internal corruption and decay. In short, while the decades leading up to the Civil War witnessed intense struggles between antislavery abolitionists and proslavery secessionists for cultural and political authority, there was fundamental agreement on both sides that there existed a class of poor whites in the South that was not, in its present condition, morally and culturally prepared for democratic self-governance. Moreover, the explanations offered by both sides supported, in different ways, one of the ideological pillars of mid-nineteenth-century American politics: white supremacy. For proslavery apologists, poor white trash were biologically corrupt; for abolitionists, they were degraded by the slave system. In both cases, the racial supremacy of other, more respectable whites was rescued from all doubt.

One of the results of this firm consensus between otherwise warring cultural and political factions was to symbolically construct a widely shared reality that would soon permeate America's social and cultural institutions. As a shared symbol, it began to achieve social effects. Primary among these effects was the symbolic violence that produced the social category and cultural designation *poor white trash* as a stigmatized, dishonored, and despised identity. The frame and patterns of perception established through these texts helped set the stage for late-nineteenth- and early-twentieth-century reform movements that focused attention on poor whites. At the same time, as the next chapters demonstrate, this shared frame and pattern of perceptions rather quickly became institutionalized as scientific knowledge, as it was embedded in medical and public health practices that subjected poor whites to unequal treatment. Stigmatyped and outcast poor whites, previously understood as regional problems, were now increasingly viewed as a national problem, the solution to which held urgent implications for other whites, other races, and for the nation as a whole.

chapter three

"Three Generations of Imbeciles Are Enough"

American Eugenics and Poor White Trash

Our laws, which were made to regulate the lives of normal people, do not touch the degenerate problem. . . . Certainly the time has come for us as an enlightened community to set about clearing up these "backdoors of our civilization" and so to save from the worst form of contagion what remains of moral health in our rising generation.
—ELIZABETH S. KITE, *The "Pineys,"* 1913 (quoted in Rafter 1988a: 184)

The South's "poor white trash," so aptly named by the Negro, is no doubt the product of the physical and mental unfit, left in the wake of the War Between the States. Let us take stock of this rubbish. . . . Sterilize all individuals who are not physically, mentally, or emotionally capable of reproducing normal offspring.
—DR. W. L. FUNKHOUSER, *Journal of the Medical Association of Georgia*, 1937 (quoted in Larson 1995: 1)

After the Civil War, it was ideas like Hundley's, not Stowe's that took root. During the closing decades of the nineteenth century, poor rural whites became an increasingly important symbol to urban middle-class professional reformers. In 1877, as radical Reconstruction collapsed and northern troops withdrew from the South, reformers in the North were already conducting extensive field research into the causes and methods of reproduction of poor white degeneracy. A few years before, a prison reformer named Richard Dugdale had noticed that six prisoners in an upstate New York penitentiary were close relatives. Dugdale, intrigued by the notion that there might be some hereditary cause for their criminality and poverty, compared the family histories of these prisoners, whom he dubbed collectively "the Jukes." In 1877, Dugdale published a book by that name in which he concluded that while the Jukes definitely constituted an example of "hereditary pauperism," it was difficult to determine to what extent their habits of poverty were also the result of their poor environment. Dugdale was essentially inconclusive on this point and called for further research, but others interpreted his research as evidence that heredity alone could offer sufficient explanation for degeneracy.[1]

Dugdale theorized that one of the root causes of degeneracy was "consanguinity" (marriage or sexual reproduction by close relations), a situation, he argued, that was brought on not by the relative geographic isolation of rural folk, but by the "impudicity of 'the Juke' women [which was] twenty-nine times greater than that of the average of women" (28). In Dugdale's eyes, the pattern was a vicious circle: "The uncommon licentiousness of 'the Juke' stock excludes them from social recognition. The prudent housewife declines to harbor their boys as farm-help or their girls in domestic service, for fear of seeing her own children contaminated. Public opinion excludes some of the 'Juke' children from the common schools. When they reach the marriageable age, the reputable will not take them 'for better for worse,' because they see no other alternative than worse. Thus, 'Juke' blood mingles with the blood of Juke" (45).[2]

Dugdale's influential work illustrates the important shift that began to occur after the Civil War. Dugdale's scientific approach to analyzing social problems reflects both the growing power of scientific knowledge and the rise of a class of intellectuals and "experts" who would come to take on important new roles in the institutions of the newly unified nation. While middle-class reformers of the mid-nineteenth century made particular use of poor white trash for their political and ideological battles and for bolstering their own nascent identities, the middle-class professionals of the late nineteenth and early twentieth centuries had their own practical purposes and uses in mind. Dugdale's research represented the beginnings of a eugenics reform movement in the United States that, building on the ideas of southerners, would frame the poor white problem as a "problem of degeneracy."

The epigraphs to this chapter illustrate two of the major solutions to the problem of degeneracy put forth by eugenicists in the early decades of the twentieth century. The first is drawn from a study of the poor white inhabitants of New Jersey's Pine Barrens published in the *Survey*, a leading social science journal of public policy, in 1913.[3] Throughout the essay, the author, Elizabeth Kite, a eugenics researcher, repeatedly noted the ineffectiveness of laws intended for "normal people" when applied to the people she called "Pine Rats." These degenerates, presumed to be beyond the reach of the law, were symbolized through Kite's vaguely scatological metaphor of "backdoors" as beyond, behind, and outside of civilization as well. The moral and social threat posed by these "lazy, lustful, and cunning" people was evidenced by the "sexual immorality" practiced by "the male of the species" and was clearly a "profound menace to social order" (Rafter 1988a: 165–66, 170). Kite offered no explicit solutions to the problems she identified, but in concluding her study she remarked upon the "folly" in permitting such people to vote, go to school, or otherwise participate in civil society, strongly implying that she believed segregation and institutionalization were the best means for dealing with this problem population. Segregation and institutionalization were seen by some eugenic reformers like Kite as less intrusive and less objectionable than the mode of control favored by more radical eugenicists: compulsory sterilization.

Within a few decades, Kite's timidity seemed out of place. The strength of the sterilization movement in the United States was such that by the early 1930s, eugenic reformers routinely performed involuntary sterilization (ovariotomies for women and vasectomies or castration for men), believing it to be the only sure way to stop the propagation and proliferation of the "unfit." By this time, segregation and institutionalization of the unfit as advocated by Kite were seen as less effective, less economical, and less desirable than the surgical solution. In the second epigraph, Funkhouser's comments, taken from a medical journal article titled simply "Human Rubbish," suggest the degree to which, by the late 1930s, it had become commonplace, respectable even, to advocate for consigning entire segments of poor rural white populations to lives of institutionalized abjection and state-sponsored sterilization.

A principal concern in the pages that follow is to understand how the term *poor white trash* came to symbolize white degeneracy, and how that perception became institutionalized as a banal social fact, resulting in the indignities of segregation and institutionalization and the harm of involuntary sterilization. This process of symbolization and misrepresentation drew upon techniques being developed in the social sciences at the turn of the century. Professional scientists, in turning their analytical gaze toward poor rural whites, crafted bold and precise lines of race, class, gender, and sexuality, thus accomplishing some of the boundary work necessary for the formation of their own group and individual identities, and boosting them in their drive for higher status, prestige, and social advancement. In this way, poor rural whites played a crucial role in the self-fashioning of turn-of-the-century white middle-class American identity, a role that has been consistently overlooked by historians and sociologists of the middle class.

The first part of this chapter focuses on eugenic field studies, of which *The Jukes* and *The Kallikak Family* are perhaps the most widely known.[4] The field studies are remarkable for their singular focus on poor rural whites. The prevailing historical interpretations of eugenics in the United States have emphasized hostility toward urban immigrant populations as a major driving force in the movement, and undoubtedly it was. Yet this was not the only or even the primary force at work. As one historian has perceptively asked, "Why, if [eugenics] reformers were reacting to immigration and the growth of cities, did *none* of the [field studies] trace bad immigrant or urban families?" (Rafter 1988a: 13).[5] These early examples of American social science claimed that "degenerate" poor white families biologically transmitted morally unacceptable and socially and culturally inappropriate qualities to generation after generation. While the field studies get short shrift in most historical accounts of eugenics, they are of great significance, not only for the influence they had on the subsequent development of social science in the United States, but also for their baleful influence in other parts of the world, including, most notably, Nazi Germany.[6] To date, too few have paid close attention to how the field studies construct their object of analysis — the poor rural white. They do so by drawing distinctions about morality, sex, race, and status.

The second part of the chapter examines the policy implications eugenicists drew from their empirical findings and charts the rise and success of the eugenics movement in actually changing and creating social policies regarding poor whites.[7] Key figures in the eugenics movement led efforts to legislate the involuntary sterilization of those who were determined by this fledgling science to be "unfit" or "feeble-minded." Debates over the appropriateness of using eugenics as a guide for social policy played out and reached a climax in *Buck v. Bell*, a 1927 Supreme Court ruling that upheld the right of states to involuntarily sterilize those it deemed unworthy for sexual reproduction. Reviewing the case reveals how boundaries of gender and sexuality enforced and reinforced middle-class ideals of what it meant to be and to act *white*.

The Progress of Eugenics

To understand the role that eugenics would play in shaping perceptions of different social collectives, including poor white trash, requires look-ing at the emerging discussions among European and American intellec-tuals and scientists that shaped nineteenth-century discourse about sci-ence and society (Bieder 1986; Degler 1991). By the 1880s, Darwin's theory of evolution offered a scientific framework for European and American ideas about the natural basis of the social order. The prevailing ideol-ogy — that those who achieved social dominance were biologically su-perior — seemed to fit remarkably well with Darwin's theory of natural selection in the animal kingdom. Biological determinism was not seen as contradicting the principles of democracy.[8] Many theorists began to argue that, just as the natural order evolved according to the principle of the survival of the fittest, so too the social order developed accord-ing to a struggle for existence and supremacy. Social Darwinists, as these theorists came to be called, combined Darwin's theory with elements of Herbert Spencer's evolutionary history to rationalize and legitimize so-cial inequalities and hierarchies of domination. While many leading So-cial Darwinists such as Lathrop Stoddard (1920), Madison Grant (1916), and David Starr Jordan (1915) relied upon popular sentiments about in-feriority and superiority and offered little in the way of empirical evi-dence for their claims, Social Darwinism took an explicitly scientific form in the work and thought of the British scientist Francis Galton.[9] Galton, a cousin of Darwin, had conducted extensive research into pat-terns governing heredity and was convinced that human characteristics — especially intelligence and moral character — were biologically trans-missible and inheritable. "Reputation," he famously argued, "truly indi-cated ability, [and] the lack of it just as reliably bespoke the absence of ability.... neither outcome depend[s] upon social circumstance" (quoted in Kevles 1986/1995: 4).

In 1883, Galton coined the term *eugenics* to describe his theories of human heredity and eugenic research quickly attracted an international audience. One of Galton's disciples and the leading scientist in the emergent field in the United States was Charles Davenport. In 1904, Davenport, a Harvard-trained biologist with a strong interest in experimentation, successfully persuaded the newly endowed Carnegie Foundation to fund his research and establish a leading-edge center for the experimental study of human evolution in Cold Spring Harbor, Long Island. In 1910 the laboratories at Cold Spring Harbor added a new center, the Eugenic Records Office (ERO). Funded by Mary Harriman, the wife of the railroad magnate R. E. Harriman, the ERO quickly became the premier center for eugenics research in the United States, and, arguably, in the world (G. Allen 1986). For the next thirty-odd years, Davenport's office conducted eugenical surveys, published monthly newsletters and bulletins, and generally acted as an international clearinghouse for scientific and popular knowledge regarding eugenics and hereditary disease.[10] Each summer, the ERO conducted intensive training sessions to prepare young men and women to become eugenic "field experts," highly trained in identifying phenotypical differences through direct contact with and observation of families.[11] Most of the trainees were young women, fresh from elite East Coast colleges and universities, seeking to start their careers as scientific researchers. As the growth in institutions and training facilities for the feeble-minded during this era demonstrates, eugenics quickly became a marketable form of knowledge and expertise (Kevles 1986/1995: 96–112, 164–75). Throughout the Progressive Era, increasing numbers of white people, men and women, tapped this market, advancing their professional careers through the detection and treatment of "mental defectives," who were, in the South at least, disproportionately found among poor rural whites. Once trained, the new eugenicists were given a *Trait Book* and sent out into the field, where they surveyed and studied, among others, "albinos in Massachusetts; the insane at the New Jersey State Hospital in Matawan; the feebleminded at the Skillman school, in Skillman, New Jersey; the Amish in Pennsylvania; the pedigrees of disease in the Academy of Medicine records in New York City; and juvenile delinquents at the Juvenile Psychopathic Institute of Chicago" (Kevles 1986/1995: 55). Eventually, some fifteen or more of these studies were written up and published as eugenic family studies.

Broadly conceived, the eugenics research initiated and carried out by the ERO followed the pattern set by Galton in his attempts to find a biological basis for human difference and social distinctiveness. The explicit purpose of these investigations was twofold: to generate records detailing genealogical information about individuals in the various institutions, and to amass data for the ERO's own strategic purposes, which fell under the rubric of "negative eugenics" (i.e., preventing the proliferation of "bad stock" and minimizing the contamination of "good stock" by bad).[12] Chief among these negative strategies would be legislative reform campaigns aimed at restricting foreign immigration, mandating state institutionalization of the biologically unfit, and legalizing eugenical involuntary sterilization. As scientifically minded researchers, eugenicists were chiefly interested in constructing empirical descriptions and analyses of many if not most of the social ills of their time. They sought the origins of social and economic problems like poverty, unemployment, and crime in human biology and heredity. They posited the existence of "degenerative germ plasm"—bad genes that carried unwanted social traits such as pauperism, laziness, promiscuity and licentiousness, inbreeding, restlessness ("vagabondage" and "nomadism"), and delinquency.

Often, researchers began just as Richard Dugdale had in his by now world-famous study *The Jukes*, by locating siblings and close relatives who were all in prisons or asylums. Using direct interviews, courthouse birth and marriage records, and physicians' files and recollections, they traced family networks back one or two generations, creating complex maps and charts of kinship and familial relations, always making note of the different histories of "deviance" encountered along the family tree. The goal was to find the origins of the "cacogenic" influence, the bad genes and gene mixtures that were the root of the problem. The source of the bad genes was often identified as marriage by first cousins (consanguinity) or sexual reproduction as a result of incest. Less frequently, the cited cause was miscegenation: cross-race sexual relations with "halfbreeds," people of mixed racial descent or with so-called tri-racial isolates.[13]

In terms of public policy, eugenicists voiced two major concerns. The first was economic: they argued that the social costs of dealing with the degenerate offspring through charity and institutionalization in prisons, poorhouses, and psychiatric institutions would drain the wealth of the

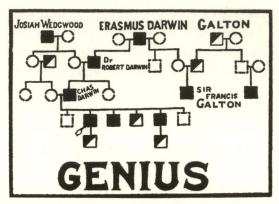

Cousin marriage did not injure the children of Charles Darwin. He married his cousin Emma Wedgewood. Four of his sons rank among the great men of England. The black squares indicate a Fellow of the Royal Society—a high scientific honor. Many of the greatest and healthiest men of genius that ever lived have been the result of a long series of cousin marriages where the stock itself was healthy and strong.

Consanguineous marriage may have been bad for the lower classes, but it was apparently good for the elite. From Albert Edward Wiggam's *The Fruit of the Family Tree* (1924), a popular introduction to eugenics.

nation. The second concern had to do with reproduction, public health, and "social hygiene." If left undetected and unsupervised, eugenicists warned, degenerates would perpetuate their defective germ plasm and spread their vice and immorality throughout their families, communities, and nations. While eugenicists advocated a wide range of practices to address these concerns, the most important and controversial was undoubtedly eugenical sterilization. By the turn of the century, due in large part to the widespread acceptance of the results of eugenics research as credible, accurate, and authoritative, the eugenics movement had garnered enough philanthropic funding and public support to enable practitioners to carry out the final eugenic solution on the so-called defectives: involuntary sterilization of both men and women.[14]

Although its influence as a scientific paradigm persisted well into the 1930s and early 1940s—some would say it persists today—eugenics as a social movement peaked in the 1920s, when urbanization, industrialization, and massive immigration sparked cultural anxieties and political unease about national identity, shifting racial and social hierarchies, and gender roles.[15] Through its methodologies of craniometry, intelligence testing, bodily measurement, and refinements in statistical analysis, the eugenical science of the 1920s seemed to offer objective, scientific, and reassuring answers for the Anglo-American elite to troubling questions about the relative social worth and value of different populations of recent immigrants, most of whom were non–northern Europeans. The direct influences of eugenic propaganda on the passage of the 1924 Immigration Act, which established national quotas and ushered in a long era of immigration restriction, and the 1924 Virginia Racial Integrity Act, a broad statue that forbade interracial marriage, have been firmly established (see Kevles 1986/1995: 46–47, 94–95, 106–7).[16]

However, the major legislative achievements of the eugenics movement included a set of involuntary sterilization laws that targeted not immigrants or people of color, but poor "feebleminded" whites. What united many eugenicists was a primary concern with "race betterment"; they feared the threat posed by poor rural white "degenerates" as much or more than they feared the presence of other races and ethnicities, miscegenation, or intermarriage among immigrants and "native" whites. Racial and national boundaries were of course central to eugenic ideology, but empirical eugenic research that focused on immigrants, blacks, Indians, Asians, and ethnoracial minorities was almost nonexistent compared to the number of studies of poor rural whites. One reason for this lack of concern was undoubtedly the fact that eugenicists were unified around a common ideology of racial supremacy: the racial inferiority of people of color was seldom in doubt for eugenicists — or the educated populace as a whole, for that matter.[17] Poor whites, however, once again posed a serious problem of classification and categorization, as they always have. This time the categorization problem was framed in explicitly biological and medical terms: how could authorities distinguish between a white person who was merely poor by circumstance and one who was biologically predisposed to poverty, crime, and low social standing? To answer empirically this question, which had profound implications for how lines of nation, race, class, and sexuality would be drawn, eugenic researchers developed the field studies.

Science and the Rise of the Professional Middle Class

Historians generally agree that the professionalization of Anglo-American science took place in the nineteenth century (Bledstein 1976; Haskell 1977; and Brubacher and Rudy 1976). The timing was due, in part, to an extraordinary number of scientific discoveries and innovations, but it was also due to transformations in the social and epistemological status of secular knowledge. While the intellectual border war between science and religion was far from over, secular forces were advancing and religion was, for the moment, in retreat. The most crucial force here was the growth of public education, particularly in the form of graduate schools. Graduate schools, an outgrowth of the land grant colleges of the 1860s, were adapted from the German university system and emphasis was placed upon research as a profession. Beginning in the 1850s, American universities started conferring the Doctor of Philosophy degree upon students who completed a rigorous course of study and demonstrated their ability to conduct original research. In 1850, there were only eight graduate students in the entire United States. Between 1850 and 1900, that number grew to 5,668, and by 1930 it had skyrocketed to 47,255 (Brubacher and Rudy 1976: 193).[18] Correspondingly, the number of professional organizations grew rapidly. One estimate is that between 1870 and 1890, over two hundred different learned societies were founded, many of them as offshoots of the American Association for the Advancement of Science (Bledstein 1976: 86). The growth in scientific research organizations and institutions of higher education reflected the need for educational mechanisms whereby scientists as an occupational group might form their community, define their interests, delineate their class status, and encourage and ensure their social growth and reproduction. These sorts of status-conscious organizational operations are, in fact, the hallmarks of professionalization. One clear result was the consolidation of economic interests, institutional power, and social prestige around specific bodies of knowledge and experts.[19]

Professional groups emerged not merely according to the needs of capitalist elites, but in part as a moral reaction against the excesses of the unbridled laissez-faire capitalism of the area. Through the articulation and institutionalization of boundaries that marked their moral superiority,

professionals carved out a new niche between labor and capital. Through
a discourse of intellectual merit, they targeted both the lower classes and
the business elites. This was particularly the case with Progressive Era
professionals, whose group identity and status claims rested on the in-
sistence that the attainment of accredited knowledges was a prerequisite
to membership in the professional and moral elite. Many professionals
saw themselves as the true standard bearers of American democracy—
an educated, intelligent vanguard of committed citizens loyal not to markets, money, or religious denominations but to cultural, scientific, and
national achievement. Yet as a group their sympathies were divided—
between rich and poor constituencies, between progressive and conservative politics, between cultures high and low—making for a collective
moral stance that was quite ambiguous and complex (Link 1992).

Overwhelmingly white and male, turn-of-the-century professionals
descended from the older American middle class.[20] They were most often
the sons of the nineteenth century petit bourgeoisie, composed of small
businessmen, merchants, independent farmers, educators, and clergy.
Sometimes, though not often, they came from the elite class, having rejected the materialistic vulgarities of their capitalist fathers. Occasionally, a member might rise from a working class or poor immigrant family
background to a position of prominence, but such mobility was relatively
rare, as it is today. The most privileged among them were the beneficiaries
of modern European educations, having earned their advanced degrees
in Germany, France, England, and Scotland. Despite the dominance of
white men, a few white women fought their way into these professions
by taking advantage of new opportunities in education.[21] By the 1890s,
over two-thirds of all universities and colleges in the United States accepted women, who accounted for 36 percent of all undergraduates and
13 percent of all graduate students. However, despite these new educational opportunities, women were still largely excluded from many professions.[22] Eugenic field research offered more opportunities for women
than most scientific specialties. Indeed, as early as the 1880s, leading male
eugenicists, including Galton in England and, later, Davenport in the
United States, viewed women as especially well suited to eugenic fieldwork. Their "natural" insights into family life and child rearing, and their
"special abilities" as listeners, quiet observers, emotional sensitivity, and
cooperative employees fit well the requirements of field-workers, who re-

lied upon brief, direct observations for their scientific findings (Rossiter 1982: 52).[23]

Social Sanitation and Hygiene

Early race scientists, such as the ethnologists of the American school, rose to prominence through their characterizations of "inferior" racial types such as Africans and Indians, offering a scientific basis for the ideology of racial supremacy. If, in 1850, professional scientists in this rising class were obsessed with inventing and classifying the nature and meanings of boundaries of racial difference, by 1880 they had shifted focus. Cutting-edge research no longer focused on differences *between* races, but instead on recognizing and delineating differences *within* races. Presumably this was because by 1880, racial science had established beyond scientific doubt the racial inferiority of people of color. Further investigations on the question were simply not needed.[24] Turning the scientific gaze to various biological and cultural distinctions among whites was an obvious next step.

In the decades following Dugdale's famous study set in upstate New York, attention shifted to poor whites in the Midwest. In 1888, the Reverend Oscar McCulloch of Indiana studied a local "case of extreme destitution," stemming from a family known as the Ishmaels, a large collection of family groups that formed, in McCulloch's memorable words, "a pauper ganglion." McCulloch claimed to have uncovered a public record of pauperism among the Ishmaels dating back to 1840, and he drew from that record to offer the following family sketch: "In this family history are murders, a large number of illegitimacies and of prostitutes. They are generally diseased. The children die young. They live by petty stealing, begging, ash-gathering. In summer they 'gypsy,' or travel in wagons east or west. We hear of them in Illinois about Decatur, and in Ohio about Columbus. In the fall they return. They have been known to live in hollow trees on the river-bottoms or in empty houses. Strangely enough, they are not intemperate" (Rafter 1988a: 51). This quick sketch is remarkable for the way it breathlessly combines nearly all the traits and characteristics stereotypically associated with poor rural whites. Laziness, criminality, promiscuity and licentiousness, nomadism, animal-like behavior, miscegenation, disease, and fecundity all appear here in a kind of scientific litany.

What caused the Ishmaels' lamentable set of circumstances? McCulloch offers three distinct factors: "First, the wandering blood from the half-breed mother, in the second generation the poison and the passion that probably came with her. Second the licentiousness which characterizes all the men and women, and the diseased and physically weakened condition. From this result mental weakness, general incapacity, and unfitness for hard work. And third, this condition is met by the benevolent public with almost unlimited public and private aid, thus encouraging them in this idle, wandering life, and in the propagation of similarly disposed children." The biological factors—"wandering blood," disease, and so on—lead to the conclusion that nothing can be done to improve this state of nature, and thus to the realization that public aid and charity, by granting a means of survival to the Ishmaels, actually encourage their deviance and must be stopped. McCulloch asks: "What can we do? First, we must close up official out-door relief. Second, we must check private and indiscriminate benevolence, or charity, falsely so called. Third, we must get hold of the children" (Rafter 1988a: 51–54). McCulloch's conclusions were hardly original. Periodic calls for these sorts of reforms regarding treatment of the poor have a long history (M. Katz 2001). What was novel was that, in keeping with the goals of the new eugenics movement, McCulloch was claiming to offer *scientific* evidence of the incorrigibility of poor rural whites.

In 1897, an academic named Frank W. Blackmar published an article in the *American Journal of Sociology* calling for tighter discipline and greater control over rural youth. Blackmar, a Johns Hopkins–trained professor of history and sociology at the University of Kansas, based his claims on a study of two family groups living in the vicinity of Lawrence, Kansas, who went by an unusual name:

> To the family, now numbering but ten persons, living in these two habitations the name "Śmoky Pilgrims" has been given; chiefly on account of their dusky color and their smoky and begrimed appearance. Possibly the sickly yellow color, on account of the Negro blood in the veins of part of the family, may have suggested the name. By this name they are known to the people of the town. They represent a family or tribal group with loose

habits of family association. They are known as people seeking odd jobs of
work, with an air of fear lest possibly they may find them; as petty thieves
and beggars, in part as prostitutes, and in general as shiftless, helpless, and
beyond hope of reform. (Rafter 1988a: 60)

Blackmar echoed Dugdale in reporting the reputation of the family as
an indicator of the quality and nature of their blood. But in his observations, he went beyond noting social reputation and directed his attention
to the body. Due to what he asserted was the influence of race mixing,
the skin he saw was somehow "smoky," "dusky" colored, and "sickly yellow" all at the same time. Like the antebellum figure of the dirt-eater, the
Smoky Pilgrims apparently carried the telltale marks of their degeneracy
on their skin.[25]

As with McCulloch's wandering Ishmaels, the rural poor of the West
presented a problem for researchers like Blackmar in part because they
seldom stayed in one place. Their "wandering blood" was, Blackmar reasoned, a genetic legacy left by intrepid, white explorers, but that honorable legacy was now corrupted and devolved. As Blackmar notes:

If the city has its paupers and criminals, the country has its tramps and
vagabonds. The tramp has become a perpetual hanger-on of town and
country life. As a rule he likes the city environs best, but he can be found
everywhere. The tramp family is of comparatively recent development.
Everywhere in the West may be seen the covered wagon drawn by poor
horses and conveying from place to place a family group that lives chiefly
by begging and by what it can pick up along the way. This is a different
species from the family of movers that travels from place to place with a
definite purpose; although the former class may be said to have come from
the latter. They are a product of the method of settlement of the West. Moving on and on, with ever repeated failures, they are finally outclassed in the
race for land, and lose place in the ranks of self-support. (Rafter 1988a: 57)

Here we encounter again, this time clothed in the language of social science, the figures of the failed frontiersmen, the dregs of white settlement
described by previous observers from the eighteenth century on. Blackmar's description of them as "outclassed in the race for land" is a phrase
that, for modern readers, is heavy with double meanings and irony. As
white settlers (part of the "race" for land?), they were quite simply out-

"classed." Left without land as the frontier closed, they never achieved self-sufficiency and were forced into a kind of restless movement. That Blackmar, a trained sociologist and historian, recognizes these facts but discounts the social and historical forces behind them, choosing instead to focus on biological explanations, speaks both to the seductive power of durable stigmatypes and the growing influence of eugenics as a new paradigm in social science research.

Blackmar ended his study with a comment on the dilemmas of social welfare at the close of the nineteenth century:

> Considered in themselves, from the standpoint of individual improvement, they seem scarcely worth saving. But from social considerations it is necessary to save such people, that society may be perpetuated. The principle of social evolution is to make the strong stronger that the purposes of social life may be conserved, but to do this the weak must be cared for or they will eventually destroy or counteract the efforts of the strong. We need social sanitation, which is the ultimate aim of the study of social pathology. (Rafter 1988a: 65)[26]

These early field studies by McCulloch and Blackmar had strong policy implications and helped set the research agenda and reform for Charles Davenport and the field-workers of the ERO, who were specifically concerned with tracking both the economic and the social costs of poor white degeneracy. In 1912 and 1913, three influential ERO-sponsored eugenic family studies appeared in print: Florence Danielson's and Charles Davenport's extensive study *The Hill Folk* and Elizabeth Kite's articles "Two Brothers" and "The 'Pineys.'"[27]

The following excerpt from Kite's "Two Brothers" gives the reader some of the narrative flavor of the study: "One of them, the inheritor of the homestead farm, whose broad acres overlooked a lordly river, was a man respected by all who knew him, intelligent, well married, with children who in themselves or in their descendants would cast nothing but honor upon the family name. The other, feeble-minded and morally repulsive, lived on a mountain-side in a hut built of rock fragments so loosely put together that more than once the roof slid from the walls." The shoddy construction of the hut was mirrored by its reputation as a place of loose morality: "For a quarter of a century this hut existed as a hotbed of vice, the resort of the debauched youth of the neighborhood, and from its walls has come a race of degenerates which, out of a total of four hundred and eighty descendants, numbers in almshouse cases, in keepers of houses of prostitution, in inmates of reformatories and institutions for the feeble-minded, in criminals of various sorts and in feeble-minded not under state protection, 143 souls" (Rafter 1988a, 76). Kite drew a picture of the sharpest possible contrast by relying upon a by now well established and deeply familiar comparison: on the one hand, the noble farmer/smallholder; on the other, poor white trash, living in a perpetual state of immorality and vice in a mountainside hut, corrupting the youth and issuing forth degenerate spawn who were to become nothing more than burdens to the state.

One of the most accomplished and prolific of the eugenic researchers, Kite also authored "The 'Pineys,' " the most inventive of all the family studies in its construction of the historical past of poor rural whites. In describing the despised inhabitants of the Pine Barrens region in New Jersey, Kite drew upon local legends, regional histories, and the rarefied air of her own fervid imagination to sketch the contours of their ancestry. Like Dugdale, McCulloch, and Byrd before her, Kite was struck by the "sexual immorality" of "The Pine-Rats," seeing it as one of their primary distinguishing characteristics. In Kite's eyes, these rural whites were less like Byrd's promiscuous, comic lubbers and more like the violent and lawless crackers that so upset the colonial order. As evidence of the Pineys' biological predisposition toward violence, Kite quoted a local historian who claimed that in the eighteenth century, the area was rife with Tory militiamen and outlaw bands of criminal refugees.[28] Hidden away in shrubby recesses and shifting dunes, these raiders posed a constant threat to respectable and law-abiding white people. They were, in Kite's mind, the original seed of the bad germ plasm that subsequently infected the entire area in the nineteenth century and that threatened to spill beyond their bounds in the twentieth. It was not merely the Pineys' idleness or their degenerate blood that posed a moral threat, but rather their very existence:

> But the real Piney has no inclination to labor, submitting to every privation in order to avoid it. Lazy, lustful and cunning, he is a degenerate creature who has learned to provide for himself the bare necessities of life without entering into life's stimulating struggle. . . . [However,] into the degenerate

human problem enters an element which has no force where it is a question of mere physical degeneracy. It is this moral element which entering in makes the human degenerate such a profound menace to social order as to demand the careful consideration of those interested in the preservation of the high standards of our commonwealth. (Rafter 1988a: 170)

As I have mentioned, the nativist hostilities toward immigrants that many historians have argued were primary in the eugenics movement are noticeably absent in the family studies, including "The 'Pineys.'" Although the immigration act of 1917, which ushered in the first great era of restrictive immigration policy in the United States, was just five years away and America's nativism and xenophobia were nearing an all-time high (Higham 1988), in Kite's study, immigrants were actually described as superior to poor rural whites in terms of their family structure and their readiness and ability to work hard. As Kite argued,

No study of the component forces of the Pines would be complete without mention being made of the thriving Jew colonies established at different points, and of the Italian communities. A superficial observer has often been led to believe that there is much similarity between these people and the native denizens of the Pines, but no one who knew them intimately could ever be so deceived. Whatever resemblance there is, is indeed superficial, such as: large families, often unsanitary and crowded conditions of living, small and incommodious dwellings; but beneath the surface we find on one hand, loose disjointed living, with attendant lack of intelligence, absence of ambition, dearth of ideals of every sort; on the other solid, compact organized existence; the father head of his home, protecting his wife and daughters, teaching the same attitude to his sons; both parents training their offspring to thrift and industry. (Rafter 1988a: 172)

The last and in some ways the most unusual of the eugenic family studies was published in 1926. Written by Arthur Estabrook, a eugenics researcher at the Carnegie Institute in Washington, D.C., and Ivan McDougle, a sociologist, *The Mongrel Virginians* was similar to other eugenic family studies in its method and mode of argumentation, but its intensive focus on "race mixing," rather than consanguinity, represents a marked departure from the previous studies.[29] Whereas the studies that preceded it focused on poor rural whites, who may or may not have been of mixed racial descent, *Mongrel Virginians* concerned itself with a small mixed-population group in the Blue Ridge Mountain foothills of western Virginia that Estabrook dubbed the Win (White-Indian-Negro) tribe. In assessing their social status, Estabrook noted that "the white folks look down on them, as do negroes, and this, with their dark skin color, has caused a segregation from the general community. They are variously described as 'low down' yellow negroes, as Indians, as 'mixed.' No one, however, speaks of them as white [although] a few claim to be white" (Estabrook and McDougle 1926: 14).[30]

Unlike Dugdale, Davenport, Kite, or any of the earlier eugenic field researchers, Estabrook and McDougle were explicitly motivated by a concern over racial miscegenation. They presented their research as evidence of the need for strengthening and enforcing antimiscegenation laws, particularly in the South, but throughout the United States generally. The appendix to their study, in which they concluded that "mongrelization" was "an ever increasing social problem in the South," gave the entire text of the Virginia Racial Integrity Law of 1924, a law that allowed local registrars of vital statistics to record the "racial composition" of individuals and, in the case of mixed blood, to ascertain and record in "what generation such mixture occurred" (Pascoe 1996). The explicit goal of the law was to prohibit marriages between whites and nonwhites, although, in a formulation that attests to the difficulties of ascribing chromatic identities, the former category included "people who have one-sixteenth or less of the blood of the American Indian."

Estabrook's and McDougle's study may be unique among the family studies because it identified miscegenation as the chief problem of race degeneracy, but it shares with other field studies a deep-seated concern about the sexual behavior of poor whites. The antimiscegenation laws the authors proposed were not directed at "respectable" whites — it was a given that any white person who sought respect from other whites would not condone marital or sexual relations with a person of another race. Antimiscegenation laws were directed primarily at people of color and at low-status, disreputable whites, the poor white trash who refused to uphold the color line.

While all the family studies present a number of problems of interpretation, their historical significance as prime examples of boundary work should be clear. Using a variety of methods of knowledge production drawn from the emerging social sciences, middle-class professionals constructed the degenerate poor white as a biologically inferior type, one that could be distinguished on the basis of such characteristics as distinctive skin color; a nomadic and vagabond way of life; promiscuity and licentiousness (especially among the women); propensities toward violence and criminality; a broken family structure and a recurring history of miscegenation. That such characteristics fit precisely the long-established framework of stigmatypes attached to poor whites might lead us to conclude that eugenic field researchers were merely using science to confirm their own prejudices. Yet the boundary work performed here involved much more than just bad science or the intellectually lazy perpetuation of old stigmatypes. The symbolic boundaries eugenicists used to elevate themselves above the liminal whites they studied became widely shared scientific perceptions, which would soon become social boundaries with profoundly discriminatory effects. For poor whites, some of the most pernicious, invidious, and damaging distinctions imposed by eugenicists were those that focused on intelligence and cognitive skills, areas of human ability that these professionals regarded as key to establishing and organizing a just and meritocratic democracy.

The Feebleminded Menace

By the end of the first decade of the twentieth century, the rhetoric and scientific research of eugenic reformers began to focus more intensely on feeblemindedness as a social problem and a social burden. The feebleminded, once thought to be the responsibility of community almshouses and charities, were increasingly figured as a national problem, one that required the intervention of state and federal governments. *Feebleminded* was originally a lay term used more or less synonymously with *village idiot*, although the former was thought to be more polite. As the nineteenth century drew to a close, *feebleminded* began to take on more scientific, yet still imprecise, meanings. In governmental and scientific usage, it became an umbrella term that encompassed not only a broad range of mental deficiencies, but also a range of socially deviant behaviors thought

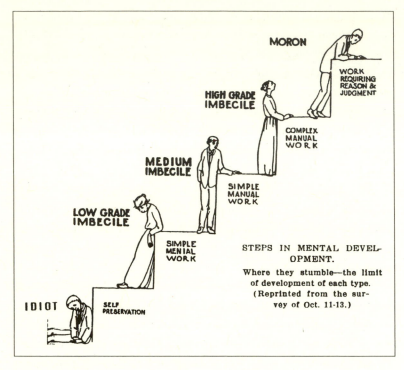

The hierarchy of feeblemindedness. From the *Survey* (1915), the premier social work journal of the era, which also published a number of eugenic field studies.

to be associated with low intelligence and insanity. The 1880 U.S. Census offered what many considered to be the first reliable count of the feeble-minded population and the resulting rate—153.3 feebleminded people per 100,000—and sounded the alarm for social reformers everywhere.[31]

As the twentieth century began, controversial new methods of intelligence testing permitted further refinement of the category. The most important development in this regard was the gradual adoption of the Binet-Simon intelligence test, which was used to determine a person's "mental age."[32] Henry H. Goddard's *The Kallikak Family: A Study in the Heredity of Feeblemindedness* (1912) used intelligence testing to establish the criteria for identifying and differentiating "mental defectives." Those whose mental age was one or two, he classified as "idiots"; those who scored a mental age of three to seven he termed "imbeciles"; and those whose mental age ranged between eight and twelve he identified as "morons"; a neologism he coined from the Greek word for "dull" (Kevles 1986/1995: 78). Goddard's study quickly became accepted as solid, empirical proof of the hereditary nature of intelligence, and many came to believe, as Goddard so succinctly put it, that feeblemindedness was "a condition of mind or brain which is transmitted as regularly or surely as color of hair or eyes" (quoted in Kevles 1986/1995: 79). Goddard's findings sparked increased medical interest in mental deficiency, and physicians and psychologists intensified their efforts to discover the etiology of feeblemindedness. After the unparalleled success of *The Kallikaks*, the modification and standardization of intelligence tests, such as the Stanford-Binet test and the widespread adoption of Lewis Terman's "intelligence quotient" (I.Q.) as a standard measure of mental ability, led to a sharp increase in diagnoses of feeblemindedness and a sharp rise in the institutionalization of those deemed mentally defective.

Mental defectives—the idiots, imbeciles, and morons who were collectively labeled feebleminded—were seen as not merely lacking intelligence, but as lacking in morals as well. By "morals," reformers had in mind a series of qualities and norms, but foremost in their minds were concerns about sexual behavior. Feebleminded women and men, given free rein, would, reformers feared, engage in immoral sex without any understanding of the consequences of their actions. Controlling the sexual reproduction of the feebleminded was, reformers believed, the only successful way to prevent future cases of mental defect. In Goddard's view, the sexual danger was compounded by two simple facts: many "high grade morons," although they were carriers of hereditary mental defects, appeared "normal" on the outside. To the extent that they remained undetected in the general population, they posed a hidden dysgenic threat. Second, by Goddard's own calculations, the feebleminded were "multiplying at twice the rate of the general population" and this uncontrolled fecundity would soon overwhelm the better classes. Their invisibility, their apparent normalcy, and their fecundity—this was the essence of what Goddard (1912: 71, 104) ominously termed "the menace of the feebleminded."

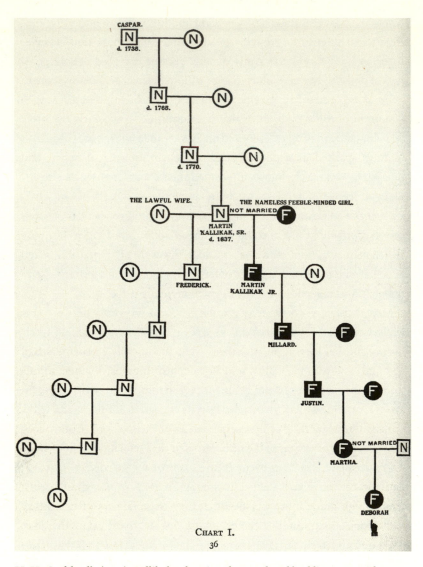

CHART I.
36

H. H. Goddard's (1912) *Kallikaks*, showing the good and bad lineages, with a very helpful key to chart the degeneracy (Chart II on facing page). Normals are—what else?—white.

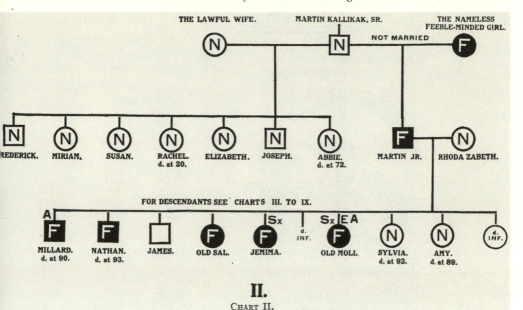

II.
CHART II.

N = Normal.   F = Feeble-minded.   Sx = Sexually immoral.   A = Alcoholic.   I = Insane.   Sy = Syphilitic.   C = Criminalistic.   D = Deaf,
d. inf. = died in infancy.   T = Tuberculous.   Hand points to child in Vineland Institution.   For further explanation see pp. 33–35.

Rural Idiots in America

Goddard and other eugenics researchers and reformers believed that feeblemindedness was not distributed evenly or randomly throughout the U.S. population. Feeblemindedness, they contended, was concentrated in certain populations and in certain regions. Recent immigrant groups, they argued, posed a particular threat in this regard. But they raised the alarm about rural white populations as well and sought new methods of analysis to make their case, turning to area survey methodologies. The publication in 1918 of "The Feeble-Minded in the Rural County of Ohio," a study more popularly known as "The Happy Hickories," introduced area survey methods to eugenics researchers in the United States. The author, Mina Sessions, who, like Elizabeth Kite, had been trained by Charles Davenport and Harry Laughlin at the ERO summer institute, expanded the definition of feeblemindedness to include not only those who could not support themselves, but also those who supported themselves badly, such as squatters and the unemployed. Using this expansive category, Sessions concluded "the percentage of feeble-

THE FEEBLE-MINDED

OR THE

HUB TO OUR WHEEL OF VICE, CRIME
AND PAUPERISM

Cincinnati's Problem

The Menace of the Feebleminded (1915). Juvenile Protective Association of Cincinnati. It wasn't just the rural south that feared the threat. Industrializing cities in the midwest also reacted with alarm.

minded at large in the rural districts was double the percentage in the urban districts" (Rafter 1988a: 255).

Sessions's claims echoed a theme that had been introduced by Florence Danielson and Charles Davenport in their 1912 study *The Hill Folk* (Rafter 1988a: 81–163) which was perhaps the most exhaustively researched and certainly remains the most visually impressive of all the family studies. Page after page of carefully coded tables and intricate kinship and genealogy charts elaborated in excruciating detail what the authors considered to be the "sociological importance" of the research—namely, that they were "dealing with a rural community such as can be found in nearly if not quite every county in the older states of the union, in which nearly all of the people belong to the vague class of the 'feebleminded'—the incapable. The individuals vary much in capacity, a result which follows from the complexity of their germ plasm." The authors concluded the only answer was reproductive control: "Some have capacities that can be developed under proper conditions, but for many more even the best of environmental conditions can do little. They must remain a drag on our civilization; a condition for which not they, but society, is responsible. It is to be hoped that a presentation of the facts will hasten the so much desired control by society of the reproduction of the grossly defective" (Rafter 1988a: 84–85).

In addition to the influential field studies, eugenicists pointed to other compelling evidence that rural areas were havens for morons and "high-grade defectives." In 1917, the results of widespread intelligence testing in the Army indicated that new recruits (the majority of whom came from rural or semirural areas, or had parents who did) were astonishingly dull-witted: 47.3 percent of test takers were judged to be feebleminded. Among southern states, demographically more rural and, in the wake of African American migration, more white than many areas in the North, the numbers were even more alarming: 50 percent of southern white males were graded as "imbeciles."[33]

In southern states, the combined effect of these studies was to direct reform efforts and funds toward rural areas and to focus on the poor whites in those regions as the population most in need of care and control.[34] Professional associations such as the short-lived but influential Committee on Provision for the Feeble-Minded and the American Association for the Study of the Feebleminded were enormously effective in getting out the message that combating the menace of feeblemindedness in the South required a swift expansion of state institutions to provide the expert care and control that local charities and almshouses could not (Trent 1994; Noll 1995). Anything less than the permanent, total institutionalization of the feebleminded was characterized as a half measure that would result in further increases in the delinquent, dependent, and defective population. Segregation and institutionalization of the "feebleminded" was under way. In 1904, 17.3 feebleminded people per 100,000 of the general population had been institutionalized. By 1923, the figure had climbed to 46.7, an increase of nearly 300 percent. The increase was especially remarkable in the southern states, where approximately 50 people per 100,000 were institutionalized by 1937 (Noll 1995: 4, 39). Still, the southern institutionalization rate of 50 per 100,000 was quite low compared to the New England and mid-Atlantic rates of 96 and 97 per 100,000, respectively. This disparity was due to a number of factors, including the relatively late development of southern institutions: between 1914 and 1923, institutions for the feebleminded were founded in nine southern states where none had existed before. Also, unlike the northern states, where a small but significant portion of those institutionalized were classified as nonwhite, southern institutions were overwhelmingly white (Trent 1994: 177).[35]

Overall, however, the growth of segregated and institutionalized populations spurred and enabled further growth in the young professions dedicated to caring for and controlling them; the early part of the twentieth century saw massive growth in the fields of medical psychology and social work (Walkowitz 1999). Reformers followed a logic of containment that resulted in the expansion of their authority and power.[36] However, many within and outside these professions saw permanent institutionalization as both an imperfect solution and an unnecessary financial burden to the state, and movement toward another less costly and more radical solution began.

The Surgical Solution: *Buck v. Bell*

Opponents to segregation as a solution to the problem of feeblemindedness generally favored controlling reproduction through involuntary sterilization. Sterilization was a prime example of "negative eugenics"— the collective name given to techniques for preventing the proliferation of poor hereditary stock. In the United States, it gained widespread support over the first three decades of the twentieth century. In 1907, only one state, Indiana, had passed a sterilization law. By 1926, the year the decisive case of *Buck v. Bell* was heard before the U.S. Supreme Court, the number of states with such laws had jumped to twenty-three.[37]

While few sterilizations were carried out in the first decade after 1907, from 1917 to 1927 the number of institutionalized feebleminded people reported to have been sterilized in the United States rose from 1,422 to 8,515.[38] In part the increase was tied to the sharp increase in the diagnosis and institutionalization of the feebleminded discussed above. However, it also reflected a greater reliance by physicians and custodians on surgical rather than segregationist solutions to solving the problem of institutionalizing the feebleminded. Increasingly, in the eyes of many reformers, the chief value in sterilization was that "higher grade morons" could be safely released back to their families and communities, easing the economic burden on the state and freeing up institutional space and resources for more severely defective patients. They saw sterilization as an efficient, practical, and convenient solution to their problems and for many, the procedure simply became routine part of institutional care.[39]

However, such pragmatic and economic concerns, which appealed to

many superintendents and custodians of state institutions facing over-
crowding and escalating costs, were less important to committed eugenicists, who held loftier goals. As Harry H. Laughlin, Davenport's assistant at the ERO and a major proponent of eugenic sterilization, argued
in 1926, the

> primary purpose is to prevent reproduction by the most degenerate and
> defective human family stocks of the particular state which is applying it.
> As the principles of eugenics become more definitely incorporated into the
> general policy of the state, eugenical sterilization will have to be applied
> still more consistently to the lowest natural or hereditary physical, mental,
> and temperamental or moral levels; because, as a rule, such inadequates
> and producers of inadequates in the body politic are not capable of obey-
> ing, on their own initiative, laws concerning mate selection and human re-
> production. These lowest human strains must, therefore, be taken in hand
> by the state, for the promotion of the general welfare. (Laughlin 1926: 2)

By the 1920s the "lowest human strains" were relatively easily identified. Intelligence and psychological testing could quickly determine the
quality of hereditary stock, just as Galton had predicted in the 1880s,
and these scientific methods were seen as authoritative and compelling,
if controversial.[40] The logic of containment was giving way to the logic
of biological eradication.

Controversies over the laws led to the overturning of several state stat-
ues between 1911 and 1922, and eugenicists grew determined to draft a
model law and use it as a test case before the highest court in the land. In
1923, Laughlin helped draft such a bill for the Virginia legislature where
it was met with almost unanimous approval, passing 75–2 the following
year. In the fall of 1924, a superintendent at Virginia's State Colony for
Epileptics and Feebleminded ordered the sterilization of a young white
woman named Carrie Buck, who had been committed earlier that same
year. Buck's guardian appealed, and the case went before the county Circuit Court in April 1925. There, the sterilization order was upheld and
the statute, the Eugenical Sterilization Act, declared valid.

Carrie Buck, an eighteen-year-old white woman from Charlottesville,
Virginia, was judged by the superintendent of the state institution, A. S.
Priddy, to have a mental age of nine and deemed to be of "social and
economic inadequacy." Her institutional records described her as having

led a "life of immorality, prostitution, and untruthfulness" bearing "one illegitimate child, now six months old, now supposed to be a mental defective." Buck's moral and intellectual weaknesses were said to be a direct inheritance from her mother who, in addition to exhibiting all the character traits ascribed to Carrie, "was maritally unworthy; having been divorced from her husband on account of infidelity" and who had a "record of prostitution and syphilis" and "one illegitimate child and probably two others inclusive of Carrie Buck" (quoted in Laughlin 1929: 16–17). Having established not only that Buck was the "degenerate offspring" of a morally defective parent, but that her young baby was likely to be mentally defective as well, the defense argued that she was therefore clearly a "potential parent of socially inadequate offspring," the category that allowed the statue for *compulsory* sterilization to come into effect. Although due to her illegitimacy her genealogy was difficult to ascertain, the defense rested with the simple but damning assertion that "these people belong to the shiftless, ignorant, and worthless class of anti-social whites of the South" (quoted in Laughlin 1929: 17). Carrie Buck was not just an example of bad family germ plasm — she was representative of an entire social group, the degenerate poor whites of the South. This apparently clinched the case.

Again, Carrie Buck's guardian appealed, this time to the Virginia Supreme Court of Appeals. The defense called in expert testimony not only from Laughlin, but also from Arthur Estabrook. In his testimony, Superintendent Priddy spoke of the economic good sense of the law and the moral uplift that would be the result of sterilization:

> If the purposes of the act chartering this institution are to be observed and carried out, that is to keep her under custody during her period of childbearing, she would have some thirty years of strict custody and care, under which she would receive only her board and clothes; would be denied all the blessings of outdoor life and liberty, and be a burden on the State of Virginia of about $200 a year for thirty years; whereas, if by the operation of sterilization, with the training she has got, she could go out, get a good home under supervision, earn good wages, and probably marry some man of her own level and do as many whom I have sterilized for disease have done — be good wives — be producers, and lead happy and useful lives in their spheres. (Laughlin 1929: 25)[41]

As in the Circuit Court trial before, Buck's lawyer argued that the Virginia Sterilization Act did not provide due process of law; that it imposed cruel and unusual punishment; and that it violated the Fourteenth Amendment, denying Buck equal protection under the law. However, no actual testimony was offered on behalf of Buck, and the Court of Appeals again upheld the ruling. In the fall of 1926, two years after Priddy had ordered Buck's sterilization, the case was heard before the U.S. Supreme Court. There, Buck's lawyer pursued the same legal strategy that had failed in previous hearings of the case, but in his argument he took note of the far-reaching social and political implications of the statue: "If the Virginia Act of Assembly under consideration is held to be a valid enactment, then the limits of the power of the state (which in the end is nothing more than the faction in control of the government) to rid itself of those citizens deemed undesirable according to its standards by means of surgical sterilization have not been set." He added that the real danger was not from the feebleminded, but from the professional doctors who would be empowered by the state to invent new categories and to target new social groups for control. "We will," he warned, "have 'established in the state the science of medicine and a corresponding system of judicature.' A reign of doctors will be inaugurated and in the name of science new classes will be added, even races may be brought within the scope of such a regulation and the worst form of tyranny practiced" (quoted in Laughlin 1926: 49). The Supreme Court justices were unmoved by this concern. In writing for the eight-to-one majority, Justice Oliver Wendell Holmes ruled, "It is better for all the world, if instead of waiting to execute degenerate offspring for crime, or to let them starve for their imbecility, society can prevent those who are manifestly unfit from continuing their kind. The principle that sustains compulsory vaccination is broad enough to cover cutting the Fallopian tubes. Three generations of imbeciles are enough."[42]

Carrie Buck's case is emblematic of the ways that "shiftless, ignorant, and worthless" lower-class white women were viewed by the middle-class white men who supervised, treated, and sterilized them. Of the 1,000 sterilizations carried out in Virginia in the decade immediately following Buck's case, 609 were performed on women. Of all the sterilizations reported between 1917 and 1941, 22,307 were done on women and 15,780 on men, a ratio of approximately 1.5:1.[43] The women were assessed not only by their mental age, but also by their sexual histories, reputations, and crimes. While men were sterilized in large numbers, there is little evidence that their sex lives were subject to the same level of scrutiny and pathologization. Controlling the sexuality and the reproductive power of lower-class women through the imposition of coercive policies of reproductive control was a major focus and a lasting consequence of eugenic reform (Roberts 1997; Briggs 2002; and Ordover 2003).[44] Through these policies and reforms, the boundaries that had symbolically marked poor white trash as a stigmatized outgroup now became institutionalized as social boundaries — legal barriers with the power to control, exclude, and deny. Differences of gender, sex, race, and class came together in a powerfully discriminatory way to justify the eradication of the feebleminded poor white trash by sterilizing them without their consent.

Eugenics is an early chapter in a long story of scientized prejudice in the United States, a story in which scientific evidence for racial, class, and gender hierarchies became popular and entered public discourse on a broad scale.[45] Over the course of the latter half of the nineteenth century, the analytical object of scientized prejudice and the focus of popular discourses about inferiority and natural hierarchies shifted from people of color — primarily blacks and Indians — to poor white Americans, "foreigners," and immigrants. This shift culminated in the 1920s with the implementation of the Johnson-Lodge National Origins Quota Act and the U.S. Supreme Court ruling in *Buck v. Bell*. Taken together, these legal actions marked both recent immigrants and feebleminded poor whites as inassimilable, as threatening outsiders-within to be excluded from the national body.

The eugenics movement played an integral part in the emergence and solidification of a new class of professionals in the United States. Their rapid social advancement was sustained intellectually through a commitment to public service and moral reform and sustained institutionally by legislative reforms at the federal, state, and local levels that granted them new and expanded powers over lower classes. However, the difficulties and challenges associated with the social reproduction of this historically new class gave rise to specific fears and anxieties about the biological reproduction of lower-class others. In the imagination of the professional middle classes, their newly gained status and prestige were fragile achievements.

Eugenics was the crucial vehicle for nationalizing and deregionalizing the stigmatypes of southern poor white trash. Previous chapters in this book aimed to track how particular words and phrases—fragments of historical meaning and signification—described, portrayed, and ultimately constructed poor white trash as a stigmatized and despised social group in the South. Both abolitionists and southern secessionists played active roles in shaping these collective representations and each used the image of poor white trash to advance their own arguments about slavery. However, there is little evidence from before the end of Reconstruction that poor white trash was considered to be a problem social group that the nation as a whole needed to address for its safety and welfare.

With the advent of eugenics, this situation changed. What had begun as a distinctively regional term emanating from the upper South soon became transregional, with meanings that were recognized in faraway places. As *poor white trash* traveled and entered into local dialects, it formed a chain of associations that symbolically linked local poor whites to those in other rural places. A large part of the cultural success of the eugenics movement lay with the way in which it used this chain of associations to group together the local images of poor rural whites in New Jersey, Ohio, New York, Pennsylvania, Kansas, and everywhere else. It incorporated and expanded upon the shared perceptions of southern poor whites as immoral, lazy, dirty, criminal, filthy, and perverse and offered an explanation that could be generalized to the entire group. That the stigmatyping images of poor rural whites was, by the late nineteenth century, firmly established as a shared cultural schema ensured that eugenicists did not have to work very hard to make their case. The power of this shared perception, coupled with the rising reformist power of the professional middle class, resulted in efforts to achieve a rare and extreme form of exclusion: the biological eradication of an entire population through coercive reproductive control.

chapter four

The Disease of Laziness

Crackers, Poor Whites, and Hookworm

Crusaders in the New South

For purposes of placating primitive and suspicious peoples, medicine
has some decided advantages over machine guns.
—GEORGE VINCENT, president, Rockefeller Foundation, 1918
(quoted in E. R. Brown 1976: 900)

Ideas about dirt have serious political implications.
—STARR 1982: 189

In the midst of the profound success of the eugenics movement, a different approach to addressing the poor white problem was undertaken in the South. The campaign to eradicate hookworm disease, a campaign concentrated in eleven southern states between 1909 and 1915, challenged eugenic public policy. To the question of whether or not "poor whites" could be useful, productive citizens and workers, eugenicists answered a resounding no. Hookworm crusaders, however, answered with a defiant yes. While eugenicists pressed their argument that the solution to southern poverty, economic backwardness, and the degradation of the white race was the institutionalization and sterilization of feebleminded poor white trash, a small but determined group of physicians and educators proposed a radically different solution. Refusing the idea that poor whites of the South were racially degenerate or dysgenically mixed, they argued instead that poor whites were suffering from chronic disease, the effects of which were commonly mistaken for degeneracy. Moreover, they argued, sick poor whites could be treated, cured of disease, and rehabilitated as productive laborers and citizens, granting health and prosperity to their local communities and the South and nation as a whole. The culprit, they argued, was not defective germ plasm. It was the hookworm. Determined to prove their case, hookworm doctors and educators conducted preliminary infection surveys that gave clear, irrefutable evidence of the widespread presence of the dreaded worm throughout the South. In 1909, on the basis of these surveys, and with financial assistance from a northern philanthropist, the Rockefeller Sanitary Commission to Eradicate Hookworm Disease (RSC) was founded. The hookworm crusade was born.[1]

While the hookworm campaign may have improved the health of some poor rural whites (and some blacks) by granting them a partial reprieve from the ravages of a debilitating internal parasite, it was far more effective in creating and legitimating powerful new social boundaries. Through the rhetoric of the hookworm campaign, poor white trash were partially refigured as pure white Americans, as a group that deserved higher status and greater prestige than that accorded to southern blacks. Along with their refiguration as definitively white, however, poor whites were simultaneously presented as working-class—as a laboring group whose abilities and attitudes made them suitable not for middle-class occupations, but for the industrial and agricultural jobs of the New South.[2] With the hookworm campaign the social status of southern poor whites had indeed begun to change, as doctors and educators negotiated and imposed new boundary lines. In turn the new boundaries helped transform existing social relations and consolidate mechanisms of social closure and symbolic domination—of poor whites over blacks and of middle-class whites over poor whites.

Of Worms and Dirt-eaters

The hookworm is an extremely unpleasant intestinal parasite. While it has been part of human history since ancient times, causing chronic disease (chiefly anemia) and occasional death, its existence was not detected and verified by western medicine until 1838, when physicians in Europe located it in peasant autopsies. Although they had discovered the presence of the worm, they could not connect it with any specific disease; for the next four decades, physicians had no way of diagnosing the presence of the worm in living humans. In 1877, as Dugdale was publishing his pioneering study *The Jukes*, two Italian physicians demonstrated that hookworm could be observed as tiny eggs passed in human feces; this breakthrough gave doctors a simple method of clinical diagnosis. Three years later, an outbreak of infection among miners and tunnel workers in Switzerland gave physicians an opportunity to study the distinct pathologies associated with infection. A search for an appropriate remedy — a chemical vermifuge that would expel the worms from the body — began in earnest. Some physicians reported success with large doses of thymol, a derivative of the herb thyme, and this remedy in the end proved to be the most often used, even as it remained a controversial (because sometimes deadly) treatment. While knowledge of successful methods for diagnosis and treatment was increasingly widespread, the route of infection remained a mystery and so did prophylactic remedies. At the close of the nineteenth century, an epidemic of "tunnel disease," as hookworm disease was then known, raged across Europe, afflicting chiefly miners, brickmakers, and tunnelers, those whose daily labor brought them into close, unavoidable, and regular contact with soil and dirt. From this point on, the story of hookworm and its victims would be deeply associated with soil and dirt.

Early theories that hookworm larvae were inhaled through dirty, dusty air were proven wrong when in 1898 a physician in Cairo inadvertently infected himself. He spilled some of the hookworm cultures he was working with on his hand and quickly developed an itchy rash.[3] He theorized that the hookworm entered through the dermis — especially the tender parts like those between toes and fingers — and that the larvae then passed through the bloodstream to the lungs, migrating through the alveoli and bronchial passages to the throat. There, he conjectured, it was swallowed and traveled through the stomach to the intestines where it colonized the intestinal lining, living up to ten years, sucking blood and reproducing at an enormous rate, with females laying up to 10,000 eggs per day. The eggs then passed out of the victim's body through feces; if they found a home in warm, moist soil, they hatched to infect again, burrowing into the skin of any unsuspecting victims who might come into contact with the polluted soil. The hypothesis regarding the route of infection was eventually proven correct in every detail, and by 1900 the anatomy and lifecycle of the hookworm (now known to doctors by its scientific name *uncinaria*) was known in Europe, where researchers and physicians began tracing, cataloguing, and classifying its numerous debilitating effects (Dock and Bass 1910; Chandler 1929). For the first time, scientists had a clear sense of how the disease was spread: it required contact with human feces. For those few who were educated in the etiology of hookworm infection, the disease was now firmly linked not just to dirt, but also to human excrement and waste.

The first diagnosis of hookworm in the United States occurred in St. Louis, Missouri in 1893. The patient was a bricklayer originally from Westphalia, a biographical detail that was to prove a significant factor in initial public reaction to the disease. Following the discovery, many diagnoses were made in Texas and other states, but close observation revealed a unique species of hookworm in the United States, one whose anatomy differed from its European counterparts. In 1902, Charles Wardell Stiles, a zoologist with the United States Bureau of Animal Industry, following the lead of a former student then stationed in Puerto Rico, became convinced that the newly identified hookworm species was the major cause of various forms of anemia endemic to the South and to other warm, humid regions around the globe. Stiles began conducting health surveys throughout Virginia and North Carolina. Initially, he found nothing to support his hypothesis, but upon turning further south into South Carolina and focusing on regions that would provide the best environmental conditions for the hookworm—those where warm, sandy soils were predominant—Stiles found the evidence he needed. He wrote, "I found a family of 11 members, one of whom was an alleged 'dirt-eater.' The instant I saw these eleven persons I recalled . . . the dirt-eaters of Florida. A physical examination made it probable that we had before us eleven cases of uncinariasis, and a specimen of feces from one of the children gave the positive diagnosis of infection with *Uncinaria americana*. There were hundreds of eggs present" (1903, quoted in Ettling 1981: 34). That upon seeing the condition of this family Stiles recalled the dirt-eater stigmatype is quite significant. In Stiles's own narrative of discovery, the distended and strangely pigmented bodies of dirt-eating poor whites signaled the presence of the disease.

Anxious for more evidence, Stiles pressed further into the region:

Inquiring for the largest plantation in this sand district, I was directed to a place in Kershaw County, South Carolina. There were about sixty white

Dr. Charles W. Stiles,
conquering hero,
outfitted in full military-
scientific regalia. From
The World's Work (1912),
Walter Hines Page's
widely circulated monthly
periodical.

"hands" on this farm. Going to a field I found about twenty at work. . . . A physical examination showed that they corresponded to cases of uncinari-asis. A family of ten members was selected and examined microscopically and found to contain hundreds of eggs of *Uncinaria americana*. The owner of the plantation informed me that it would be a waste of my time to exam-ine the remaining forty "hands" as they were in exactly the same condition as the twenty already examined (1903, quoted in Ettling 1981: 34–35)

Stiles's mention of "sixty white 'hands'" suggests that there were black workers on the plantation as well. Indeed, it would have been quite rare for a South Carolina plantation of that size to have employed only white workers. But Stiles did not look for evidence of hookworm among blacks, nor did he say why he examined only whites. Stiles was well versed in the scientific literature regarding hookworm and its connections to soil and feces; as a southerner himself, he was also well acquainted with the clay-eater stigma that surrounded poor whites in the sandy districts. Did these factors—based in part on science and in part on collective representa-tions of poor whites—predispose Stiles to look to poor whites as the most likely hosts for the worm? Or was the narrowness of Stiles's inquiry based

AN INFECTED FAMILY
A TYPICAL GROUP OF HOOKWORM PEOPLE

"Two million men and women who are maimed, stunted, kept back, are inefficient, and children to whom red-blooded life is denied—all these wretched and a burden, not by any necessity of heredity or by any willful defect of character, but because they are sick." From *The World's Work* (1912).

on existing boundary lines of color and class that, as a white southerner, Stiles intuitively understood? Whatever the reasons, the research protocol established by Stiles of searching for evidence of hookworm disease primarily among poor whites had enormous consequences for how the disease and its sufferers were constructed by scientists, physicians, public health reformers, and other influential hookworm crusaders. Yet as hookworm campaigners followed the patterns of research and representation already established, so too did larger historical forces pattern their actions. As the founding of the Eugenics Record Office in 1910 reflected the newly found status of medical and biological sciences, the launch of the RSC in 1909 occurred at a historical moment when physicians and public health professionals were achieving new levels of cultural authority and social status. The key to this transformation was newfound power to construct shared reality through definitions of fact and moral virtue (Starr 1982), a power derived in part from moral panics and symbolic crusades about degeneracy and disease.[4]

Science and the Professionalization of Medicine and Public Health

Throughout the nineteenth century, the establishment and growth of medical schools and organization for physicians had enabled the professionalization of medicine. In 1800, there were a mere four medical colleges in the United States. By 1877, the year Dugdale published *The Jukes*, that number had jumped to seventy-three. Between 1880 and 1902, the year Stiles discovered the worm he dubbed "the American Killer," the number of institutions devoted to medical training climbed from 80 to 154 (Burrow 1977: 15; Starr 1982: 79–179). Organizational growth was equally impressive. Between 1847 and 1902, the number of national organizations devoted to medical practice and research rose from one to sixteen, and by the end of the first decade of the twentieth century, over 275 medical journals were being published regularly (Shortt 1983: 53).

Physicians were now a sizable group within the burgeoning professional middle class, but their ranks were growing so quickly that they were essentially flooding the field, driving down the value of their own services. As the cost of living rose, doctors' incomes stayed virtually flat. Influential and well-connected physicians turned to politics, lobbying to institute new controls on licensing and to legislate stricter controls over access to the profession. Increasingly, many physicians sought as well to expand their public roles and to take a larger part in the nascent field of public health. They turned toward public health reform in an effort to strengthen their relationship to the needs of the state. In particular, they sought to enlarge the powers of state boards of health, seeing these as the key avenues for the advancement of their own political and economic agendas. By the close of the first decade of the twentieth century, physicians and their professional organizations had successfully mounted campaigns to enact legislation expanding the powers and responsibilities of state boards of health; to standardize medical inspection of schools; and to institute certification procedures for the dairy industry (the "pure milk" crusade). In addition, they fought for and won federal pure food and drug legislation and federal requirements regulating the collection of vital statistics at the state level. As a result of these efforts, governmental agencies came to institutionalize the boundary lines that elevated physicians above other professionals and granted physicians unique powers over other citizens. Both the eugenics movement and the hookworm campaign exemplified the strategy of securing and advancing the class status of medical doctors through expanding the regulatory powers of the state (Burrow 1977: 88–102; Starr 1982: 180–234).

Public health as a profession distinct from medicine emerged more slowly (Rosen 1958). Partly this was due to a dramatic shift in scientific debates about the origins of illness and disease. In the decades following the Civil War, departments of health were established in larger cities and towns to deal with epidemics, guided by a consensus that "filth" and "miasma" contributed a great deal to illness and disease. Consequently, these departments soon took control of most aspects of basic public sanitation, such as garbage collecting, street cleaning, and the regulation and monitoring of food. As the paradigm shifted away from miasma and filth theories toward the more promising germ theory, health departments placed new emphasis upon educating the public and treating individuals.[5] Due in part to this paradigm shift, the period between the end of the Civil War and World War I was an era of "modernization" in both the medical and public health professions. Modern germ theory, which provided a universal understanding of disease, brought the professions more closely together than ever before. Yet within germ theory there were two distinct and competing paradigms: a reductionist, biomedical model and a holistic, ecological model. The biomedical model minimized environment and social circumstances and stressed biological laws, placing emphasis upon the individual as the primary locus for education and change. The holistic model viewed links between the individual and the social environment as crucial factors in both cause and cure, placing emphasis upon institutional (not individual) change as the appropriate goal of reform. Within the emerging field of public health, these two models often clashed, but in the hookworm campaign, the biomedical model was established early on and essentially remained unchallenged, with predictable results (Kunitz 1988).

During the period 1910–13, as various state boards of health entered the hookworm fight, efforts to counter the disease began with sanitary and infection surveys, followed by campaigns for cure and prevention. The infection surveys, directed primarily at rural white children between the ages of six and eighteen, revealed the presence of hookworm in every one of the nearly seven hundred counties surveyed. Infection was incredibly widespread. One historian has estimated that, between 1865 and 1910, as much as 40 percent of the population of the South harbored the parasite (Ettling 1981: 2). As in the preliminary reports, "soil pollution"—the practice of open-air defecation—was judged to be the chief mechanism of infection. Physicians, public health inspectors, and educators began working county-by-county to limit soil pollution, emphasizing the proper construction and use of outhouses. These professionals, engaged in their own battles for professional advancement, downplayed or ignored social issues such as racial inequality, poverty, unemployment, and other social disparities. They envisioned treating hookworm disease in a largely individualistic fashion, focusing on improving personal hygiene and sanitation. In light of the dominant biomedical model, this strategy made a great deal of sense: it focused on identifying the vectors of infection and then sought to eradicate the disease by eliminating the vectors. One result of such a strategy, however, was the legitimization and authorization of the general view that the habits and customs of poor rural whites caused infection and disease and that diseases were the *cause* of poverty. As this model became dominant through the educational efforts of the crusade, any thought that perhaps poverty might be a factor in the causation of disease was pushed further and further from view. In short, as we will see, few hookworm campaigners ever seriously considered issues of social inequalities.

The Lazy Cracker Disease

The research Stiles carried out in South Carolina was a product of these sociohistorical shifts. Upon returning to Washington, D.C., Stiles wrote in the conclusion of his report that hookworm disease was one of the most important diseases in the South and "that much of the trouble popularly attributed to 'dirt-eating' . . . and even some of the proverbial laziness of the poorer classes of the white populations are . . . manifestations of uncinariasis" (1903, quoted in Ettling 1981: 35). Convinced of the significance of his findings, Stiles immediately began to seek a larger audience for his research. His ambitions in this regard led him to experiment with different names for the hookworm: in addition to dubbing the parasite *Uncinaria americana*, Stiles also coined the more sensational term *Necator*

americanus, meaning "the American Killer."[6] However, the name that became most popular and widespread among the general public, the name
that would resonate with the popular press and appear in most popular
accounts, came from an enterprising reporter. While lecturing before the
Sanitary Conference of American Republics in Washington, D.C., Stiles
remarked upon his findings in the South and the next day was surprised
to read the headline in the *New York Sun*: "Germ of Laziness Found? Disease of the 'Cracker' and of Some Nations Identified." The story brought
Stiles instant notoriety and established the hookworm as "the germ of
laziness" in the public imagination.[7] With this added boost of publicity,
Stiles began to seek financial support for his research.

In January 1909, after several long, frustrating years, he eventually
found a sponsor willing to fund a campaign that would combine scientific research with efforts to fight the disease. Northern billionaire John D.
Rockefeller donated $1 million and established the RSC, launching a mas-
sive public health campaign in eleven southern states, the first of its kind
in size and scope. The goals of the commission were threefold: to make
a geographic survey of the southern states and determine the extent and
degree of hookworm infection; to cure those suffering from the disease;
and to remove the source of the disease by putting a stop to "soil pollution," or open-air defecation (Rockefeller Sanitary Commission 1914: 6).

The formal announcement in October 1909 of Rockefeller's financial
contribution made front-page news in the *New York Times*. By this time,
nearly a decade after Stiles's discovery, hookworm doctors had widened
the scope of their research and found evidence of the disease across all
social groups in the South. Consequently, members of the RSC tried to
make clear in accepting Rockefeller's gift that hookworm disease was not
a problem related solely or even primarily to southern poor whites: "Two
millions of our people are infected with this parasite," they wrote. "It is
by no means confined to one class; it takes its toll of suffering and death
from the intelligent and well to do as well as from the less fortunate."[8]
The remainder of the *Times* article, however, reiterated the now familiar link between the hookworm and the southern poor white, describing the worm as "the parasite to which the shiftliness and laziness of a
certain class of very poor whites in the Middle South known locally as
'Crackers,' 'Sandhillers,' or 'Pinelanders' is attributed." The article goes
on: "The sufferers had no idea what was the matter with them, and in

Courtesy of Dr. J. L. Nicholson

A FAMILY OF "POOR WHITES" IN NORTH CAROLINA, ALL INFECTED WITH HOOKWORM DISEASE

"The 'Poor Whites' turned into an invalid population by the hookworm. One's first and strongest impression of the 'poor whites' is of their shiftlessness." From *McClure's Magazine*, 1909. Note the bare feet.

some instances their disinclination for work or exertion of any kind led to their being said to have the 'lazy sickness.'" Despite efforts by the RSC to broaden the focus to include other populations, the poor white remained the unofficial poster child for the crusade. This pattern of reporting held true in three more front-page hookworm articles that appeared later that month in the *Times*, one of which was a report on the Mississippi Medical Association's annual convention, where Stiles declared that "over two million southerners" suffered from the disease.[9] A second story reported again that the disease afflicted not only poor whites, but college students at the University of Georgia as well—perhaps as much as 30 percent of the student population—"many of whom were sons of the best southern families." However, this article assigned blame for the disease and delegated responsibility for the cure. The writer cautioned, "The wealthy and educated men of the South must realize that they and their wives and children are not immune to the hookworm's ravages. In their own defense, they will now bestir themselves about the condition of the poor whites. It is eternally true that the enlightened classes can advance only by carrying along with them the less enlightened and unfortunate classes. Some two millions of poor whites afflicted with this 'lazy man's disease' will benefit by the discovery of the prevalence of this scourge, for that will lead to remedial and preventive measures."[10] In short, the "poor white" was seen as both agent and pathway of infection. The editorializing of this northern urban newspaper was unmistakably intended for southern elites: take responsibility for the less fortunate of your race, and in so doing you may also save yourselves. Such direct appeals to the self-interest of the "enlightened classes" quickly became a central and lasting rhetorical strategy of the hookworm campaign.

These and other northern prejudices about the Old South, some of which were discussed in earlier chapters, figured largely in the *Times* coverage of the crusade. Of all the regional stigmas associated with the South, the one that lent the most legitimacy and authority to the hookworm crusade was the long-standing northern perception of the South as a region of death and disease. From the colonial period well into the late nineteenth century, the South was widely represented as a sickly region where malaria reigned as the chief endemic disease, frequent yellow fever epidemics killed thousands—black, white, rich and poor alike—and infant mortality rates were the highest in the nation.[11] Countless social observers, relying on poor understandings of miasma theories or a passing familiarity with colonial medicine, held forth with strong opinions about the negative health effects of southern tropical climates. So poor was the reputation (and to a lesser extent, the reality) of the South when it came to health that northern insurance companies charged higher premiums to their southern customers.[12] Some argued from a religious or spiritualist perspective that the diseases were mainly supernatural in origin—a kind of Divine Scourge. Others argued that the cause of disease lay in personal, individual behavior and that health could be ensured and maintained through proper diet, exercise, and discipline. A third group blamed individuals not for their behavior or bad habits, but for their "bad blood." The eugenics movement, as I discussed in the previous chapter, placed the blame squarely on degenerative germ plasm passed down from generation to generation, corrupting entire bloodlines, always threatening to spill out of the bounds of isolated poor rural white communities and into the general white population. A fourth view blamed environmental factors, drawing upon miasma theories and theories of contagion, claiming that rural farm life was filthy and foul. This view led to early public health interventions based on hygiene and sanitation and was of crucial importance during the hookworm campaign, when cleanliness became a national obsession.

The Diseased South

This nineteenth-century icon of the Old South as a region of death and disease—part gloomy myth and part social reality—took on a distinctively new shape through the hookworm crusade, even as it retained many of its older elements. In the late summer of 1908, readers of the *New York Times* opened the front section of the paper to find, under the ominous headline "A 'Vampire' of the South," the following story:

> The uncinaria, or hook worm, the cause of "lazy sickness" according to their State Board of Health, afflicts from 150,000 to 200,000 Georgians. *The Atlanta Constitution* calls this parasitic legacy of the African slave trade "a southern Vampire." . . . The State authorities are hampered by the unbelief of the people and by the very simplicity of the plan by which they hope to destroy the plague, the death rate from which they calculate to be greater than that from tuberculosis and pneumonia combined. The uncinaria is picked up in its embryo stage by barefooted children, and from the integument of the foot reaches the vital organs through circulation. The children grow into sickly, bloodless, indolent, and stupid adults. The ignorance of the negroes and poor whites precludes the cure, which can be had in one or two doses of thymol. Prevention of re-entry of the hookworm into the system is accomplished by wearing shoes. The State provides free diagnosis and treatment. Perhaps Georgia and other southern States may in time pass laws making the wearing of shoes compulsory.[13]

This melodramatic, Gothic tale, one worthy of Poe, had worms of death lurking behind every turgid phrase. The article offered a multitude of symbolic meanings to its readers. First, there was the horror of vampire hookworm itself: a bloodthirsty parasite, it was a survivor left over from the Old South era of African slavery. Sleeping, as vampires must, in the soil, it emerged only to suck the lifeblood of its ignorant, hapless victims. The hero, the State Board of Health, entered the story fight-

ing the "unbelief," "superstition," and "ignorance" of the people with
rationality and scientific knowledge. This hero was poised to save the
hookworm's victims—the afflicted children of the South who had been
tragically transformed into zombie-like grotesques, "sickly, bloodless,
indolent and stupid." These haunting, monstrous images would have
resonated deeply with northern readers who were avid consumers of
southern Gothic tales and who were predisposed to view the entire South
and especially its poor whites as tragic, backward, ignorant, full of death
and disease.[14]

As a factual account, the *Times* article made several potent but completely unsupported claims about the nature, causes, and outcomes of the
disease. The hookworm, it claimed, was brought to the South from Africa,
Trojan horse–style, smuggled inside the bodies of slaves. The hookworm
was identified as the cause of "lazy sickness," an ill-defined but widely ascribed condition thought to afflict primarily the poor whites and blacks
of the South, robbing them of energy and ambition, leaving them idle
and shiftless, and delivering them into lifelong poverty and dependence.
The *Times* also claimed that the victims of the hookworm were victimized not only by disease and the poverty it caused, but also by their
own idiocy and superstition. The vampire hookworm, according to the
article, survived and thrived through "the ignorance of negroes and poor
whites" alike, due to their potentially criminal habit of not wearing shoes.
Through rational intervention and judicious legislation, the article suggested, southern states could win the battle against lack of awareness and
physical disease and could finally put to rest the bloodsucking, undead
ghosts of the terrible past. Dramatically and effectively, the *Times* article
established symbolic and social linkages between blacks and poor whites
and assigned responsibility for the disease to both. It also suggested a
symbolic chain of reference between vampirism, parasitism, and slavery
that fit well with a common northern perception of the slave south—the
idea that southern whites were themselves parasitic vampires, living off
the blood and sweat of African slaves. Northerners' collective representations of the South were strongly affirmed, even as new information was
added to the cultural schema.

The unsupported claims of the article were repeated in much of the
subsequent reportage in the *Times* and elsewhere. However, as a rhetorical mode, Gothic melodrama was soon discarded in favor of one that was

religiously moralistic, evangelical, and optimistic. The hookworm campaigners themselves were partial to viewing their work as redemptive, as were most of the era's public health professionals. In their evangelical zeal, crusaders relied upon a message of the essential morality of cleanliness, a message that was especially effective in stirring religious sentiment and that meshed well with evolutionary models of human perfectibility that were prevalent in the sciences. The stitching together of religious and scientific models—a rare achievement in the early twentieth century—created a compelling vision of heroic combat against physical and moral corruption.[15] Typical of this blending of science and morality was the language used in the very first circular written by Stiles and published by the RSC, a tract on "Soil Pollution as Cause of Ground-Itch": "Soil pollution is the act of defiling the soil or rendering it unclean: it also refers to the condition of the soil caused by defiling it. The word '*pollution*' means about the same as the words 'defilement,' 'uncleanness,' and 'impurity' " (1910: 5–6). Stiles pointed out that "the Bible warns against soil pollution" and, in classic fundamentalist "proof text" mode, directed his readers to Deuteronomy 23, verses 12 and 13, which read as follows: "Thou shalt have a place also without the camp, whither thou shalt go forth abroad; and thou shalt have a paddle upon thy weapon; and it shall be, when thou wilt case thyself abroad, thou shalt dig therewith, and shalt turn back and cover that which cometh from thee." Stiles's homily was followed by a "Health Catechism" structured in a question-and-answer format common in religious training that concluded with a spiritual crescendo: "In olden times the heathen sacrificed the blood of their children on the altars of unknown gods. Shall we continue to sacrifice the blood of our children to the miserable hookworm?"[16] By relying on conventional moral sentiment and infusing prevention strategies with an aura of spiritual duty, moral obligation, sanctity, and purity, hookworm campaigners shared and helped shape the prevailing middle-class ideology of the moral basis for social reform and placed personal sanitation and hygiene in the center of early-twentieth-century social reform efforts. This relentless focus on individual responsibility served quite well to direct attention away from the profound social inequalities—poverty, illiteracy, Jim Crow discrimination, and regional underdevelopment—that made it difficult, if not impossible, for poor southerners, both black and white, to avoid the hookworm.

The rapturous language of the crusade. A poster (ca. 1910) from the Rockefeller Sanitary Commission's hookworm eradication campaign in North Carolina. From *The World's Work* (1912).

Chasing Dirt: The Sanitarians

Empirical discoveries in germ theory certainly helped fuel the hookworm crusade, but anxieties about and obsessions with cleanliness and sanitation derived from other, less scientific concerns (Tomes 1990). The middle-class compulsion to "chase dirt" went well beyond what sanitation science called for, answering a need for a way to differentiate and separate the healthy from the sick, the worthy from the unworthy, and the "American" from the "un-American." In effect, the sanitary codes of the early twentieth century functioned much like the biblical dietary laws in Mary Douglas's classic analysis of Leviticus—they modeled the forming of the national body through close attention to and regulation of the physical body.[17]

An early-twentieth-century Ransy
Sniffle, alive and apparently eating
dirt somewhere in the Carolina
Piedmont. "This weird, abnormal
appetite is now regarded as a
symptom of the disease, exhibited
when the infection is severe and the
digestive derangement has become
pronounced." From *McClure's
Magazine*, 1909.

Courtesy of Dr. Weston
A DIRT-EATER FROM A SOUTH
CAROLINA COTTON-MILL

Dirt not only symbolized disease (sanitarian reformers invented and
promoted the catchphrase "dirt = disease"), it also served to help designate class, social status, and group belonging (Williams 1991). The
middle-class fixation on dirt gave moral significance and cultural legitimacy to a social hierarchy based on a division of labor that placed some in
close contact with dirt and positioned others out of dirt's way. The mental
labor of the educated middle classes was thus seen to be *naturally* superior
to the manual labor of the working class and the poor. The prohibition
against dirt provoked disgust toward the poor, but also evoked a kind
of perverse fascination with their immoral habits (Stallybrass and White
1984: 191–202). Nowhere are the cultural effects of the taboo against dirt

more clearly demonstrated than in the middle-class fascination and disgust with the stigmatyping figure of the poor white dirt-eater discussed earlier in this book. While dirt eating—a practice known to physicians and anthropologists as pica or geophagy—existed, albeit rarely, among both blacks and whites in the South, early accounts of dirt-eating focused exclusively on "the most degraded of the 'poor white trash' [who] lived in the barren and sandy areas of the southern states, especially the Carolinas and Georgia (Twyman 1971: 44)."

Eating dirt is a symbolically transgressive act and expresses a deviant desire: it signals a desire to pollute oneself and to take pleasure in impurity, desires that upset the moral order of boundary maintenance. Dirt-eaters were thus assumed to be morally and socially deviant, as was the poor white class to which they presumably belonged. Media accounts of the hookworm campaign, especially in its initial stages, repeatedly linked the hookworm disease to the figure of the dirt-eater, and hookworm scientists insisted (incorrectly) that geophagy was a result, not a cause of the disease.[18]

Along with the many newspaper accounts and wire reports about hookworm in the early 1900s, there were dozens of articles published on the subject in the weekly and monthly magazines that adorned the parlors in tens of thousands of American middle-class homes.[19] In October 1909, the same month that Rockefeller announced his gift and established the RSC, an article on hookworm disease appeared in one such magazine, *McClure's*. It began with an anecdote about a North Carolina country doctor who observed a poor white ("a mere skeleton, ghastly pale") clinging to a hitching post. The doctor queried the poor white about his condition, only to discover that the man planned to treat himself with some iron filings and vinegar, a common home remedy for anemia. The anecdote, which served to exemplify poor white disregard for the expert advice of doctors, was a fitting prelude to the writer's subsequent characterization of poor whites as "a Great Abnormal Race of the South."

> Feeble, slow-moving creatures, you recognize them at once by their lustreless eye and a peculiar pallor — "the Florida complexion" — their skin is like tallow, and you seem to be looking through a semi-transparent layer into an ashy or saffron layer beneath. If you speak to one of these saffron-hued natives, especially to one of the children, you are generally met by a very

curious, fish-eyed stare, without a gleam of intelligence back of it, and you
wait long before you get a reply. The reply, when it does come, is very likely
a repetition of your own words and you go off saying "Stupid!" to yourself.
(Carter 1909: 617)

The passage neatly illustrated one of the stigmatizing webs of significa-
cations, spun by the hookworm campaigns, that clung to southern poor
whites at the turn of the century: dirt-eater=hookworm disease=idiocy
and feeblemindedness.[20] The symbolic nexus of dirt, disease, and ignorant poor whites appeared in countless documents related to the campaign. It appeared across all the most significant domains of representation—sciences, education, government, and journalism. Campaigners
depended upon it again and again in their education and reform efforts.
The dominant image of the poor rural white as hookworm sufferer established in popular journalism and scientific and medical research was frequently cited by historians and sociologists of the South, who reiterated
the image—quite uncritically and authoritatively—in scores of articles
and monographs.[21] In a remarkably short time, dirt, disease, and the
southern poor white were thus firmly linked in the national imagination.
The hookworm campaign greatly reinforced the power of these negative
linkages by backing them with the authority of science and the policies
of the state. So effective was the boundary work of the campaign that
the perception that hookworm disease and southern poor whites were
intimately and biologically linked—the idea that the hookworm and the
southern poor white somehow shared the same past and the same destiny and that the eradication of the one would lead to the elimination or
amelioration of the condition of the other—remained forcefully strong
in public and scientific opinion for many subsequent decades.[22]

Why did a campaign to improve the public health of all southerners
and to eliminate a deadly pathogen come to be figured as a crusade to save
southern poor whites from themselves, from poverty, from apathy, from
national neglect? How did the emphasis upon death and disease give way
to a focus on salvation and improvement? Answers to these questions can
be found by analyzing the emerging rhetoric of poor white uplift and by
looking to the economic forces affecting the so-called New South, in particular the forms of labor discipline related to capitalist transformation.

Two boys, one "too weak to work" and the other "almost an idiot." Hookworm infection often caused severe anemia, resulting in symptoms that were taken as signs of hereditary indolence and feeblemindedness. From *McClure's Magazine*, 1909.

Courtesy of Dr. Weston, Columbia, S. C.

TWO BOYS FROM FARMS IN SOUTH CAROLINA, BOTH INFECTED WITH HOOKWORM DISEASE. THE LARGER SLEEPS MOST OF THE TIME, AND IS TOO WEAK TO WORK IN THE MILL. THE SMALLER IS A DIRT-EATER AND ALMOST AN IDIOT; NOTICE HIS SWOLLEN STOMACH

Worms and Work

One's first and strongest impression of the "poor whites" is of their shiftlessness, [but] when the cure is complete, the South will take her place with the North and West in agricultural and industrial prosperity, for her two million sick whites will be two million able workers. — CARTER 1909: 618

The need for a more efficient and productive work force in the South was a theme that dominated many aspects of the hookworm campaign. That efficient, productive workers would be white was, in the minds of New South boosters, a given. The quote above clearly articulates the view that the ultimate justification for intervening in the lives and habits of the poor whites of the South was the unleashing of tremendous economic development that would follow. Many hookworm crusaders, particularly southern boosters, considered inefficient productivity due to sick and weakened workers to be the primary cost associated with the disease.

In order to understand these concerns, it helps to recall the rapid transformations in the southern economy that were taking place in the aftermath of the Civil War. Such dynamism and change was the result of many different forces, but chief among them were the abolition of chattel slavery and the penetration into the region of northern capital and industrialism. Between 1860 and 1880, agricultural output in the South declined precipitously.[23] But between 1880 and 1930, the South's growth in manufacturing and industry outpaced all other regions of the United States. Such rapid economic growth was not without corresponding social upheavals. During this era, the entire region was transformed from a relatively simple agrarian society of caste and class in which whites were mainly independent producers and blacks mainly slaves to a more complex and more highly differentiated social hierarchy of status and prestige. For blacks, emancipation and Reconstruction had given way to new forms of unfree labor under Jim Crow. Chattel slavery was now ended, but super-exploitation continued under post-Reconstruction relations of agricultural production, as interlocking systems of sharecropping, tenant farming, and debt peonage became the central mode of small farming. Not only blacks, but also poor whites and recent immigrants from Europe and Mexico were forced into this mode as well. Millions were reduced to serflike conditions where a small white elite dominated different groups of black and white sharecroppers, indebted tenants and permanent debtors virtually enslaved through peonage (Ayers 1992; Daniel 1985, 1990). As historian David Carlton (1982) has explained, "the biggest losers in this process were the poorer whites (the blacks having little to lose) and not being docile, they fought back. As a result, the period between the end of Reconstruction and World War I was one of intermittent, sometimes violent contention among whites over the emerging shape of their society" (7).

The hookworm crusade was one of these intermittent struggles, although it was markedly different from the labor struggles Carlton had in mind. The nature of the struggle over hookworm was cultural and not political or economic. Couched in the language of religious and moral reform and implemented through the practices of medical science and the state, the crusade was not a violent or particularly coercive operation. Its emphasis on efficiency and worker productivity, however, made it extremely attractive to New South boosters and industrialists, and to northern financiers and capitalists like John Rockefeller.

An example was the interest generated among northern capitalists and financiers by southern cotton mills and the textile industry of the Piedmont region. This interest was especially intense during the 1890s, when depressed cotton prices and declining regional advantage forced layoffs and shutdowns in scores of New England textile mills. Between 1880 and 1900, when mills in New England were declining, the number in the South rose from 239 to 400, an increase of 67.4 percent.[24] Most impressive of all was the growth in employment in the mills: during the same two decade period the population of mill workers swelled from approximately 17,000 to a little under 100,000, an increase of almost 600 percent.

Yet northern business elites remained skeptical about future prospects for the industry, which they saw imperiled by the lack of a stable, dependable workforce. Public health historian E. Richard Brown has argued that the RSC was specifically intended to increase worker productivity and integrate the "backward" South into an industrial economy controlled by northern capitalists. As evidence, he has pointed to a letter from Frederick Gates, a chief adviser of the RSC, to Rockefeller, wherein Gates noted that the stock prices of cotton mills in North Carolina were worth less than those in other areas because of the "inefficiency of labor in these cotton mills, and the inefficiency of labor is due to the infection by the hookworm which weakens the operatives" (quoted in E. R. Brown 1976: 899). Gates predicted an increase in efficiency of 25 percent if the mill workers were cured.[25] One of the real triumphs of the Rockefeller health programs both at home and abroad, Brown concluded, was the way in which they "reduce[d] the cultural resistance" of locals, better enabling the "domination of their lives and societies by industrial capitalism." The hookworm campaign demonstrated that "medicine was an almost irresistible force" in softening any indigenous resistance. In the words of one of the directors of the Rockefeller Foundation, "for purposes of placating primitive and suspicious peoples, medicine has some decided advantages over machine guns" (quoted in E. R. Brown 1976: 899). Brown's argument usefully illuminates some of the cultural effects of economic motivations, highlighting the fact that the campaign was motivated by desires to do more than altruistically heal the sick (E. R. Brown 1979).

More evidence for this interpretation may be found in the preoccupation with labor efficiency and worker productivity that dominated much of the popular press surrounding the southern hookworm crusade. For example, writing in *The World's Work*, Walter Hines Page (1912), a New South partisan, lauded the efforts of the RSC. Page, himself a southerner and a close friend of Gates, had played a major role in bringing Stiles's research and campaign to the attention of the Rockefeller Foundation (Tullos 1978: 40–45; Ettling 1981: 97–102). Page asserted that hookworm was the main cause of inefficient labor, not just in the South but in the entire world. Citing a letter from a physician who had established a free dispensary for the treatment of hookworm, Page quoted, "For the benefit of workers, we [dispense] each Sunday morning. By so doing, we do not take them away from their labor . . . I never invested a little money in anything that has ever given me half the pleasure I have gotten out of our hookworm crusade. There has been a remarkable increase in the intelligence of these people, rosy cheeks and bright eyes have taken the place of pallor and leaden eyes. . . . Many of them are going to be fine citizens someday" (512). In a phrase that reflected the peculiar blend of religion and economics that characterized the hookworm crusade, Page likened the dispensary fieldwork of the RSC to an industry that "show[ed] the efficiency of an admirable business organization and the fervor of religious propaganda" and further remarked that "the hookworm stands in the way to salvation" (513). To Page, the moral, economic, and civic implications of the hookworm campaign were clear: to improve the physical health of the southern poor whites was to return them to useful labor, opening the door for moral uplift, economic rebirth, and civic renewal throughout the entire region.

Uncertainty about whether the formation of the New South would help or hinder national economic and political development had provoked serious reconsideration of the region and its inhabitants by northern elites. The results for southern poor whites were equivocal at best. To be sure, masses of poor people were dewormed and the pace of construction of sanitary outhouses moderately increased. However, the more prominent and durable effects of the hookworm campaign rendered poor rural whites of the South more exploitable for the forces of industrial capital-

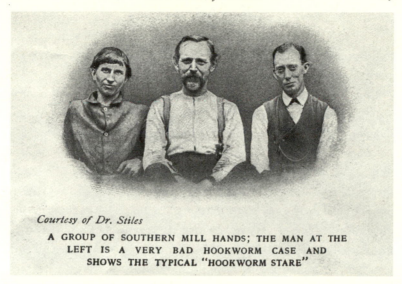

Courtesy of Dr. Stiles

A GROUP OF SOUTHERN MILL HANDS; THE MAN AT THE LEFT IS A VERY BAD HOOKWORM CASE AND SHOWS THE TYPICAL "HOOKWORM STARE"

"Retardation of development due to hookworms has caused a great deal of unmerited criticism to be heaped on the southern cotton mills." *McClure's Magazine*, 1909. Note the symptomatic fish-eyed stare of the one to the left. Poor white cotton mill operatives were widely stigmatyped with the label "lint-heads" — due to the clinging cotton dust of the humidified textile factories, the cause of the deadly brown lung disease — but they are regarded as unmistakably "white."

ism, subjugating their bodies and their personal habits to new forms of inspection, surveillance, and discipline. As a result, great masses of southern poor whites morphed into *lintheads*, the stigmatizing and derogatory term applied to southern textile workers from the Piedmont to Alabama. In a social promotion largely denied to blacks, the hookworm campaign helped transform the poor white from lazy dirt-eaters into mill hands — stigmatyped, but decidedly white.

"Purely Anglo-Saxon"

By 1910, the year the RSC began its most intensive work in the South, the eugenics movement had already managed to pass compulsory sterilization laws in six states, and proposals for such laws had already been discussed by eugenicists in several southern states. Southern legislators resisted these laws for a relatively longer time than did their northern counterparts, but eugenics was by now a powerful social movement, with leading intellectuals, politicians, and scientists among the ranks, and it was gaining new adherents every day (Larson 1995).

In the eyes of the hookworm crusaders, eugenicists were misunderstanding and miscategorizing the southern poor white. Poor whites, they thought, were not to be confused with racial degenerates or "mongrels," nor were they racially similar or inferior to blacks. Rather, poor whites were merely sick. In insisting upon the racial integrity and superiority of the southern poor white, hookworm crusaders challenged the increasingly dominant view that poor whites were, biologically speaking, a race of "feebleminded degenerates." As Marion Carter (1909) had written in *McClure's*, "the 'poor whites,' shiftless, ignorant, poverty pinched, and wretched, are of pure Anglo-Saxon stock — as purely Anglo-Saxon as any left in the country." Opposing the prevailing eugenic assessment of the poor white was a difficult and daunting task, but hookworm crusaders took to it with their customary religious zeal. They did not, however, tackle the issue head-on, taking instead a more oblique angle of attack and rarely, if ever, naming their adversaries. Crusaders were well aware of the fact that through well-established stigmas about dirt-eaters and lazy crackers an entire segment of the southern poor white population was commonly perceived as different on the basis of both behavior and physical appearance, particularly with respect to the shape of the body, the head, and the color of the hair and skin.[26] Everyone agreed that poor whites were lazy, dirty, stupid, and diseased. Eugenicists contended they were racially distinct as well. If this was true, would expensive social reform efforts work or would they founder on the "immutable" realities of racial inferiority? As RSC crusaders were keenly aware, the economic and cultural stakes were quite real, and the answer to the question would in large part determine the success or failure of their campaigns. Nothing less than the identity of the poor rural white was at stake, an identity that was as much about race and class as it was about national belonging.

The hookworm crusade manifested its preoccupation with establishing the boundaries of racial and national identity in several ways. There were the frequent assertions of the pure "Anglo-Saxon stock" of the poor white. There was the curious fascination expressed regarding the triangular relationship between the poor white, the black, and the hookworm —

suggesting a desire to differentiate and segregate the poor white body from that of the black and to scribe more boldly what was often, for the poorest people of the South, a very thin line. And by transforming the initial reputation of hookworm from a "foreign" disease to one of "native" origins, hookworm crusaders symbolically recast its poor white victims into the role of pure American workers for the New South. In these ways, the southern poor white figured in the minds of middle-class Progressive Era reformers and capitalist elites as more fully and more properly "white" and "American" than ever before. Consider the following passage, an especially vivid account from the *New York Times*, describing people with hookworm: "The people themselves, of pure Anglo-Saxon stock, though always poor were found as a rule to have yellow skin, wrinkled and waxy, hair dry and lusterless, eyes without color, and expressions stupid and melancholy. Besides emaciation these people often manifested a peculiar dropsical condition of the face and other parts of the body."[27] Close, clinical attention to the symptomatic body of the poor white/hookworm sufferer was a common feature of the stories in the *Times*, and it was echoed in magazine journalism. The reader's imaginative gaze was directed over the poor white body, to notice the hair; the unusual disposition; the sluggish movement; the dull expression; the abnormal shape; and finally, the skin. The skin was the most conspicuous of all, for it was layered, with a waxy, slightly opaque top layer, beneath which lay a yellow, ashen layer. Although the body went by many different names (*cracker, sandhiller, barrenite, poor white trash*), its distinctive nature was marked, made visible, in part by its skin. This mode of perceiving the defiled body of the poor white was, as we have seen, well established, with history that reached well back before the Civil War.

Hookworm crusaders sought to confront these modes of perception indirectly. Rather than refute eugenical science's claims about racial degeneracy of the miscegenated poor white, they ascribed a different reason for the oddly colored skin and the disturbing distinctiveness of the body. For example, Walter Hines Page (1912) noted, "The southern white people are of almost pure English stock. It has been hard to explain their backwardness, for they are descended from capable ancestors and inhabit a rich land. Now, for the first time, the main cause of their backwardness is explained and it is a removable cause" (509). The now familiar poor white paradox reappeared once more—how could it be that, given their superior racial ancestry, these whites were so backward? Page's simple answer was, of course, the hookworm. He further lamented the toll hookworm disease had taken on specific communities:

> As for the effect of the disease on the intellectual and moral qualities of a people, consider this picture of a dark Virginian neighborhood. The people had for generations been set apart by marked peculiarities from the people surrounding them. They made a dark spot on the map. A nickname of reproach was given to them. They were even regarded by some of the neighboring communities as a distinct race. They lived in abject poverty; they were of very low mental power; they had lost the normal moral perception of the surrounding communities; they lived in promiscuous immorality that is almost incredible. It was a country slum of the worst type. (512)

The imagery here was visual and chromatic: the "dark" neighborhood; the "marked peculiarities"; the "dark spot," suggesting a kind of racial stain. However, Page again reassured his readers that all the depravity and degradation was due not to defective blood, but to disease. As evidence, he cited the annual medical reports of the RSC:

> This whole population has for generations borne the burden of a heavy infection. The community has been islanded and isolated, with cumulative results—physical, intellectual, economic, and moral; from generation to generation there has been a lowering of vitality, physical, and mental. One result has been the deadening of the moral sense and the loss of self-respect. But the clearing of the moral atmosphere has already set in. The results are not only gratifying; they are stirring. I predict that within five years the whole face of this country will be changed and one will see here a new people and a new earth. (512–13)[28]

For Page, one of the most prominent and well-respected southerners of his day, the hookworm crusade promised regeneration through medical intervention. The removal of infection would lead to restoration of the poor white body and to a "clearing" of the atmosphere of moral contagion. In short, in a prophetic vision, the RSC proclaimed that lifting the "burden" of hookworm infection would restore the morality, honor, and self-respect of the benighted community, bringing the truly white and middle-class virtues of intelligence, self-respect, and sexual discipline.

OLD HOME OF HOOKWORM VICTIMS

THE CABIN IN WHICH AN INFECTED FAMILY OF
SIX PERSONS LIVED, NO MEMBER OF WHICH, FOR
FOUR GENERATIONS, HAD BEEN TO SCHOOL OR DONE
A FULL DAY'S WORK

THEIR NEW HOME

SIX MONTHS AFTER TREATMENT THIS HOUSE WAS
BUILT BY THE SAME FAMILY WHO NOW WORK
HOPEFULLY AND SEND THEIR CHILDREN TO SCHOOL

Home improvement. An entire family restored to health, work, education, and white respectability. From *The World's Work* (1912).

Interracial Pollution

The crusaders also performed boundary work by posing a triangular relationship between poor whites, blacks, and the hookworm. Both the scientific and popular literature on hookworm were replete with references to the idea that hookworm was originally "an African disease" (Reisman 1903: 612). It was not the poor white that was the source, but the African slave. What hookworm campaigners essentially argued was remarkably similar to the eugenicists' theories of cross-racial contamination as the root of the poor white problem. Yes, crusaders agreed, the poor white *was* the victim of cross-racial contamination, but not, as eugenicists argued, as the result of interracial pollution through sexual contact. It was, instead, soil pollution that had enabled the corrupting worm to be passed from black to white. Crusaders, acutely aware of the moral value and symbolic power of racial pollution to southerners, considered using this idea to whip up enthusiasm for the campaign.

For most of the campaign, it was assumed that soil pollution was the only significant vector of infection. However, in 1914, the final year of the campaign, Stiles began to take note of antifly crusaders' research on insects as carriers of disease. Stiles began using new bacteriological tests for *E. coli* that made it possible to detect whether or not a person had swallowed even minute quantities of human excrement. Using these tests, Stiles investigated some 2,372 randomly selected cases from twelve different localities in three different southern states. He quickly reached the conclusion that a significant vector of many diseases in the South was indeed the ingestion of human feces. In Stiles's reasoning, the lack of sanitary outhouses throughout the South resulted in a situation where flies bred and fed at the outhouses and then deposited excrement on food. Once he had verified this as a scientific fact, Stiles moved quickly to use it in the campaign. He and other crusaders were seeking ways to "create a sentiment which will lead the people of the better class to seek examination for hookworm disease. By making the idea 'fashionable' among the better class of people," they reasoned, "the most highly infected class will be more easily reached and will seek examination and treatment."[29] Stiles prepared an open letter, calling it a "Confidential Letter to the Most

Prominent Citizens." "Fight Flies, Filth, and Fever!" the letter began. It went on to explain the scientific findings in clinical detail.

> Our studies . . . demonstrate beyond question that of the 2372 persons tested. . . . 17.9% (namely, practically 1 person in every 5) has [*sic*] given us positive proof that he or she has actually swallowed human excrement. Our experiments show that one of the most common methods of bringing about this condition is through the means of flies; the flies breed and feed at the privies, soil their feet and bodies with filth, carry the filth to the food (as at stores, or in dining rooms and kitchens) with which it is swallowed. Our test does not show us whether the contamination in a given person comes from the privy of a white person or a negro neighbor, but as the two races are living in such close proximity, it is clear that each race is eating not only its own excrement, but also that of the other race. In justice to the Mothers in the South, it is our serious moral duty to protect them and their children from this totally unnecessary source of so much disease.[30]

After reading Stiles's circular, the campaign's Board of Directors suppressed it and would not permit Stiles to release it, an act that further alienated Stiles from the RSC. Apparently, the directors considered the scientific facts to be too scandalous and concluded the letter would hurt rather than help the campaign. The crusaders, in order to gain the support of white elites, had carefully constructed the disease as passing from black to poor white to middle- and upper-class white. Any deviation from that path of infection might be seen as insulting and dishonoring to higher-status whites. The threat of racial contamination and defilement—a miscegenating and polluting exchange of bodily wastes, however unintentional—simply provoked too much horror, disgust, and disbelief.[31] In the historical context of Jim Crow discrimination, the startling implications of this message—that segregation was not working, could never work, to fully protect whites from black pollution—could have easily turned white elites against the campaign.

In 1939, long after the RSC had ended its campaign, one of the Rockefeller Foundation's directors prepared an institutional history of the campaign years 1909–14. An early draft of the document was sent to Stiles for review. His very first comment in a long and querulous reply was that the document contained unacceptable references to *poor white trash*. "The expression 'poor white trash,' he wrote, "is probably of negro origin and is an exceedingly offensive one in the South."

> I would suggest the substitution of some other expression, namely, the tenant white or the poorer white population of the whites in lower brackets of income. It is to be recalled that these "poor whites" are that part of the population who have borne the brunt of the effect of slavery. Their financial condition made it impossible for them to own the better land and slaves, hence, they entered into economic competition with slave labor; their poverty prevented them from supplying themselves with conditions that would protect them from the imported African diseases; thus, a vicious circle was formed, namely, their poverty resulted in disease and their diseases resulted in poverty. They were not responsible for their conditions and the expression "poor white trash" is as unjust when applied to them as the expression "poor white trash" would be if applied to Tubercular patients in the slums of New York. They are exceedingly sensitive people and if the Rockefeller Office were to use the expression "trash" as applied to them this would react unfavorably on the Rockefeller Office. Thus, from their point of view and from the point of view of the Rockefeller Office I would suggest the elimination of this term.[32]

Stiles, in looking back, gave voice to a number of ideas and concepts that had been virtually absent in the work of the RSC three decades earlier. In these comments, he not only acknowledged a causal link between poverty and disease, he also advanced a social theory of the origins of southern poor whites, offering a slight variation on the old abolitionist argument: that the poor whites of the South were victims who suffered due to the slave system and disease, and were thus undeserving of being called "trash."

Americanizing the Hookworm

The transmission of diseases among races was an explicit concern of white American nativists in the first two decades of the twentieth century, as was the health menace posed by foreign-born groups. Immigration, medicine, and public health interacted to shape prejudices and policies that expressed xenophobia. Alan Kraut (1994) has argued that this symbolic linkage of specific populations to diseases allowed for "medicalized nativism": a situation where "the entire group is stigmatized . . . being reduced from 'a whole and usual person to a tainted, discounted one,' because of association with disease in the mind of the native born" (3). However, not only the foreign born were stigmatized in this way. The same patterns of stigmatization applied to those groups of native-born "Americans" who were not fully assimilated to "the established order's cultural preferences and priorities" — those who lived in rural or hinterland areas into which the "established order" had not yet penetrated.[33] As the "African origins" story demonstrated, however, the hookworm was originally perceived as an outside agent, an imported threat, and an ironic legacy of the slave trade. Similarly, the outbreak among Swiss rail workers in 1880 that lent it the name "tunneler's disease" also branded it as a disease of immigrants in the United States. The fact that the first recorded case of hookworm in the United States was found in a European immigrant bricklayer enhanced this perception. Early newspaper reports show that, especially in New York, the disease was linked with both immigrants and southerners. In a January 1910 article, Dr. Harlow Brooks, who claimed to have treated a considerable number of cases during the fall of 1909, explained how he believed the hookworm had reached New York and indicated how he thought it would spread. The first case

> was that of an Irishman who worked as a rock driller in the reservoir at Brewster . . . [and] it has also been found in the cases of laborers who have come from Italy and other countries. We have received some cases from the South too . . . It is likely that the infection may become generally more spread here eventually, especially among those who work in the earth. Hundreds of men have flocked here recently to take positions in subway or in water works construction and quite a number of them have brought the hookworm along.[34]

Among the archival records of the RSC, there are many examples of queries about the link between hookworm and immigration (see RSC 1911). In response to a "legal question" about "whether or not, within the meaning of immigration laws, the disease known as hookworm is regarded as contagious," Wycliffe Rose, the director of the RSC, responded that the disease has been and is being transmitted by immigration. The importation of coolie labor from India has been instrumental in spreading the disease in Ceylon, the Malay States, Siam, Natal, British Guyana and some of the British West Indies. Microscopic examination of a ship load of coolies at San Francisco showed heavy infection, whereupon the authorities there have taken action against receiving infected immigrants . . . prevent[ing] . . . steamship companies from transporting Chinese laborers afflicted with hookworm disease through the United States.[35]

Drawing too many parallels between the poor white inhabitants of the South and other colonized populations posed a problem, however. If part of the crusaders' efforts were to persuade elites about the racial purity of poor whites, then it would weaken their argument to suggest that poor white southerners had much in common with colonized, racially inferior peoples. In other words, perceptions of the disease as "foreign" or "un-American," associated with black slaves and undesirable immigrants, might work against the goal, important to southern boosters and northern business elites, of making over the southern poor white into an authentically white, working-class American. Making such fine distinctions required careful boundary work. In their writings after 1909, hookworm crusaders exhibited a tendency to portray the hookworm not only as a southern problem, but also as a national "American" problem. For Page, one of the most prominent southerners in the crusade, hookworm was as fully southern as could be: "It is not malaria, it is not the warmth of the climate, it is not the after-effects of slavery, it is not a large 'poor white' element of the population—but it is the . . . hookworm [and it] has probably played a larger part in our southern history than slavery or wars or any political dogma or economic creed" (1913: 509). Other writers, including Stiles, were careful to claim hookworm disease as an unfortunate but lasting legacy of the Old South, one that held important implications for the entire nation.[36] The hookworm was, after all, not the "southern" but the "American" killer. Crusaders struggled to find ways to symbolically domesticate the disease—to establish it as an endemic, indigenous pestilence—and thereby establish the pure "American-ness" of its poor white sufferers.[37] Consider the proposals put forth by William Weston, a South Carolina physician, who worked extensively in Piedmont cotton mills and tirelessly preached the Progressive ideal that the

South must be economically, socially, and politically integrated into the American system. Full integration required a stable, dependable workforce (one presumed to be white), and Weston explicitly rejected calls for increased immigration to the South. Instead, he maintained, the indigenous poor whites of the South constituted the ideal workforce, for these native foreigners "speak our language [and] are familiar with our laws and customs." Once the un-American deviance — the laziness, the filthiness, the immorality — of poor whites was eliminated by freeing them of the hookworm, Weston argued, they would rise to assume "the responsibility of citizenship" (W. Weston 1908, quoted in Marcus 1989: 115).[38]

Weston was just one of many who saw the hookworm problem as an issue of national significance and as a primary social and economic issue for the New South (see Tullos 1989 for more examples). For many observers, the hookworm itself had become an apt metaphor for the entire undeveloped South: an alien element within the land, a foreign body within the national body, one that through its unproductive and inefficient relationship to capitalism threatened to suck away the lifeblood of the entire nation. Crusaders used the language and sentiment of patriotic nationalism and white racial supremacy to rehabilitate the image of the region and its poor white inhabitants.[39]

By 1915, the RSC was officially closed and its efforts were redirected to other parts of the globe under the auspices of the International Health Board (IHB) of the Rockefeller Foundation. The crusade was widely hailed by public health and governmental officials as a complete success. In 1927, the same year that Carrie Buck was surgically sterilized without her consent in Virginia, the RSC announced confidently, "It is fair to state that the hookworm disease has almost disappeared from the United States" (quoted in Stiles 1939: 305). This was a highly dubious claim. When one considers the high rates of reinfection and Stiles's own publicly stated reservations about the effectiveness of the campaign, it remains far from clear that the campaign crusade should be counted much of a public health success at all. Rather, what made the RSC appear so successful was its innovative approach to the seemingly intractable problem of the southern poor rural white. One of the true successes of the crusade was the way it repositioned and redefined the social role of southern poor rural whites without posing any major challenge to the emergent racial and class formations of the New South and the way it confirmed northern perceptions of the South as a region rife with sickness and disease, while simultaneously proffering a cure.

"A Matter of National Concern"

When it was launched in 1909, not every southerner greeted the RSC with open arms. Many were outraged at the suggestion that the region and its inhabitants were diseased and backward. Many saw the RSC as yet another episode in a long history of nefarious attempts by northern capitalists to manipulate or destroy southern ways of life. The day after the press release announcing the formation of the RSC, Bishop Warren Candler of Florida launched a crusade of his own, protesting that "for some reason, self-appointed philanthropists have taken it upon themselves to discover and proclaim conditions in the South calculated to create further prejudice against the States and people of the South, to divert immigration, and to alarm the resident population." Candler fulminated against both Rockefeller and Stiles, satirizing them as arrogant men who, in his words, "would take charge of both our heads and our stomach, and purge our brains of ignorance and our bowels of worms."[40] Candler prophesied that the hookworm campaign, like the campaign against pellagra, would fail in its stated objectives and that it would accomplish little more than increasing northern prejudice and stigmatization toward the South.[41]

Public expressions of southern animus and suspicion toward the campaign continued throughout the fall and into January 1910, when Governor Hadley of Missouri, replying to a letter of inquiry from the head of the Business Men's League of St. Louis, refused to send any delegates to the hookworm convention slated to assemble in Atlanta later that month. The paper noted that Hadley ridiculed the purposes of Rockefeller's campaign and that "while he had sent delegates to nearly every convention under the sun, he drew the line at hookworm."[42] Complaints, suspicion, and distrust were certainly not limited to Methodist bishops and governors. In North Carolina, rumors circulated widely that Rockefeller was expanding his interests in shoe manufacturing and retail and that the campaign was an elaborate monopolist scheme to outlaw bare feet and legislate the wearing of shoes (Cassedy 1971: 166; Link 1990).

Although theirs were the voices of the minority and the choirs of cru-

A PRELIMINARY TO THE WORK OF HEALING

MICROSCOPISTS (AT THE SMALL TABLE AT THE RIGHT) EXAMINING SPECIMENS FOR THE COUNTRY FOLK. IN SUCH GATHERINGS, NEARLY 100 PER CENT. OF THE PEOPLE ARE INFECTED WITH HOOKWORM DISEASE.

White uplift through disease control. A Rockefeller Sanitary Commission dispensary, c. 1910. "Every man who knows the people of the Southern states sees in the results of this work a new epoch in their history . . . and in our national history. The Southern white people are of almost pure English stock. [Until now] it has been hard to explain their backwardness."

saders would drown out their protests, Candler and others spoke to legitimate worries: would the campaign not adversely affect northern attitudes toward southerners? Given the campaign's focus on sanitation and education and the accompanying moral overtones, would not northerners continue to see the poor whites of the South as more or less uniformly dirty, ignorant, and immoral, perhaps even more so? Would not the success of the campaign require scare tactics and the creation of a moral panic about the epidemic proportions of the infections? Was this kind of public health, they seemed to be saying, worth the cultural price?[43] The larger cultural effects of the crusade included the penetration into the rural South of middle-class values of cleanliness and hygiene; the consolidation and enhancement of the professional authority and economic and political power of the medical and public health establishment; the beginnings of the process of "whitening" and Americanization of the crackers, dirt-eaters, and poor white trash of the South; the medicalization of the processes of racial delineation, separation, and segregation that characterized the Jim Crow South; and the modeling and shaping of a properly receptive, docile, and efficient southern white industrial worker. Perhaps Candler and his fellow southern resisters were not so far off in their reactionary assessment of the crusade.

The South needed its workers, and this capitalist imperative, perhaps more than any other force, explains why the South—and not the West, which also experienced high rates of hookworm infection—was singled out for the crusade. The South was the ideal place to harness the discourses of race and nationality and to impose the middle-class cult of cleanliness and hygiene. As one prominent physician, an editor of *American Medicine*, H. Edwin Lewis (1909) contended, the disease was "a matter of national concern" because it was an identifiable and "removable cause of part of our own racial deterioration." Although poor whites were clearly "suffering from their notorious neglect of cleanliness," Lewis believed a physician-led education campaign would eradicate "the lack of intelligence" that prevented poor whites from "learning how to be as clean as [members of] civilized communities should be." He called upon doctors and educators to end "the defective development which has apparently removed [poor whites] from national control" (quoted in Marcus 1989: 117).

Hookworm crusaders took an active and aggressive attitude toward defending and restoring the racial purity of the poor rural whites of the South. By portraying them as victims, "not responsible for their condition," crusaders established the basis for viewing the uplift of poor whites as a social cause. By insisting that these poor white victims were of pure Anglo-Saxon descent, crusaders sought to evoke sympathy where before there had been scorn and disgust. Through their efforts, the terms *lazy crackers* and *poor white trash* entered the national consciousness and imagination in a new way. Organized groups of poor whites began to confront the stigma of racial inferiority and white liminality.[44] For the first time, in the eyes of many, the poor whites of the South became a worthwhile cause.

chapter five

Limning the Boundaries of Whiteness

The domain of social life is essentially a domain of differences.
— MARCEL MAUSS, quoted in Lamont and Fournier 1992: 1

Social identity lies in difference, and the difference is asserted against
what is closest, which represents the greatest threat.
— PIERRE BOURDIEU (1984: 479)

Erskine Caldwell's *God's Little Acre* (1933) opens with an ironic and satirical scene. A bedraggled band of southern poor whites are digging for gold. As it turns out, they have been digging, unsuccessfully, for over fifteen years. They have torn up the ground around their ruined settlement and burrowed through sand, dirt, and clay in search of the elusive yellow metal. These characters, led by the comically grotesque figure of Ty Ty Walden, are dirt poor, fallen farmers whose futile mining efforts are destroying what little is left of their land. According to one of Ty Ty's neighbors, Pluto, local folk wisdom says there is a secret to finding the gold: you need "a diviner." "What you folks need is an albino to help you out," he says. "A man ain't got as much of a chance as a snowball in hell without an albino to help."

Puzzled, Ty Ty replies, "What in the pluperfect hell is an albino, Pluto?"

"He's one of these all-white men who look like they are made out of chalk or something just as white," Pluto replies. "An albino is one of these all-white men, Ty Ty. They're all white; hair, eyes, and all, they say. . . . It's the all-whiteness, Ty Ty" (9–11). Caldwell's meaning is transparently clear: If the Ty Ty Waldens of the world were ever to strike it rich and enjoy wealth and success, they needed to have pure whiteness on their side. Pure whiteness always brought the gold—without it, you got nothing but dirt. Caldwell, the acid satirist of southern poor whites, gives us a vignette that serves as a fitting conclusion to this book.

I began this book by making the case that *white trash* is more than just an ordinary slur. Of course, in the mundane sense, it is inescapably that and always has been. *White trash* and its related slurs exhibit the general features shared by symbolic markers of stigma and dishonor. Primary among these features are effects of symbolic distancing and social exclusion through moral disapproval, resulting in "us/them" dichotomies that both enable and enact different forms of inequality, prejudice, and discrimination. Consequently, such terms are crucial markers of status and prestige and serve to establish thresholds of inclusion and respectability. As such, they are important symbolic resources in the struggle to attain social closure.[1]

My purpose has not been to construct an exhaustive, encyclopedic account cataloguing historical utterances of these terms, although this book offers a wide range of examples. Rather I sought to focus, whenever possible, on specific moments and places where poor whites became the subject of sustained or intense public scrutiny and debate. To this end, I selected a number of specific historical periods when *white trash* and its related terms appeared to cluster in the archives. In each case, I sought to identify the many meanings that circulated around these terms and to identify not only who was being named, but by whom. Furthermore, I described and analyzed these moments as examples of boundary work and asked about their social and cultural effects. What emotions did these interpretations evoke? What kinds of collective actions were taken based on these interpretations? Who gained in status and prestige and who did not? In this way, I sought to link the process of symbolic boundary making to the collective expression and institutionalization of power, domination, and inequality.

My major theoretical aim in this book has been to test some of the core ideas in both whiteness studies and boundary studies and to explore through them what we might learn about mechanisms and effects of social differentiation. My methodological aim has been to join historical methods with sociological methods to treat meanings and interpretations of boundaries as primary grounds of social action.[2] At the intersection of interdisciplinary models like boundary theory with interdisciplinary fields like whiteness studies, we can expect to see new insights and new intellectual and political agendas emerge. As I hope this book has demonstrated, such an exchange can be fruitful for both areas of research.[3]

The Strange Career of *White Trash*

A unifying thread that runs through the chapters in this book has been the effort to understand and analyze some of the ways that *white trash* and its linguistic kin have historically been used as boundary terms that have not only marked out a despised and stigmatyped white other but enabled the articulation and rearticulation of white as a bounded cultural identity.[4] While *white trash* exemplifies some very general features of social differentiation, it has its own unique and peculiar history. Its deep origins lie within fifteenth-, sixteenth-, and seventeenth-century English bourgeois conceptions of the poor as immoral, lazy, and criminal.[5] Those origins were left unexplored by this book, which picked up the trail in North America, in the eighteenth-century British colonies of Virginia and North Carolina. There, the figure of the lazy lubber as popularized by William Byrd in 1728 established a basic frame of the colonial poor white as a picaresque curiosity, an ethnological oddity to be classified somewhere below native Indians in the natural order of things. Excluded from land ownership, faced with few opportunities, the impoverished lubber dwelled both literally and figuratively in the colonial borderlands. Geographically and politically, lubbers occupied the boundaries and frontiers, staying out of sight of administrative and judicial powers. Culturally and socially, they lived on the margins, beyond the reach of even the few civilizing colonial institutions that existed at the time. Economically, they survived by squatting, in blatant disregard of colonial property claims, and by crossing over the colonial color lines, grouping and allying themselves with other marginalized and despised social groups like Indians and runaway slaves.[6] They eked out a subsistence existence by engaging in both primitive agriculture and herding, a hybrid survival strategy that further alienated them from the planter elite. To many observers, they must have appeared as neither fish nor fowl—anomalous creatures that prompted emotional reactions ranging from amusement to disgust and its close companion, desire.

Byrd's descriptions suggest that these lubbers were viewed primarily as symbolic threats to the still unstable social order. Their social practices and lifestyles were so at odds with the tidewater plantation ideal and their numbers thought to be so few that colonial patriarchs took little serious note of them, except perhaps when doing so could bolster their own self-image as superior white men. This perception of the nature of the threat began to change in the tumultuous decades leading up to the American Revolution. The survival strategies of poor colonial whites grew to include organized raiding and thieving and began to cause serious trouble for colonial authorities and Indians alike. The symbolic threat of the lubber materialized as an economic and political one, and a transmogrified figure, the cracker, appeared on the cultural landscape. The cracker's reputation drew upon the earlier image of the colonial poor white but added new elements of violence, cruelty, treachery, and criminality, all of which triggered the repressive apparatus of both the colonial government and local vigilantes. Where the lubber had been dismissed as a social cast-off, the cracker was targeted for arrest, imprisonment, vigilante terror, and death. Amusement, disgust, and desire had been replaced by fear, hatred, and extrajudicial violence. Had revolutionary fervor not swept the colonies in the 1770s, the colonial campaign against the cracker may have well deteriorated into an extended internal border war.

Within a few decades after the close of the revolutionary period, the image of poor whites changed once again. With the merging of formerly warring colonies into the United States of America, what had started in the South as a regional stigmatype now became a significant national fixation. Poor white trash entered the national drama of unification and took center stage, alongside blacks. While there had been little commentary about the origins of the crackers or speculation about the causes of their criminality, poor white trash became the subject of extensive public debates in the antebellum period. Social observers of all kinds agreed that poor white trash lived in deplorable and degenerate conditions — indeed, it was those very conditions that seemed to define them as trash. But from the 1840s to the end of Reconstruction in the 1870s, the same social observers hotly debated the reasons for the degeneracy of poor white trash. These debates reflected the emerging conflicts over the shifting boundaries of race, class, politics, and culture that erupted in the Civil War.

On one side, northern abolitionist reformers argued that the existence of poor white trash in the South was evidence of the moral corruption and debasement that a slave society visits upon all its members. End slavery, they argued, and the poor white trash would rise to their rightful place as respectable white citizens and industrious workers. On the other side, southern proslavery apologists argued that a "degenerate" class of poor whites in the South existed not because of social or economic factors, but rather as the result of "natural inferiority," the inherited depravity that comes from generations of "defective blood." As proof, they pointed to the existence of white trash in non-slave states.

When it came to thinking about poor whites, Americans now had a wide variety of different stigmatypical images to choose from, as well as a set of opposing explanations. That is to say, they had a sufficiently complex cognitive schema, a contradictory set of representations that could be used to make adequate sense of the conundrum of poor whites. Within this interpretive frame, poor white trash were poor and trashy either because they were victims of social and economic exclusion, or because of tainted heredity. These differing interpretations over the meaning and cause of poor white trash intensified in the decades leading up to the Civil War and they continued to shape culture and politics during Reconstruction. As its cultural influence grew, this schema effectively established an interpretive framework for understanding poor whites that would take on new significance and cultural authority in the early-twentieth-century encounter with science, medicine, and public health.[7]

By the Progressive Era of 1920s, though the basic framework remained unchanged, a new set of theories had taken shape to explain the existence and persistence of this despised social group. Two groups of educated, middle-class reformers vied for the professional and cultural authority to explain the problem of the poor white to the rest of the nation. On the one hand, eugenicists like Dugdale had argued since the late nineteenth century that the source of poor white trash depravity was "defective germ plasm"—hereditary impurities that resulted from incest and from racial and class miscegenation. On the other hand, beginning in the early 1900s, a small but increasingly powerful group of medical doctors and educators, led by Dr. Charles Stiles and backed by the Rockefeller Foundation, argued that poor white trash suffered not from hereditary impurities, but from a recently discovered and eradicable parasite, the American hookworm.

Both groups of professionals assumed that the nation's poor white trash posed a significant set of social, economic, cultural, and political problems. However, professionals differed both in their interpretations of the problems and in the actions they took to solve them. Eugenicists advocated confining the problem through segregation, institutionalization, and involuntary surgical sterilization of the "feebleminded." Hookworm campaigners argued instead that southern poor whites, once cured of the "laziness disease" brought on by the hookworm, would regain the superior moral, intellectual, and cultural qualities that were their racial birthright. While eugenics campaigners were broadly successful in their efforts to portray poor rural whites as inherently inferior and dysgenic, it was the efforts of hookworm campaigners that symbolically opened the door to development of a southern, white working class—a "whitening" of southern poor whites. For in the years that followed the hookworm campaign, the poorest whites of the New South began to shed some of the stigma that had formerly been attached to their condition. In doing so, they gained a new measure of respectability as workers and Americans that had previously eluded them.[8] The boundary lines that limned whiteness were being redrawn once again.

In all of these periods, changing perceptions of poor whites were tied to important historical shifts and transformations in class structures, in racial taxonomies, in gender relations, in political economy, in reform movements, and in the status and content of social scientific and medical knowledge. As historical situations changed, so did the symbolic boundaries that served to establish social categories of both inclusion and exclusion and the social boundaries that inscribed the dominant categories with power and privilege. A major theme of this book has been that for the historical periods under consideration, one of the most important and consequential social categories was the category *white*.

Whiteness Studies Revisited

I define *white* as a social category, not a racial category. Of course, it carries unmistakable racial meanings, but as I have argued in this book, to see it as racial and nothing more is to misapprehend it. *White* and *whiteness* speak to much more than color and race. We know this because the grounds on which lubbers, cracker, and poor white trash have been excluded from belonging in the category *white*, the reasons given for their lack of whiteness have encompassed far more than just ideas about racial difference. The social domination that whiteness enables is of many different forms and relies on many different kinds of social difference. Why subsume all of these disparate mechanisms under the signs of race or white supremacy? It requires us to elevate one form of social difference, race, to the level of analytical preeminence. Why do this?[9] If it is a mistake to reduce race to class, as so many have argued (Roediger 1991; Omi and Winant 1994; Winant 1994; Wray and Newitz 1997), surely it is also a mistake to reduce manifold forms of social difference to race. The idea that *whiteness* is "about race" is simply not adequate to account for the case of *poor white trash*, a boundary term that speaks equivocally and ambivalently to the question of belonging and membership in the category *white*, and one that mobilizes a wide array of social differences to do so.

I offer two suggestions for charting new directions and approaches in whiteness studies. The first is theoretical and conceptual and the second concerns method. First, we should acknowledge that whiteness need not be analytically precise to be useful. Reconceptualizing whiteness as a flexible set of social and symbolic boundaries that give shape, meaning, and power to the social category *white* focuses the attention of whiteness studies exactly where it belongs—on the processes and agents that generate symbolic boundaries and grant them social power. These are precisely what I have targeted in this book. Second, students of whiteness should focus on how white majorities are made not just on the basis of race, but through successful attempts to control and define multiple boundaries of social difference. There are many interpretive methods available that enable us to bring this focus to our research, and I need not enumerate them here. The point is that for whiteness studies the methodological focus should be on the strategies majorities use to articulate and institutionalize their own schemas of social difference and hierarchy. I have chosen to track the movement of this latent, invisible power by gauging the impacts and effects of shifting boundary terms and stigmatypes, but I could have approached this question in other ways.

Boundary Theory Revisited

We are a class of beings that classify. In classifying, we introduce differences, draw boundaries, and create categories that are not inherent features of things themselves. We use these conceptual constructs to make sense of the world, to render discrete and bounded the flow of raw sensory information. In the social world, the classifying process enables us to place ourselves and others in relation to one another as we stake out the boundaries of our individual and group identities. Boundary theory is devoted to analyzing and understanding these classifying processes and their manifold effects (Zhao 2005; Zerubavel 1991). Here, I will briefly assess the major gains and shortcomings associated with this theoretical approach.

Group boundaries are inescapable, permanent features of social life, as are the boundaries that give shape to the self. With regard to group and identity formation, boundaries come into existence through three major mechanisms: (1) The observation and documentation of differences that exist among humans. These may be perceived differences in anatomy; religious beliefs; skin color and hair type; language; economic status; mental and physical abilities; region—in short, anything at all. (2) The construal and interpretation of those differences as socially significant by attaching to them shared meanings and collective representations. (3) The division of people into social groups based on those shared meanings and representations. Initially, this is an intersubjective process of attaching social significance and social meaning to differences that may or may not be significant in terms of how they affect individual agency and action. But after a time and under the right conditions, the process of making these differences socially salient—of making them not just visible, but focal points of difference to which our vision is drawn again and again—can lead to the formation of objective social boundaries that exclude and divide and to practices that render human relationships unequal.

From the point of view of this study and from the point of view of boundary theory, what is most interesting is that boundaries can exist and produce social categories whether or not there are actual people inhabiting those categories or not. Group formation—in the sense of symbolic boundaries calling forth and creating a social collective—need not occur in order for group-like effects and interactions to be observably present. The attribution of "groupness" to a particular collection of individuals sets the process of social differentiation in motion. Group effects like boundary work, intergroup conflict, and status differentiation can and do occur whether or not there are "real" groups standing behind these processes. In other words, even when those perceived as a social group don't coalesce around their ascribed identity "as they should" (that is, as our theories expect them to), others act "as if" they have.

As I have shown throughout the book, giving names like *cracker, white trash,* and *poor white* to light-skinned people of low status didn't often result in the formation of bounded groups of poor whites that acted as collectives, but the perception that such groups did exist often had the effect of mobilizing others to take dramatic social action. Social differentiation can occur whether the perception of social difference is valid or not (Brubaker 2004). It is the definition, imposition, and reiteration of the boundary that makes the difference.[10] The resulting social divisions can seem so "real" and "natural" to those living amid them that there is a strong tendency to believe they are timeless biological or scientific facts, rather than social facts that have been assembled and built up through human effort. The recognition of this tendency reroutes our thinking around the seemingly intractable problematic of essentialism versus antiessentialism and primordialism versus circumstantialism endemic to identity analysis today.[11] This, then, is the first major gain: boundary theory provides a theory of group formation and social differentiation that does not require us to choose between subjective or objective realities, while still allowing us to observe and document the existence of various group effects. We need not have the discussion, for instance, about whether or not race is "real" (see, for example, the debate between Bonilla-Silva [1997] and Loveman [1999]).

A second major gain is that we can use boundary theory as a model for comprehending and comparing through a single marker of difference varied processes of social differentiation — class, race, ethnicity, gender, sexuality, nationality, and so on. We can refuse to view each of these areas as distinct and monadic categories of identity and we can refuse to study them in isolation from one another, only to have to then search for reconstructive models that will allow us to reconnect them and grasp their "intersectionality."[12] Instead, we can use boundary theory to analyze interrelated, simultaneously occurring and recurring processes of identification and group formation — processes that historically have been central to the development of stratified human communities and societies. This synchronic approach — embedded in accounts of historical change — enables us to observe the intersection and simultaneity of various aspects of social identity without stating in advance that this one was a conflict about gender roles, this one a conflict about class, and this one about race. We are led instead to observe the historical construction of group boundaries and then to observe how those same boundaries may serve as a foundation for or a reflection of a particular gender/sex regime, a particular class structure, a particular ethnoracial taxonomy, or a particular hierarchy of status. Boundary theory can also help the researcher avoid the unfortunate tendency — still prevalent in current analyses — to privilege one form of domination, say, racism, class domination, patriarchy, or heteronormativity, as paradigmatic for other forms or modalities of domination. In boundary theory, what is of primary analytical importance is the boundary and its associated mechanisms. *Class*, *race*, *gender*, and *sexuality* can be understood as ways of foregrounding and objectifying certain aspects of the boundary and its manifold operations, but none by itself constitutes the boundary in its entirety.

If these are some of the advantages, what are some of the shortcomings of boundary theory? Here I offer two caveats: one theoretical and one methodological. First, merely cataloging various boundaries and noting the kinds of identity work they do is insufficient for understanding their role in enabling social domination and its attendant hierarchies of inequality. In order to grasp this dimension of power and domination, some concept of social closure or boundary work is required. These notions are essential to boundary theory, for they direct our attention to the strategic actions taken in order to secure privileges, institutionalize social advantages, and create the social boundaries that favor the dominant. Without them, boundary theory proffers no theory of power.

In terms of method, boundary theorists need to develop more precise ways to conceptualize the important differences between *categories, properties*, and *boundaries* and to devise appropriate methods for studying each of these distinct but related entities. How do we distinguish between the category *white*, the criteria for *whiteness*, and the boundary terms like *white trash* that mark the limits and edges of the category? The potential advantage is that by isolating and focusing on the differences among categories, properties, and boundaries, we may be able to offer fuller, more comprehensive accounts of the logic used to determine group membership and belonging, both at the level of everyday practices of differentiation and at the level of technical, institutional administration of difference.[13] Most important, such a focus may help us to better recognize the hidden roles that boundary markers like *poor white trash* play in precipitating important transformations of social categories and the criteria used to establish belonging in them. I say most important because boundaries, not the categories they delimit or the properties they are believed to represent, are the place where change and flux have the greatest impact. In everyday terms, boundaries and margins are where all the action is.[14]

Analyzing Social Differentiation: An Incomplete Project?

If, as Mauss asserts in the epigraph to this chapter, social life may be characterized as a realm of differences, then how are those differences created? How are they maintained and transformed? How do they come to be the bases of inequalities? If the goal of social analysis is to understand the social world, why not seek a unified theory of social differentiation? Why not use boundary theory as a starting point for such an intellectual endeavor?[15]

The search for a unified theory of social differentiation—a way of bringing together class, race, gender, and sex analysis into a single comparative frame—may not initially appeal to those whose analytical style has been shaped by poststructuralism. That philosophical stance has made us skeptical of grand narratives, made us wary of speaking about social totalities, and inclined us to focus on local knowledges, structures rather than structure. Admittedly, constructing a theory of anything can be a little scary when one is surrounded by deconstructionists. But after decades of theoretical civil war between structuralists and poststructuralists, objectivists and subjectivists, we can sense the beginnings of a truce — or perhaps it is a stalemate. No one has really won, but both sides have tired of the fight (Wray 2004). Perhaps the conditions are ripe for a new peace in which, having learned from pragmatist, interactionist, and poststructuralist insights about the historical and contingent nature of structures and the situational and emergent nature of meaning making, we can return to the unfinished classical project of social analysis — understanding social differentiation and inequality as a single dynamic composed of multiple subprocesses. This would be an exceptionally challenging intellectual journey, and I have done no more than sketch out some possible routes and paths. Any such journey will necessarily involve leaving behind the relative safety of sclerotic, discipline-bound knowledges and risking total failure to boot. Combining warring analytical approaches involves transgressing disciplinary boundaries, committing treason against those to whom we were once loyal, and subverting the political expectations of all sides. Yet it seems to me that we should shoulder this work gladly, because it is precisely the sort of intellectual intrigue that is both the burden and the reward of interdisciplinary work.

Notes

Preface and Acknowledgments

1. Throughout the book, italics are used when a term is referred to as a term, and quotation marks are used to enclose objectionable terms at their first use, but not thereafter.

Introduction

1. On *nigger* as a "troublesome word," see R. Kennedy 2002. It is unlikely that over the course of history *white trash* has inflicted as much human suffering and anguish as *nigger*—few ethnophaulisms in the American lexicon have. Yet the term *white trash* has performed much of the same symbolic violence. While *white trash* remains a "fighting word" in some circles, it continues to be used colloquially and humorously by different outgroups in ways that are impossible to imagine with *nigger*. The meanings of *nigger* have been hotly contested, but African Americans have largely gained control over the word. Poor whites have not been similarly mobilized by *white trash* (although the same cannot be said for *redneck*—see Kirwan 1951; Reed 1972, 1986; Roebuck and Hickson 1982; Huber 1995; and Goad 1997). See J. Katz 1988: 268 for brief but cogent remarks on the different ways these words operate in "cultures of insult." See also S. Smith 2006.

2. See, however, the *Ethnic Prejudice in America* series published by Meridian Books in the 1970s, especially Selzer 1972 and Wu 1972. See also Harkins 2004.

3. Among the classic sociological and anthropological works on shared representations and symbolic orders are Durkheim 1915/1965 and Lévi-Strauss 1966. In terms of the logic of structures, *white trash* is both the raw and the cooked, abstract categories that should not be mixed. The conflicting emotions and cognitive dissonance that attach to such admixtures are so intense that often they must be defused through humor and wit. So amusement

is also one of the reactions evoked, but I would suggest that this is because people so often rely on satire, irony, and parody to render the term safe for linguistic exchange. See, for example, Kipnis and Reeder 1997. On the moral significance of contempt, anger, and disgust, see Rozin 1997.

4. When race has been discussed in these studies, it has usually been in the context of trying to explain or understand the putative extreme racism of poor whites. Historical research that has viewed poor and nonslaveholding whites primarily through the lens of class and status includes Buck 1925, 1937; Phillips 1929; Brewer 1930; Hollander 1934; Mell 1938; Owsley and Owsley 1940; Owsley 1949; Genovese 1967, 1975, 1977; Hahn 1978, 1983; Flynt 1979, 1989; and Burton and McMath 1982. For social science analyses of poor whites based on class and caste, see Davis, Gardner, and Gardner 1941; Dollard 1937/1949; and Cox 1948/2000. For influential nonfictional portraits of poor whites that do not conform to traditional historical or social scientific genres, see Agee and Evans 1939/1960 and Cash 1941/1991. See Anderson 1920/1993 for a neglected literary portrait. For late-twentieth-century ethnographic and documentary accounts about poor whites, see Gitlin and Hollander 1970; Coles 1971a, 1971b; Howell 1973; MacLeod 1987/2004; and D. Foley 1994. Recent historical scholarship includes Bolton 1994; Cecil-Fronsmen 1992; N. Foley 1997; Newby 1989; Tillson 1991; and Feldman 2004, and recent ethnographies include Bettie 2003; Kefalas 2003; and Moss 2003. For a dated but comprehensive bibliography on southern poor whites, see Flynt and Flynt 1981.

5. The body of research known as whiteness studies is now quite large. For important early works, see Saxton 1990; Roediger 1991, 1994; Morrison 1992; Harris 1993; Frankenberg 1993; and T. Allen 1994. By the mid-1990s, a second wave of research engaged these earlier works and expanded both the range of topics and the disciplinary breadth of whiteness studies: see Lott 1995; Haney López 1996; Rogin 1996; Hill 1997; Frankenberg 1997; Wray and Newitz 1997; N. Foley 1997; and Hale 1998. For recent work, see Hill 2004 and Roediger 2005.

6. For examples of writing on whiteness in other national contexts, see Ware 2004 on Brazil; Ware and Back 2002 on the United Kingdom; Anderson 2003 on Australia; and Steyn 2001 on South Africa.

7. To add to the confusion, debates over the analytical status of concepts like race, class, gender, and sexuality have been mired in philosophical discussions about essentialism versus antiessentialism and structuralism versus poststructuralism. Moreover, there is an unfortunate but widespread tendency to argue for the analytical preeminence of one or more of the four categories over others. I revisit this point in chapter 5.

8. For an early critique, see Newitz and Wray 1997. For a more recent critique, see my coauthored introduction in Brander Rasmussen et al. 2001. Historians have been among the most vocal critics, in part because of the

dominance of historian David Roediger's work in the field. In addition to Arnesen 2001, see Fields 2001 and Kolchin 2001. For an extended critique directed more toward social scientists, see Hartigan 2005.

9. For a novel approach to analyzing social differentiation that does not foreground boundary theory, but that incorporates interactionist perspectives, see Mark 1998.

10. Beginning in the late 1980s, an interpretive sociology of culture began challenging the dominant quantitative and positivist approaches. Driven in part by developments outside sociology, in disciplines as divergent as anthropology, ethnic studies, philosophy, and literary criticism, as well as developments internal to sociology, the study of how culture produces and organizes human difference has reached new levels of theoretical sophistication and methodological coherence. For useful overviews, in chronological order, see Wuthnow and Witten 1988; Lamont and Fournier 1992; Bonnell and Hunt 1999; and Jacobs and Spillman 2005. The rise of boundary theory has been a significant part of this development (see Lamont and Molnar 2002).

11. As Brubaker (2004) puts it: "It is not that the notion of social construction is wrong, it is rather that it is today too obviously right, too familiar, too readily taken for granted, to generate the friction, force, and freshness needed to push arguments further and generate new insights" (3). For provocative critiques of constructionism, see Hacking 1999 and Michaels 1998. I have argued elsewhere that current analyses have for a long time been hamstrung by competing liberal and left political agendas (Wray 2004). If the intensity of these conflicts is now waning — and I am not entirely convinced it is — it is not because there is any newfound consensus between the warring factions, but because the combatants have exhausted themselves and emptied the conflicts of any productive meaning. Whiteness studies, it must be noted, owes its very existence to traditional models of identity analysis and has, accordingly, inherited some of these same problems. Whiteness studies represents, in a sense, identity theory come full circle. The long universalist history of treating the particular experiences and social realities of whites as the norm was followed by decades of close attention to the particular experiences of minority social groups. This period was in turn followed by a period where analysts began to set critical sights on the majority and to reveal its purported universality as in fact a particularity. One could argue, as I do here, that having completed the circle, it is time to step out of it, reassess it, and consider establishing another intellectual trajectory. For useful critiques of some of the intellectual and political limits of current analytical idioms of race and ethnicity, see W. Brown 1995; Stoler 1997; Wacquant 1997; and Gilroy 1991, 1993, 2000. See Lamont 2000 for an example of how boundary theory can engage questions of ethnoracial domination while providing an alternative framework to existing analyses. For a radical call to entirely abandon identity as an analytical concept, see Brubaker and Cooper 2000.

12. Cognitive psychologists speak of these shortcuts rather loosely as being a kind of "cognitive schemata." See DiMaggio 1997.

13. Lamont's phrase suggests both "shared representations" and "cognitive schemas."

14. Tilly (2004) notes: "People everywhere organize a significant part of their social interaction around the formation, transformation, activation, and suppression of social boundaries. It happens at the small scale of interpersonal dialogue, at the medium scale of rivalry within organizations, and at the large scale of genocide. Us-them boundaries matter" (213). Tilly's quote, besides speaking to the issue of the variability of scale of social interaction, also speaks to the kinds of action that occur at and around the boundary. Although sociologists from Durkheim to Parsons have relied on different notions of boundary action, Gieryn's (1983) concept of *boundary work* has been one of the most useful to emerge from boundary theory. Gieryn uses the term rather narrowly to designate the efforts of scientists to police their professional interests, and at times in this book I use it in this restricted sense. At other times I follow Michèle Lamont and Marcel Fournier's (1992) broader deployment of the term, which encompasses all efforts by people to differentiate themselves from others.

15. However, if symbolic boundaries are to be reproduced and maintained, they require active policing and reiteration. Left untended, symbolic boundaries can lose their salience — sometimes leaving a faint semantic or historical trace, sometimes disappearing under sedimented layers of new symbols, new distinctions, or new symbolic systems. By focusing analytical attention on *white trash* as a palimpsest, we can uncover and reconstruct a few of these untended and forgotten symbolic boundaries.

16. Etymologically, the word *race* means to make a line. It derives from old French (Rase), Italian (Razzo), and Spanish (Raza) words, which can be traced to an Old High German word (Reiza) meaning line of mark, which is akin to the English word *write*. *Race* is essentially a buried metaphor for a boundary line or a line marking descent. See the entries under *race* in *Webster's Revised Unabridged Dictionary* (1913) and the *Encyclopedia Britannica, Eleventh Edition* (1911).

17. I am deliberately borrowing here from the language of symbolic interactionism — a major intellectual tributary in boundary theory. For an overview of interactionism, see Fine 1993. Since interactionism implies a need to capture meaning-making in process, historical sociologists with an interactionist perspective have few methods with which to investigate exactly how the boundaries that delineate social reality are agreed upon, built up, and legitimated. Careful analysis of archival materials is key. Works that have been particularly helpful to me in this regard include Somers 1994; Kane 2000; Beisel 1997; and Gusfield 1963/1986. Regarding utterances as objects of analysis, see Bourdieu 1991.

18. The efforts of a labor union, for instance, to secure greater prestige or better working conditions for its members are a classic instance of boundary work, as are the efforts of any socially dominant group to retain its dominance by shaping social institutions in ways that favor the group. For a recent overview of the literature on boundary mechanisms, see Tilly 2004.

19. Other examples of boundary terms would include *mulatto* and *half-breed*, but neither connotes the mixing of unmixables the way *white trash* does.

20. When applied to archival research, an obvious problem with this method appears: the elite bias in primary sources. Archives tend to offer unrepresentative samples of historical experience, as they preserve only the meanings produced by interactions among elites, authorities, and literate social groups. The farther back one reaches in time, the worse the problem becomes. While for this book I conducted extensive archival research to retrieve and reconstruct linguistic interactions among elites, I have tried to mitigate the elite bias by turning to slang: that segment of speech long considered to be illegitimate and impolite, troublesome and undignified. Historical slang may be interpreted as an archive of the secret language of despised social groups who symbolically resisted, reconfigured, and challenged oppression through inventive informal speech. Slang is often heterodox, a way of attempting to speak against power, to speak from below. This understanding of slang as the return of repressed elements within legitimate, serious discourse, as a symptom of the great unsaid, suggests that it may be a valuable resource in the attempt to capture local, historical meanings. On the social significance of heteroglossia, see Bakhtin 1984. On slang and group conflict, see I. Allen 1990, 1993. On the limits and powers of heterodoxy, see Bourdieu 1991 and Stallybrass and White 1986. For a concise overview of contemporary lexical research into American slang, see Nunnally 2001. For an interactionist, ethnographic take on language and music in white working-class cultures, see Fox 2004.

21. In addition to works already cited, this study shares elements with and drew inspiration from some of the scholarship in Appalachian studies that has powerfully critiqued the ongoing misrepresentation and colonization of the region and its inhabitants. See Lewis and Askins 1978; Shapiro 1978; Whisnant 1980; Philliber 1981; Eller 1982; Batteau 1990; Williamson 1995; and Pudup et al. 1995. For a critique of certain strands of Appalachian studies, see Wray 2006c. For a study examining the "whitening efforts" of hookworm crusaders and eugenic science in a different national context, see Anderson 2003.

22. This is a fundamental idea in sociological thought, with historical roots in the pioneering work of Durkheim 1915/1965 and Weber 1968 and contemporary expression in Goffman 1963. For more recent rearticulations of this idea, see Lamont 2000.

23. That would entail a certain circularity of logic, since the origins of morality are to be found in particular forms of social organization (Nietzsche 1887/1968).

24. Of course, emotions are also crucial in binding people to the existing social order. As Miller (1997) has noted, "An account of class, rank, or social hierarchy must be thin indeed unless accompanied by an account of the passions and sentiments that sustain it" (245). On the role of emotions in social movements, see the excellent essays in Goodwin, Jasper, and Polletta 2001. On the sociology of emotion, see J. Katz 1999.

1 Lubbers, Crackers, and Poor White Trash

1. See McIlwaine 1939: 9; Masterson 1937; and Cook 1976: 3–5. Masterson completely ignores class ideology in his analysis, but it is central for Sylvia Cook, as it is for Carr 1996. For the most recent assessment of Byrd's lasting influence, see Harkins 2004. On the symbolic and political importance to colonial projects of mapping geographic boundary lines, see Nobles 1997.

2. The Proclamation of 1763, issued by King George III, promised there would be no more settlements in the Appalachian Mountains and points west. However, there was no formal mechanism to enforce this "paper blockade." Consequently, most historians have viewed the proclamation as ineffective and as having had little historical role in shaping revolutionary America. For an opposing view, see Holton 1999. From the point of view of this book, it is only a slight exaggeration to say that the proclamation invented the cracker, for at the stroke of a pen, it criminalized the habits of settlement of hundreds, perhaps thousands, of people.

3. A difference—and its historical significance must not be understated even if it is yet to be fully understood—was that by 1700, there were everyday habits, laws, and codes that marked out Indians and blacks for differential and unequal treatment. By contrast, no such laws existed for poor whites as a group. Under the law, even the poorest and most disadvantaged whites could, in theory at least, lay claim to their white identity before the law and demand whatever preferential treatment the law afforded them. See T. Allen 1994.

4. *Stigmatype* is perhaps an odd neologism, but I coined it because *stereotype*, a tired word that connotes psychological prejudices and thought patterns, doesn't speak well to the social dimensions of cultural differentiation and because *stigmatizing boundary term* is too cumbersome and unwieldy. *Stigmatypes* speaks both to the classifying impulse—the impulse to typify— and to the hierarchicalization of categories through denigration of the other. Analytically, *stigmatype* is needed for another reason: stereotypes need not be stigmatizing. The stereotyping statement "All Asians are good at math," while a gross and offensive generalization, is hardly stigmatizing in the same

way as the statement "Girls aren't good at math." I use the word *stigma* in the sense developed by Goffman (1963). On stereotypes, see Gilman 1985; Stangor and Lange 1994; and Schauer 2003.

5. There are, of course, many other classifications and categories that help differentiate the cracker from the noncracker, and there is much more in play here than a simple set of binary terms. Nonetheless, *cracker*, like any stigmatype, has an implicit, silent partner that suggests something about the self-assigned superiority of those who are doing the naming. This implicit or latent function of stigmatypes is extremely important for understanding their symbolic operations and their social effects in establishing hierarchies of prestige. Too often, boundary terms have been analyzed with respect only to their manifest function: the marking of a distinct category of identity to which various symbolic properties, characteristics, and traits are ascribed.

6. The various texts that I researched for this chapter are among the only extant primary sources dealing with the symbolic and social differentiation of low-status and outcast whites in the eighteenth and early nineteenth centuries and represent a wide array of different kinds of sources — letters, court cases, administrative reports, and journals and diaries. I also relied heavily on secondary historical, literary, sociological scholarship. All are detailed in these notes. For linguistic evidence, dictionaries consulted include Thornton 1912; Craigie and Hulbert 1940; Mathews 1951; Flexner 1976; Barnhart 1988; and Simpson and Weiner 1989, and linguistic atlases consulted include Kretzschmar et al. 1976; McDavid and O'Cain 1980; and Pederson et al. 1981.

7. In 1676, the landed colonist Nathaniel Bacon, who favored colonial expansion into Native American–controlled areas, led an army of white settlers and African slaves against local Indian tribes, then quickly turned on the colonial government and burned Jamestown. Bacon's Rebellion marked a turning point in colonial policy toward the social control of the lower classes of poor whites, Native Americans, and the African slaves. After the rebellion, historians agree, the colonial elite took steps to divide blacks from whites, discouraging solidarity by introducing racially based legal and economic privileges that were intended to benefit even the poorest whites. As the seventeenth century gave way to the eighteenth, colonial society was becoming even more sharply divided along lines of both class and race, making for, from the elite point of view, a more stable social order. See the work of Allen (1994, 1997), for whom the origins of whiteness can be found in this bundle of economic, social, and legal privileges afforded to whites. See also Breen 1976.

8. For an obsequious hagiography of Byrd, see L. Wright 1940. For a more critical assessment, see Lockridge 1987, 1992.

9. According to the *Oxford English Dictionary* (hereafter OED), Lubberland originally appeared in 1598 — as a synonym for Cockaigne — and was used frequently throughout the seventeenth, eighteenth, and nineteenth centuries,

most famously by Ben Jonson (1614/1960) in *Bartholomew's Fair*, a popular satirical play with which Byrd was undoubtedly familiar. *Lubber* predates *Lubberland* by at least two centuries and may have come from the Old French *loboer*, meaning swindler or parasite, meanings that clearly resonate with *lubber*. On a related note, it is entirely possible that the term *landlubber* is a linguistic inversion of *Lubberland*.

10. See one of Byrd's contemporaries, Robert Beverley (1705/1947, 283, 284, and 319), who rails against the immorality of torpor and indolence.

11. Many other members of the social elite dwelt on the laziness of the outcast white. The Reverend Hugh Jones (1724/1956) also bemoaned this condition, viewing it exclusively in moral terms. See McIlwaine 1939: 11–15 and Harkins 2004: 15–17 for more examples from the colonial era.

12. "By the eighteenth century an intricate discourse on idleness had emerged, not only to draw distinctions between laboring classes but also to sanction and enforce labor discipline, to legitimize land plunder, and to alter habits of labor. . . . The discourse on idleness is, more properly speaking, a discourse on work—used to distinguish between desirable and undesirable labor. Pressure to work was, more accurately, pressure to alter traditional habits of work. . . . At the same time, the discourse on idleness is also a register of labor resistance, a resistance then lambasted as torpor and sloth" (McClintock 1995: 252–53). McClintock's remarks are in the context of British colonialism in South Africa in the nineteenth century, but they apply to British colonialism in the Americas as well. See Jordan 1968/1977: 51, 85–91. On the importance and difficulties of understanding the place of poor whites in different colonial discourses, see Stoler 1989: 134–61. The eighteenth-century Anglo-American theodicy of industriousness is well described by Bertelson (1967: 7–9, 124, 126). The classic text on the work ethic and its economic and social consequences is of course Weber 1958.

13. Byrd may have been strongly motivated by his own morality and the demands of social status to portray lubbers in a damning light, but, as a land speculator, he also had a huge financial stake in the matter. The boundary survey gave Byrd the perfect opportunity to identify the best lands for himself. Indeed, his land holdings increased by more than 150,000 acres in the years immediately following the completion of his survey, a nearly six-fold increase. See Lockridge 1987: 140 and K. Brown 1996: 252 for exact figures.

14. The scholarship on colonial social structure is voluminous. Economic and quantitative historians have employed a vast array of different archival sources to arrive at estimates of the distribution of wealth and the demographics—occupation, age structure, geographic and social origins—of various strata. Scholars have focused on economic systems of slavery and servitude. For a useful overview, see K. Morgan 2001. A great deal of this research has focused on the colonies in the tidewater region and the South, which

differ in important respects from the colonies in New England. Within the focus on the colonial South, there are works that detail regional differences in social organization between the backcountry (frontier), upcountry (Appalachia, Piedmont), and lowcountry (plantation). In this chapter and those that follow, I have tried to cite some of the relevant literature but I make no attempt to systematically sort out all the arguments. Why? The search for certainty about the exact nature of colonial social arrangement—fascinating and important though it may be—is in many ways beyond the scope of my project, which is more concerned with the intersubjective processes of boundary making and marking than it is with objectifying social relations in a sociohistorical manner. In the end, I relied chiefly on E. Morgan 1975 and Kulikoff 2000, but see also T. Allen 1994, which identifies a simpler structure in economically deductive fashion, utilizing not the Weberian notion of social groups but that of orthodox Marxist classes.

15. Historians have offered differing interpretations of the status of bonded laborers who were of European origin in relation to the bonded laborer of African descent. For contrasting interpretations of the systems of white servitude in the colonies, see the early works by Ballagh (1895); McCormac (1904); and Herrick (1926). Smith (1947) followed the lead of these earlier scholars in stigmatyping indentured servants as the dregs of Stuart England. For more modern historiography, see work by Galenson (1981), who argued that indentured white servants represented a cross-section of the English population; and Grubb (1994), who dates the total collapse of the North American system of indentured servitude to 1818–21. The historical scholarship on yeomen is particularly immense. I address it briefly in the next chapter.

16. For an overview of these laws and their political and social effects, see E. Morgan 1975: 215–70. See Parkin 1977 for more on the theory of social closure—"the process by which social collectivities seek to maximize rewards by restricting access to resources and opportunities to a limited circle of eligibles" (44). For the locus classicus of the concept, see Weber 1968: 341–355.

17. As a devout Anglican, Byrd would likely have believed in a common origin for all human beings. These conflicting ideas—that racial difference signified "species difference" and that humans share a single origin—clearly would have made it very difficult for Byrd to articulate a coherent concept of race. Therefore, while the lubbers in Byrd's narratives are portrayed as a fairly distinct social group, one that is not only culturally different but also socially inferior, the same clarity cannot be found with regard to their racial identity or to where Byrd might have placed them in a racial taxonomy. See Fischer 2002: 75.

18. For representative examples, see Byrd 1728/1929: 46, 54, 90–92. For a rare comparison of the poor whites to the lazy "Wild Irish," a comparison that must have held special resonance for Byrd's English readers, see Byrd

1728/1929: 102. For early colonists' attitudes toward Native Americans, see E. Morgan 1975: 6–20, 328–32; Berkhofer 1979; and Axtell 1988: 125–43.

19. The historical scholarship on these communities is in need of further development, but in addition to Price 1973/1996, see Craven 1971; Hudson 1971; Nash 1974; and Shuffelton 1993.

20. Of particular interest in this regard is the case of Christian Priber, a German colonist who in 1743 sought to establish a utopian commonwealth in Cherokee lands in Georgia as an asylum for "debtors, Transport Felons, Servants and Negroe Slaves in the two Carolinas & Virginia" (Mellon 1973: 319). See also V. Crane 1919 and Mellon 1960. For work that details the influence such communities may have had on the American Revolution, see Linebaugh and Rediker 2000.

21. Cited in Fischer 2002: 68–70. I follow her analysis closely here.

22. Mathews's claim may link *crackers* to English analogs explored by E. J. Hobsbawm (1959), who surveyed the "protopolitical" acts of trespassing, poaching, piracy, and thievery that sustained marginal communities. For a continuation of this line of historical interpretation, see E. P. Thompson 1975 and Linebaugh and Rediker 2000.

23. McWhiney (1988) has argued that the dominant culture of the pre-revolutionary south was "Cracker culture," one distinct from the more staid and reserved culture of the North. His argument rests on the idea that the vast majority of immigrants who flowed into southern colonies in the seventeenth and eighteenth centuries were from Celtic regions in the British Isles — Scotland, Ireland, Wales, and Cornwall — and that the cultural traditions and practices they brought with them were opposed to those of immigrants in the northern colonies of New England, whose origins lay in the English lowlands. McWhiney argues that as the cultural habits, customs, and values of Celtic immigrants spread through cultural diffusion, cracker culture became more or less uniformly shared by southern whites of all classes. On this account, crackers constitute what contemporary social scientists would call a distinct ethnic group — they were not only perceived as culturally different from English settlers, they also perceived themselves as different. In McWhiney's view, cracker values, attitudes, and practices were not just different, they were anti-English. Where the English colonists practiced agriculture, crackers hunted and practiced extensive open-range grazing and herding; where English colonists preached the virtues of hard work, crackers lived lives devoted to the leisurely pursuits of smoking, drinking, and gambling; where English colonists sought the rule of law, crackers settled disputes with deadly rituals of interpersonal violence. In addition, McWhiney argues, crackers and English colonists held sharply different attitudes about morality, education, progress, and human worth. He suggests it was these cultural differences, not a dispute over slavery, that ultimately fueled the sectional conflicts that led to Civil War.

There appears to be a good deal of explanatory power in this argument. For example, it seems to explain why planter elites like Byrd and colonial authorities like Cochrane, whose cultural sympathies lay with the non-Celtic English, looked askance at lubbers and crackers and regarded them with a mixture of fear and distaste in the pre-Revolutionary era. It might even appear to explain why, a century later, southern poor whites, who had gained so little wealth or prosperity from slavery, were unified in support of "the southern way of life" during the Civil War; that is, they saw themselves as defending a common culture that was under attack, and their cultural identity as crackers superseded any economic distinctions of class or status that might have otherwise caused them to abandon the planter elite. However, from a boundary perspective, a major flaw in the "Cracker culture" argument lies in the way it focuses on "cultural stuff" — the substance of content culture — and assumes that cultures consist of stable, unchanging core values, habits, and customs. Ethnic cultures in this view are static and durable, not dynamic processes that feature complex shifting of boundary lines, changing patterns of inclusion and exclusion, and variations in how cultural difference is socially organized and arranged. McWhiney's focus on the ethnic category and its supposed cultural content, rather than the processes of boundary making and marking, is exactly the kind of analysis I wish to avoid. See the work of Norwegian anthropologist Fredrik Barth (1969/1998), who turned the traditional concept of cultural difference inside out. It is not the possession of specific cultural traits that makes groups distinct from one another — it is the encounters, interactions, and transactions with other groups that makes cultural difference visible, meaningful, and salient. "The critical point of investigation from now on becomes the ethnic boundary that defines the group, not the cultural stuff it encloses" (15). Barth points us here to the central importance of processes of ascription and self-ascription in creating, maintaining, imposing, and redrawing ethnicity. See also Jenkins 1997.

24. The word *cracker* appears with regularity in letters, diaries, travel writings, and the popular press, always carrying some pejorative meaning and bearing some level of stigma. Thornton's (1912) historical dictionary records a 1772 usage as follows: "Persons who have no settled habitation, and live by hunting and plundering the industrious Settlers . . . The people I refer to are really what you and I understand by *Crackers*." Thornton's revised dictionary of 1939 adds a 1784 example from the *London Chronicle*, with specific reference to poor whites in Maryland: "That hardy banditti well known by the name of crackers." Thornton, along with several other authorities, offers the onomatopoetic etymology that crackers were so-called because of the way they habitually cracked their buckskin whips. Others claimed the term was short for "corn-crackers" — a reference to the notion that these folk always cracked their own corn for meal, unable or unwilling to pay the miller to do the task, too poor to eat anything else. These appear to be creative folk ety-

mologies. The most authoritative etymology of the term argues persuasively that the word is of Scottish extraction, meaning "to boast." See Presley 1976: 112–13. While the etymology of the term remains murky, there is wide consensus about its geographic origins. As Cochrane's letter suggests, it was applied first to Georgians, then to Floridians, and from there to other denizens of the colonial borderlands. See McDavid and McDavid 1973.

25. Brown (1963: 184) cites a wide array of sources to support these assertions, including a document dated 1765 that contains the word *cracker*. This predates the Cochrane citation from 1766, the one used by the OED as the earliest appearance of the term in America.

26. As Stock (1996) has written, Regulators "victimized people, for example, who had chosen a subsistence or nomadic lifestyle that conflicted with the emerging tenants of market production or who refused to work for wages despite the labor shortage. 'Having no property or visible way of living,' hunting on public land without a permit, squatting, drifting, owing money and not paying up, these behaviors separated the poorest settlers from the rest of frontier society and made them potential victims of the Regulation." In Stock's interpretation, part of the conflict was cultural in nature, and the intensity of the violent vigilantism was intended to exterminate and eliminate the threat cultural difference posed to farmers. Ongoing struggles over labor, land, and property rights are cast here as contests over culture. *Crackers* was the name given to those in the colonial backcountry who somehow challenged the dominant social order and who resisted assimilation and subordination (90, 94).

27. See Holton 1999. For more on South Carolina Regulation, see Klein (1981), who largely concurs with Brown (1963). On the Regulators of North Carolina, see Whittenburg (1977) and Kars (2002), who paints a different picture of regulation than does Brown or Klein. Kars notes that Regulators in North Carolina bore a closer resemblance to Regulators in Pennsylvania (the Whiskey Rebellion) and Massachusetts (Shay's Rebellion) than to those in South Carolina (219n2). For a novel reading of rural insurrections in U.S. history, see E. White 2005.

28. Mary Douglas's (1966/1984) studies of the sources and significance of "pollution behavior" (i.e., concerns with ritual cleanliness and purity) in a variety of cultures, primitive and modern, help explain why the clay eater would have been a particularly disturbing symbol of depravity. Her approach involved recognizing that pollution or, more simply, "dirt," was a metaphorical way of conceptualizing "matter out of place." With this perspective, Douglas argues that our ideas of social and cultural order and the boundaries we use to form and give shape to that order are revealed by cultural attitudes toward and definitions of what is dirty and what is not: "Dirt is essentially disorder. There is no such thing as absolute dirt: it exists in the eye of the beholder. . . . Dirt offends against order" (2–3). Dirt is, in essence, a violation of

boundaries and poses a danger, a risk, and a threat to the prevailing system of order. In this symbolic or metaphorical sense, dirt, rather than just being stuff out of place, actually carries great social, cultural, and political meaning. Douglas's work has certain obvious connections to the study of *white trash*. The *trash* in *white trash* is, after all, metonymic for all manner of pollution and waste. It stands in for the larger category of dirt and signals the essential impurity of both the category and those named by it. For important extensions of these ideas, see Stallybrass and White 1986 and Frykman and Löfgren 1987.

29. The figure of the clay eater is treated more fully in chapter 4. For useful historical overviews, see Twyman 1971 and Tullos 1978.

30. If, as David Roediger (1994) has argued, white workers of the 1830s and 1840s were actively engaged in distinguishing themselves from and placing their labor above black slaves and slavery, blacks, free and slave alike, were interested in distinguishing themselves from and elevating themselves above poor whites. The most famous expression of this sentiment is the often cited refrain, "I'd rather be a nigger than po' white trash." Among the dozens of sources for this saying, see Chestnutt 1899/1969: 75 and Genovese 1977. To upend Roediger's argument (one he derives rather uncritically from Du Bois 1935/1962) we can recognize that at least some blacks paid themselves and each other "a psychological wage" that allowed them to feel superior to some poor whites. It is reasonable to think that some blacks took pleasure in the symbolic demotion of certain whites, for whom they had more than one derogatory, stigmatizing name. For instance, another African American term for poor whites was *poor bukra*. While its origins are obscure—it is most likely a variation of a Gullah word meaning "white man" (Mason 1960)—its contemptuous meanings are not. From the perspective of black servants and slaves, it may have been that, in some situations, to be poor white trash was quite simply to be a white person in a position where one was defined by one's labor and where the only labor one could do was that of a black slave. In many cases, however, poor whites did work that was actually considered too dangerous for slaves, who were, after all, expensive and valuable property. This situation suggests the possibility that the working and living conditions of some black slaves were superior to that of some poor whites. For intriguing evidence on this point, see Otto and Burns 1983; Carr and Walsh 1988. More recently, Morgan (2004) has concluded emphatically that while "[black] slaves were the true poor in colonial America," they were, in some respects, "materially better off than some white people. Without question then, some whites in early America were devoid of basic necessities, and some of them were even poorer in a material sense than at least some slaves. The life expectancy of slaves, for example, was quite high for an early modern population, as was their stature. Some slaves had greater access to property, better levels of subsistence, and even opportunities to earn cash than

other slaves—and some poor whites. In some places and at certain times, many slaves experienced a material status superior to that enjoyed by poor folk" (95).

31. Carson, Donald, and Rice 1998: 76. The notebooks of Louisa Catherine Adams, wife of President John Quincy Adams, reveal that the Adamses employed seven men and six women as servants.

32. In 1800, on a trip through Maryland to take up residence in Washington, D.C., Abigail Adams, wife of then President John Adams, spoke disparagingly of "the lower class of whites" who "are a grade below the Negro in point of intelligence and ten below them in civility" (D. McCullough 2001: 553). Black use of poor white stigmatypes can be found throughout slave narratives of the era. See especially Douglass 1855/1987: 253.

33. For primary examples, see Sedgwick 1835 and Beecher and Stowe 1869. O'Leary 1996: 38–45 gives an excellent brief account of these changes in sentiment. Tocqueville (1840/1994) noted this attitude when he observed, "In democracies servants are not only equal among themselves, but it may be said that they are, in some sort, the equals of their masters" (181). On the Irish "Biddy" servant, see Dudden 1983, esp. 60–71; Sutherland 1981; Diner 1983; and Carson, Donald, and Rice 1998. On the legal status and rights of servants in this era, see Kahana 2000.

34. In this sense, *poor white trash* can be understood from an interactionist perspective as an expression of black prejudice, the result of a shifting sense of group position. See Blumer 1958.

35. All numbers are derived from Maryland decennial censuses 1790–1850, available at http://fisher.lib.virginia.edu/collections/stats/histcensus/.

36. By 1855, Frederick Douglass complained that "every hour sees us elbowed out of some employment to make room for some newly arrived immigrants, whose hunger and color are thought to give them title to some special favor." By taking these common jobs, Douglass noted, the Irish servants also "assumed our degradation" (1855/2003: 354). Note that the "famine Irish," of whom Douglass was speaking, did not begin arriving on American shores until the 1840s. See also O'Leary 1996: 130.

37. However, black, white, servant, slave, and free, also conspired together to get what they wanted and needed to survive. On interracial cooperation and competition in underground economies, see the pathbreaking work of Lockley (1997, 2001) and Forret (2004).

2 Imagining Poor Whites in the Antebellum South

1. This chapter draws upon readings of seven novels and dozens of magazines and journals. In selecting these texts, I chose those that had the greatest circulation and diffusion relying on data about circulation, readership,

and impact found in Mott 1930, 1938a, 1938b; Haveman 2004; and Tracy 1995.

2. A survey of electronics archives and historical dictionaries suggests that derogatory names for poor whites proliferated during the antebellum period, with a great deal of variety from one region to the next. Modern linguists (H. Allen 1958; McDavid and O'Cain 1981; Pederson et al. 1981; and Dorrill 1986) have catalogued several hundred different terms for poor whites in the twentieth century, but we have no similar data source for the antebellum period.

3. The images offered by both fiction and nonfiction writers are viewed as fictive constructs and are not judged here on their merits as literary inventions—nor, needless to say, are they examined with an eye toward determining their historical accuracy or degree of ethnographic verisimilitude. Instead, I explore how and from what such images were formed and what symbolic and practical purposes they served.

4. Throughout the present and following chapters, the words *South, southern, New South*, and *southerner* are frequently invoked. Like the boundary term *poor white trash*, these simple-sounding words convey complex social realities and articulate multiple layers of cultural meaning. The South is presented here as both a geographic region and a concept, a mythical place. Unless otherwise indicated, the South as a geographic region refers to the eleven states that formed the Confederacy (Alabama, Arkansas, Florida, Georgia, Louisiana, Mississippi, North Carolina, South Carolina, Tennessee, Texas, and Virginia). This book makes no attempt to deal directly with that mountainous subregion within the South known as Appalachia, the significance of which is so great that it requires separate study. As a mythical rather than geographic place, the South is much harder to locate. As Tindall (1964: 10) observed, "the infinite variety of southern mythology could be catalogued and analyzed endlessly." For additional reflections on this protean term, see Ayers 1996: 62–82; O'Brien 1979, 1988, 2004; and, most recently, Greeson 1999.

5. Marx's (1852/1963) definition of the *lumpenproletariat* included the "vagabonds, discharged soldiers, discharged jailbirds, escaped galley slaves, swindlers, mountebanks, *lazzaroni*, pickpockets, tricksters, gamblers, *maquereaus*, brothel keepers, porters, *literati*, organ-grinders, ragpickers, knife grinders, tinkers, beggars—in short, the whole indefinite, disintegrated mass, thrown hither and thither, which the French term *la bohème* . . . this scum, offal, [and] refuse of all class" (75). The last phrase resonates remarkably well with the symbolism surrounding *white trash*. Marx's depiction of the *lumpenproletariat* as a wholly regressive, unproductive, and conservative political faction (when compared to the progressive and productive proletariat and bourgeoisie) has exerted influence both subtle and profound on social scientists and historians for the last 150 years.

6. Williams (1973) argues that "the country" has been a primary concep-

tual tool in the historical development of a Western discourse around "culture." As a concept, "the country" shares central place with the concept of "the city"; the tensions and frictions produced by the ever-shifting oppositions between these two terms has enabled social domination and environmental exploitation. Williams's readings of English poetry, drama, and novels are all directed at showing how, in different historical eras, distinct ideologies developed to naturalize city/country divisions and to hide the various forms of exploitation involved. By the beginning of the twentieth century, Williams argued, the oppositions between city and country had come to share a strong affinity with the grand ideological oppositions between modern/premodern, core/periphery, industry/agriculture, capitalism/socialism, advanced/primitive, and savage/civilized that preoccupied the leading thinkers and cultural figures of the day. As Williams points out, under agrarian capitalism, these superficial comparisons mask the "continuing contrast between the extraordinary improvement of the land and the social consequences of just this process, in the dispossessed and the vagrants, and the old, the sick, the disabled, the nursing mothers, the children who, unable to work in these terms, were seen merely as negative, an unwanted burden. To see the paradox of successful production and these human consequences would be to penetrate the inner character of capitalism itself. It was easier . . . to separate the consequences from the system, and then to ascribe to social decay what was actually the result of social and economic growth" (82). In other words, one result of the economic divide and the ideological masking that accompanied it was that those dispossessed by the forces of economic growth appeared to be suffering from social decay—from declines in the traditions, morals, conduct, and attitudes that were seen as crucial resources for sustaining former communities. The process results in the cultural production of social groups classified, in Williams's words, as "human debris— the sick, the old, the deranged, the unfortunate, the runaways." The notion of the "human debris" produced by processes of uneven capitalist development shares obvious symbolic and material correspondence with the notion of white trash that is the central concern of this book. See also Williams 1985, especially the entries *culture, country* and *imperialism*.

7. In addition to "frontier" as a complicating factor, American historians have argued (contrary to what orthodox Marxism would suggest) that the historical origins of the industrial revolution in the United States were located in rural, not urban areas. On this view, the peaceful "factories under the elms" were so reassuring to nineteenth-century Americans that they did not pay critical attention to what industrialism might mean. The classic source for this interpretation is L. Marx 1964. For an interesting response to Marx, see Prude 1985.

8. For Turner, the frontier acted as a "safety valve" that allowed class con-

flict and other social disorder to be safely exported to the geographic, social, and political fringes of society. For more on Turner's thesis, see Berkhofer 1964.

9. See Saxton 1990: 78–84 and 184–95 for astute remarks on Davey Crockett
and Daniel Boone as "Jacksonian vernacular heroes."

10. Cultural sociologists have argued and demonstrated that times of upheaval and uncertainty are marked by an intense search for new meanings
and new systems of categorization. See Swidler 1986 and Wuthnow 1987.

11. I discuss the formation of the professional middle class further in chapters 3 and 4. On the market revolution, see Sellers 1991, and for differing views
on middle-class culture, see Blumin 1985; Bledstein 1976; and Ryan 1981.

12. For a brief inventory and analysis of antebellum images of barbarism
and boorishness among poor whites in the West, see Henry Nash Smith 1950.
Smith interprets the stigmatization of western farmers and frontiersmen as
simple class prejudice.

13. The historical debate, which I can address only in summary fashion
here, is in part about whether there was less antagonism or whether the antagonism was there but the opportunities for it to ripen into class-based
political rebellion were not. See Shugg 1939 for a key early statement. The
McWhiney 1988 "cracker" argument, discussed in chapter 1, downplays political antagonism and privileges shared culture as the source of cross-class
intraracial white solidarity in the Old South. The notion of a "psychological
wage" originated with Du Bois (1935/1962), was later employed by Fredrickson (1981), and has been reprised in the context of northern industrialism
by Roediger (1994). The "wage" argument privileges racism as the source
of cross-class intraracial solidarity among whites. Neither of these theories
squares very well with the disfranchisement of southern poor whites as described by Woodward (1971) and Kousser (1974) (for a contrary view, see Feldman 2004) or with the movements—however short-lived—for biracial populism and fusion in the 1890s, as described by Kantrowitz (2000a, 2000b). Note
that all sides of the debate share the fundamental assumption that absence
of "class conflict" is something that must be explained. This is an assumption dictated by, inter alia, various forms of class conflict theory. Boundary
theory suggests an alternate view: that we cannot say in advance of empirical investigation exactly which boundaries—be they moral, ethnic, gender,
class, or other—will prove most salient and determinative in social struggle.
For persuasive challenges to the dominant view that the most salient social
boundary in the antebellum South was that of race, see J. Jones 1986; Cashin
1991; Bleser 1991; Bynum 1992; and McCurry 1995. In these accounts, gender
and family relations shape all other social relations. For compelling evidence
that poor whites in the antebellum South were anything but passive in the
face of their economic marginalization, see Ash 1999.

14. Fredrickson (1981: xi) defines white supremacy as "attitudes, ideologies, and policies associated with the rise of blatant forms of white or European dominance over 'nonwhite' populations."

15. As a boundary term, *poor white* is a precursor to *poor white trash*. According to most historical dictionaries, the term first appeared in print in 1819, roughly a decade and a half earlier than *poor white trash*. Although the term sounds neutral, less pejorative than *poor white trash*, this was not actually the case, as the term carried nearly identical meanings. It was perhaps a more polite-sounding synonym with less emotional charge.

16. Tracy (1995) estimates that the fictional works of Simms and Kennedy sold nearly as well as did those of Hawthorne and Melville. The foregoing paragraphs are indebted to Tracy's excellent and immaculately researched book. See also Skaggs 1972.

17. This is the source of the dual aspect of the Turnerian figure of the heroic white frontiersmen. The notion of a rebellious, antisocial, unscrupulous, white male squatter defending self, family, and way of life from aggressive attempts to displace him and take over the land reverberates with the pejorative, stigmatizing image of the violent, paranoid, reactionary, rural poor white. Simultaneously, this same figure is idealized for having maintained "backcountry" outlaw authenticity, a cantankerously rebellious attitude, and honorable defense of kith and kin against the dehumanizing social forces of modernity. This complex rhetorical image has long served to reinforce the mythic status of the poor white male on the margins, viewed simultaneously as tragic, threatening, and heroic.

18. This view did not originate with Stowe, having been formulated in the 1830s by abolitionist novelists like Richard Hildreth. See McIlwaine 1939: 33, 47, and 88–99 for some of the most important sources of this view, both before and after Stowe.

19. For instance, Kemble followed the success of her 1835 *American Journal*, discussed in the previous chapter, with a second memoir (1863) that recounted her experience as the wife of a slave owner on a Georgia rice plantation, an experience that transformed her into a passionate abolitionist. While sympathetic to black slaves, she wrote that she considered the southern poor white "the most degraded race of human beings claiming an Anglo-Saxon origin that can be found on the face of the earth — filthy, lazy, ignorant, brutal, proud, penniless savages without one of the nobler attributes which have been found occasionally allied to the vices of savage nature" (146). Kemble's reference to Anglo-Saxons raises the possibility of the racial superiority of poor whites only to deny it, a rhetorical move that neatly expresses the ambivalent racial sentiments of abolitionists. See Clinton 2002 for more on Kemble.

20. Clearly missing here is the emphasis on criminality found in earlier accounts. A careful search through historical dictionaries yielded no nine-

teenth-century references to *cracker* (or *poor white* for that matter) that carried the aura of criminality Cochrane so clearly described in 1766. For a traveler's perspective on the pacified *cracker* of the late nineteenth century, see Dunning 1882.

21. Ms. in possession of author. Thanks to Todd Uhlman, Department of History, University of Dayton, for bringing this manuscript to my attention.

22. On the social power of disgust, see W. Miller 1997 and Nussbaum 2004. On the role of emotions in sparking and sustaining social movements and reform efforts, see Goodwin, Jasper, and Polletta 2001.

23. Fitzhugh 1856/1960: 69. Fitzhugh mentions poor whites in *Sociology of the South*, where he describes them as "a stigma on the South that should be wiped out." In this earlier work, he concedes the abolitionist point that southern poor whites suffered from a lack of education. See Fitzhugh 1854: 144, 148.

24. The book was virtually ignored until the 1940s. See William J. Cooper Jr.'s useful introduction in Hundley 1860/1979: xiii–xlv. For a more recent assessment of Hundley, see O'Brien 2004: 379–385.

25. The emphasis is Hundley's. As we shall see in the next chapter, the idea of "bad blood" among poor whites took on an enormous significance in the latter part of the nineteenth century. Hundley was certainly not alone in making a case for locating poor white trash in places outside the South. Although Hundley does not mention them, the poor whites of Missouri were given a particularly disgusting and repugnant designation. As William Cutler (1883: 336) wrote in his monumental *History of Kansas*: "The rank and file were not even what would be called the best society, even in Western Missouri. They were of that most pitiable, despicable, and often desperate class known in all the Slave States as 'poor white trash,' and in Missouri as 'pukes.' They were filthy, shiftless, debauched and lawless. . . . the virtue, amenity, refinement and intelligence of civilized life had given place to the combined vice and brutality of the three races with which they mingled; beneath, and mutually despised by all. . . . They were, without doubt, the most desperate and depraved specimens of humanity within the borders of the Republic— the very jackals of the human race."

3 "Three Generations of Imbeciles Are Enough"

1. In the foreword to this work, Dugdale (1877: 2) calls his research a study of "the debris of our civilization," a phrase that euphemizes *white trash*.

2. Dugdale's comment recalls the stereotype of sexually promiscuous poor whites, both male and female, portrayed in Byrd's *History of the Dividing Line* (1728/1929) and further elaborated and reiterated by a long line of casual observers. However, Dugdale was the first to articulate the stereotype in sci-

entific language and the first to use the scientific method to prove his case. Rather than using these methods as a means of dispelling or challenging myths, Dugdale objectified the stigmatypes of white trash sexuality that had been in circulation for at least two centuries. As we will see, the fascination with and compulsion to report upon the sexual reputations of poor rural whites was a consistent and primary feature of eugenics research. As with Francis Galton (1871, 1909), *reputation* and *character* become objects of eugenic analysis, and Dugdale peppers his report with stories from local observers—neighbors, distant relatives, physicians, and judges. Of course, the inclusion of these anecdotes and local stories in scientific journals and reports lent such stories the aura of scientific explanation, the power of which, at the turn of the century, was gaining in intensity and scope (Haskell 1977).

3. Here and throughout this chapter, I cite from Nicole Hahn Rafter's (1988b) indispensable volume and not from the original field studies primarily because the latter are scarce and hard to find. Whenever possible, I compared Rafter's edited collection to the original documents.

4. This research is based in part on an examination of archival documents at Cold Spring Harbor Laboratories (CSHL) on Long Island in New York. At the beginning of the twentieth century, CSHL was the birthplace and headquarters of the U.S. eugenics movement and site of the Eugenics Record Office (ERO), where field researchers were trained and schooled in the techniques that were used in the Eugenic Field Studies. Between 1990 and 2003, CSHL served as a center for the Human Genome Project in the United States, a collaboration between the U.S. Department of Energy and the National Institutes of Health.

5. Elsewhere, Rafter (1988b, 1997) greatly expands upon this point.

6. Nazi doctors and scientists frequently invoked the field studies and sterilization laws as inspiration for their own eugenic research and campaigns. In addition to Germany, the family studies were heavily used in eugenics research in Brazil, France, and Great Britain. For eugenics in different national and regional contexts, see, in addition to works already cited, Adams 1990 on Germany, France, Brazil, and Russia; Schneider 1990 on France; Broberg and Roll-Hansen 1996 on Scandinavian countries; Dowbiggin 1997 and McLaren 1990 on Canada; Dubow 1995 on South Africa; Farrall 1985, Mazumdar 1992, and Thomson 1997 on Britain; Kühl 1994 and Miller 1996 on the United States and Germany; Stepan 1991 on Latin American countries; Ludmerer 1972; Selden 1999; Briggs 2002; and Ordover 2003 on the United States. For helpful reviews of many of the above works, see Pauly 1993 and Dikötter 1998. For a discursive analysis of eugenics, see Hasian 1996. The eugenic family studies were in significant ways intellectual forerunners of sociobiology and human genetics research of the 1970s and 1980s. See Duster 1990 and Paul 1998: 1–21.

7. Other significant intellectual and cultural developments during this period, such as the rise of "scientific management" and the increasingly com-

plex articulation of discourses regarding national health, productivity, and efficiency, while important aspects of the historical context for eugenics, are beyond the scope of this study. On these important themes, see Kühl 1994 and Weiss 1987.

8. So much for Jefferson's troublesome sentiments about all men being created equal. For primary examples of how, in the rhetoric of eugenicists, democratic principles and biological determinism were not merely reconciled, but also rendered mutually constitutive, consult the works of McDougall (1921a, 1921b).

9. On Galton, see Cowan 1985. For recent analyses of Stoddard and Grant, see Guterl 2001: 14–67 and Hartigan 2005: 88–107.

10. See, in particular, Davenport 1910 and Davenport 1911. See also the textbook Davenport coauthored with Harry H. Laughlin, Henry H. Goddard, and others: Davenport et al. 1911.

11. Some of these techniques are described in Davenport 1913a, 1913b.

12. Examples of "positive eugenics" included proper marriage selection and increased sexual reproduction among the "socially fit." For examples of this "social hygiene" approach, see Burbank 1906; R. Crane 1910; Davenport 1913a; Popenoe and Johnson 1918; and Wiggam 1924. For an early articulation of this thinking, see Walker 1872.

13. For a review of anthropological observations on these populations, see Beale 1972. For an attempt to track the derogatory labels applied to them, see Dunlap and Weslager 1947. The term *tri-racial isolates* derives from eugenic science.

14. For a full history, see Reilly 1991: xiii, which estimates that between 1907 and the early 1960s, 60,000 "mental defectives" were subjected to involuntary sterilization in the United States. Between 1907 and 1927, about 53 percent of those sterilized were men. For more on eugenic sterilization in the South, see Woodside 1950; Gardella 1995; and Larson 1995.

15. For scholarly works that deal with the larger historical context, see, in addition to Kevles 1986/1995, Haller 1963; Pickens 1968; and Kraut 1994.

16. For a chief primary source, see Laughlin and United States Congress House Committee on Immigration and Naturalization 1921.

17. Eugenicists had heated disagreements over whether it was Nordics or Anglo-Saxons or some other Northern European group that represented the supreme racial type. To label this shared ideology "white supremacy" is historically inaccurate and potentially misleading, as during this era, it was not just color lines, but also lines of ethnicity and nationality that were being drawn. See Jacobson 1998.

18. The number of PhDs granted grew apace: from 44 in 1876 to 1,064 in 1924, an increase of roughly 2,400 percent. Also, see Ben-David 1971, especially chapter 8, "The Professionalization of Research in the United States."

19. Many historians of science have offered compelling and intricately

detailed descriptions of just how the professionalization process occurred within the ranks of specific scientific fields, but too few have considered the dynamics of social-group relations that affected and transformed the process of professionalization. Among historians, Haskell 1977 is the major exception. Sociologists and political economists have fared better at this task. See Starr 1982, Navarro 1976: 67–99, and Friedson 1970, 1982. For an extended overview of what he terms "the professionalization of the study of race," see Barkan 1992.

It is crucial to understand the intergroup relations and issues of status, power, and privilege that are at the core of the process of professionalization. Alvin Gouldner's work is an important if now neglected resource in this regard. While he was hardly the first to comment upon the rise of bureaucratic forces in modern society, his insight that a "New Class" comprised of intellectuals and the "technical intelligentsia" was entering into contention with the groups already in control of the economy — namely, the business and political elite — and emerging into the public sphere as a structurally differentiated and (relatively) autonomous social stratum, provided a novel sociological critique about the role of professionals in society. Gouldner (1979) warned against simply viewing the new class of professionals as "benign technocrats," carefully adjusting social policies to maximize efficiency, or as "servants of power," bowing and scraping to the needs of the old power elite, or even as a new "master class," using education and knowledge rather than money to exploit others. Instead, he contended, we must recognize the morally ambiguous and politically ambivalent nature of this class position. Moreover, we must recognize that the social reproduction of professionals is derived primarily from public education and that this fact in turn gives rise to the development of an ideology of autonomy — a condition of relative independence from market forces and political interests. According to this ideology, autonomy is grounded both in specialized knowledge gained through the educational system and in the moral "obligation of educated persons to attend to the welfare of the collectivity. In other words," he says, "the ideology of 'professionalism' is born" (19). Gouldner's recognition that the actual moral position of professionals is one of ambiguity, not superiority, can help us understand the ambiguous results of social reform for the poor (see also Noble 1953). Eugenic researchers and campaigners observed poor rural white family life in order to better understand how to regulate and intervene in the lives of the white poor. The results for poor whites were mixed. Identifying motives as either "good" (humanitarian) or "bad" (control-oriented) — applying the sort of trial logic that characterizes so much of the social theory and historiography on the topic — obscures Gouldner's point about the moral ambivalence of this class location and invites us to project what we now know about the horrors of eugenics back into the past. Gouldner's ideas fit well with the social closure perspective I have relied on throughout this book and finds support in Burrow 1977. Lastly, Gouldner's emphasis upon the crisis in social reproduction occasioned by the decline of the patriarchal family suggests one reason "the family" became an idée fixe in eugenics. I elaborate on this point below.

20. There was, at the same time, a very small but growing class of middle-class black intellectuals. For useful overviews, see Landry 1987 and Patillo-McCoy 1999: 13–22.

21. Historians of eugenics have noted the relatively high level of prestige accorded to white women in and through the eugenics movement. That women were particularly capable when it came to matters of social reform was not a novel idea. For classed aspects of this gendered reality, see Mink 1990. For a general treatment, see Rossiter 1982.

22. As Diane Paul (1998: 55) explains, "Universities were much readier to educate than to hire women. . . . Sex segregation was justified in part on the grounds that women had special skills—cooperativeness, emotional sensitivity, perseverance, patience, close attention to detail—that suited them for particular kinds of work."

23. The ERO proved to be a place of exceptional opportunity for aspiring young women. Of the over 250 field-workers trained by Davenport and his assistant H. H. Laughlin, more than 90 percent were women. In part, the high percentage of female trainees reflected Davenport's generally paternalistic view toward middle-class women, but it also made shrewd economic sense: these highly trained women were given extremely low pay for their services—many receiving no pay at all. Through eugenics research, young women professionals were thus accorded an unprecedented degree of authority that, while still unequal to that of male professionals, allowed them to be recognized and to market themselves as experts. To a degree, as rural poor whites became the object of systematic research by middle-class professionals, these researchers were increasingly white women. See Larson 1995: 31–32, 131–33; Rafter 1988a, 21–22; and Paul 1998: 54.

24. The first real effective scientific challenge to these ideas in the United States came from Boasian anthropology in the first two decades of the twentieth century. See Barkan 1992: 90–95 and Jacobson 1998: 100–104.

25. The close attention to the color and texture of skin suggests Blackmar's might have been a "racial" observation, leaving aside the realm of class identity. Here as elsewhere, in historical contexts such as these, answering the question of what counts as a racial observation and what does not is hardly simple or straightforward.

26. On social sanitation, see Duffy 1990, Rosenberg 1962, and Rosen 1958.

27. I discuss *The Hill Folk* later in this chapter, as both it and Kite's "Two Brothers" are important precursors to what was to become one of the most

well-known and oft-cited of the family studies, H. H. Goddard's *The Kalli-kaks: A Study in Hereditary Feeblemindedness* (1912).

28. "Associated with these regiments, possessing a semblance of military organization, real or assumed, was a disjointed band of land pirates, known as 'Pine robbers.' The worst of them were hunted down and killed, the bodies of some being hung as a warning in conspicuous places" (Rafter 1988a: 168, 170, 172).

29. This study, which addresses mixed-race populations, is omitted from Rafter's otherwise thorough collection, as is Estabrook's earlier collaboration with Davenport (1912). Neither of these studies fits well with Rafter's overall thesis. On the "mongrelized" populations of the Appalachian South, see the eugenics-influenced studies by Hirsch 1928; Manne 1936; and the notorious work by M. Sherman and Henry (1933). For a brief overview, see Wray 2006a.

30. Considered by the general population as "neither negro nor white," they were of a type that postwar social scientists have labeled "tri-racial isolates." For social science literature concerning these populations, see Gilbert 1946; Sawyer 1961; Berry 1963; and Beale 1972. See also Demarce 1993. For the most part, these studies uncritically embrace the racial categorizations promulgated by eugenics. Given the locale of study, some have concluded that Estabrook and McDougle may well have been speaking of the *Melungeons*, a group of disputed origins who claimed multiracial descent. See Henige and Wilson 1998 for the debate over Melungeon origins.

31. In today's terminology, *feebleminded* plays a role similar to *mentally retarded* or *developmentally disabled*, concepts that have retained some of the flexibility and imprecision of the earlier terms. See Trent 1994.

32. This test, which originated in France, was adapted and modified by psychologist Lewis Terman of Stanford University. Terman was a pupil of G. Stanley Hall, a prominent psychologist and eugenicist. Terman also sat on the board of the Human Betterment Foundation, a highly influential and powerful eugenics organization headquartered in Pasadena, California. See Kevles 1986/1995: 80–84; Braslow 1996; Birn and Molina 2005.

33. The Army Alpha Test, as it was called, set the score for average intelligence at 100. Idiots were those with scores below 25; imbeciles, 25–55; and morons, 55–75. No southern state even came close to meeting the "average" mark, with most states registering median scores of between 40 and 48, solidly in the imbecile category. See Noll 1995: 31.

34. However, even as late as the 1970s, the supposed link between rural poverty and "mental deficiency" was the subject of extended study. See, for example, Hurley 1969.

35. Southern institutions had overwhelmingly white populations because blacks were generally not considered worthy of the expense of welfare. This situation changed in 1939, when an all black institution opened in Virginia.

According to Noll (1995: 90), southern states either housed feebleminded blacks in institutions "designed for the care of the black insane or made no provisions at all for their care and training."

36. For a classic, unflinching account of what institutionalization meant for the institutionalized, see Goffman 1961. For a historical overview, see Rothman 1971.

37. Indiana passed the first sterilization law in 1907. It was quickly followed by the passage of laws in Washington, California, and Connecticut in 1909. Virginia passed its sterilization law in 1924, the very same year that it also passed the Racial Integrity Law. See Sherman 1988.

38. The first year for which accurate records exist is 1917. Of the 1,422 people sterilized in the first decade, over 70 percent were sterilized in California, which had by far the most aggressive sterilization program of any state. By 1941, the last year for which there are reliable records, the total number had climbed to approximately 38,000. As Philip Reilly (1987: 96) points out, there is good reason to believe that these numbers are quite low, since underreporting of sterilization was common. See also Kevles 1986/1995: 116. For more on California sterilizations, see Gosney 1929 and Braslow 1996.

39. Rothman 1980 emphasizes the routinization and efficiency of the surgery. Trent 1994 offers a somewhat more critical view.

40. Controversial because there was, in fact, very strong resistance to eugenic sterilization from, among other sources, the Catholic Church. See, in particular, Chesterton 1922 and Darrow 1926. For general scholarly discussions of the opposition, see Dikötter 1998; Kevles 1986/1995: 120; Paul 1998: 11, 17; and Reilly 1987: 118–22.

41. Laughlin's account is drawn from court transcripts and depositions and is generally reliable. The Buck story is told rather melodramatically in J. Smith and Nelson 1989 and discussed in Trombley 1988.

42. Buck v. Bell (1927). 274 U.S. 200, 47 S. Ct. 584. *Buck v. Bell* has never been formally overturned. For the authoritative legal analysis of the ruling, see Cynkar 1981. See also Soskin 1983 and Schussler 1989. New evidence in the Buck case suggests it is unlikely that Carrie Buck was "feebleminded," even by the standards of the day. Rather, her pregnancy was the result of a rape by a foster parent and she had been institutionalized to hide the crime. See Rhode 1993–94 and Shapiro 1985. In 2001, after years of protests by victims, the commonwealth of Virginia expressed "regret" over its historical role in eugenic sterilization. In an article in the *Washington Post* (Timberg 2001), historian Steven Selden is quoted as saying that "people were sterilized not because they were feebleminded, but because they were 'poor white trash.'" For an earlier, popular account that comes to the same conclusion, see Chase 1975. See also Selden 1999.

43. These numbers are calculated from Laughlin 1926 and Gosney 1929.

The gender gap here is even more impressive when one considers that during this era, vasectomies were considered low-risk, but tubal ligation, the preferred operation for women, was a major surgical procedure, posing significant risks to the patient. Also, see Reilly's (1987: 98) report that at least three women in California institutions and two women in Virginia died after undergoing involuntary compulsory sterilization. Nationally, between 1930 and the 1960s, many more sterilizations were performed on women than on men (Roberts 1997).

44. Exactly why middle-class reformers fixated so intently on sexual reproduction remains unclear, but, as I mentioned above with regard to Gouldner's view, it may have been a transcoding and projection of anxieties and fears about middle class *social* reproduction. As a strategy for social advancement, professionalization has a significant flaw: it can work against the efforts of a class to reproduce itself from one generation to the next. As Barbara Ehrenreich (1989: 82–83) has observed: "The emerging middle class had erected steep barriers around its professional domain for the purpose of excluding intruders from other classes. But, like it or not, the same barriers not only stand in the way of 'outsiders'—upstarts from the lower classes and the occasional amateur from the upper class—they also stand in the way of the children of the middle class. . . . Thus the barriers that the middle class erected to protect itself make it painfully difficult to reproduce itself." For middle-class professionals, guaranteeing that one's own offspring would maintain middle-class status was difficult, given the institutional barriers such as long, low-paying apprenticeships in the educational system, increasingly active gatekeeping by professional associations, and uncertainties about status and prestige. Such obstacles threatened to disrupt the continued growth of the middle class, creating crises within middle-class families and operating as something of an ironic contradiction within the class itself. This is true even in times of rapid expansion of the middle class. This dilemma perhaps explains why many of these middle-class professionals focused so intensely on family, heredity, and reproduction as major issues of reform: the family and the children became sites of struggle over modes of social and biological reproduction, onto which professionals projected both ambitions and fears. Such symbolic projections may have led middle-class social reformers who could not fully ensure their own social reproduction to attempt to control the biological reproduction of their lower-class others. Conceptually, this cognitive slide from social to biological was facilitated by the rhetoric of eugenics, which acknowledged few distinctions between the two. For primary sources that express an acute sense of crisis around social reproduction, see Chapple 1904 and Ellis 1912. For the classic statement on families and social reproduction, see Engels 1884/1942. See also Coontz 1988; Laslett and Brenner 1989; and Gordon 1990, 1994.

45. *Scientific racism* is an exceedingly misleading term when applied to the ideology and policies of eugenics. It has had the unfortunate effect of center-

ing racial aspects of eugenic thought and minimizing the content and practices of eugenics that involved drawing on boundaries of class, sex, and gender. I prefer to use *scientized prejudice* because it encompasses a much broader
range of social and symbolic domination than does *scientific racism*.

4 "The Disease of Laziness"

1. The term *campaign*, with its connotations of military conquest, appro-
priately describes the attitudes and ideas of those involved, and *crusade*,
which was also widely used at the time, helps capture the moral and religious
fervor that ran throughout the movement. Ettling (1981) conveys this dual aspect of the RSC exceedingly well. For other historical accounts of hookworm
eradication efforts in the south, see Tullos 1978; Eberson 1980; House 1982;
Farmer 1986; Link 1990; and Woody 1992.

2. *The New South* names not just a historical period (usually dated from
Henry Grady's 1886 speech) or an economic (G. Wright 1986) or political
situation, but also a changing set of narratives and myths that southern
boosters, politicians, and entrepreneurs invented in order to sell the region to
skeptical northern investors. See Tindall 1967; Gaston 1970; and Woodward
1951/1971.

3. This mild dermatitis, characteristic of infection, was apparently the
source for some of the more popular names for hookworm disease; for example, "ground itch," "foot itch," and "dew poison." See Boccacio 1972 and
Cassedy 1971: 159.

4. I use the term *moral panic* in the sense provided by Cohen 1972/2002
and Hall et al. 1978; that is, the mobilization of private and public interest and governmental action by arousing fears and anxieties about declining morality. See also Goode and Ben-Yehuda 1994. On the phrase *symbolic
crusade*, see Gusfield 1963/1986 and Beisel 1997. For more on middle-class
anxieties about dirt, death, and disease, see Felberg 1995 and Ott 1996.

5. As Naomi Rogers (1989: 600) has noted: "Promoters of this new approach, now less interested in broad sanitary reforms to prevent disease, were
concerned instead with diagnosing and treating infected individuals. Officials sought to make germs as fearful as filth, but unlike garbage, overflowing
sewers, or inadequate privies, germs were not visible to ordinary citizens.
Flushing streets and disinfecting buildings were dramatic methods of guard-
ing a community's health, but officials could not be observed in the act of
killing germs. Insects offered a way to resolve the ambiguities of germ theory
in relation to twentieth-century health practice."

6. "American Killer" was, of course, a misnomer. The parasite rarely kills,
instead disabling and weakening its victims, who then may or may not suc-
cumb to other infectious diseases.

7. *New York Sun*, December 5, 1902. In subsequent years, this and related terms appeared with great regularity in the press. See Boccacio 1972: 30; Ettling 1981: 35–38; and García 1981.

8. *New York Times*, October 29, 1909.

9. *New York Times*, October 13, 1909. This number was surely a wild guess.

10. *New York Times*, October 22, 1909. The echoes of southern paternalism are unmistakably clear.

11. Even as there was widespread agreement that the region was a place of disease (Deaderick and Thompson 1916), there were fierce arguments about the general etiology of disease in the South. See Patterson 1989.

12. For historical interpretations of how this perception of the "diseased South" may have limited immigration and economic investment in the region and how it contributed to the notions of southern "distinctiveness," otherness, and inferiority, see Goldfield 1976 and Breedon 1988. Savitt and Young (1978) have argued quite persuasively that diseases were crucial factors in creating an image of "southern distinctiveness"—the durable nineteenth-century idea that the entire region and its population was "other" to the North and was somehow less than fully "American." In this view, the reputation of the South as a diseased region, and southerners as diseased, was an important factor in "perpetuating the country's view of the region as inferior and reinforcing southern defensiveness and sense of isolation" (xv–xvii). See also Warner 1985 and Marcus 1988. On the notion of "southern distinctiveness" more generally, see Degler 1977. On yellow fever, see Ellis 1992; Humphreys 1992; and Rosenberg 1962.

13. *New York Times*, August 28, 1908.

14. For northern views on southern pathologies, see Cash 1941/1991.

15. Kunitz (1988), in comparing the early-twentieth-century public health campaigns against hookworm and pellagra in the South, remarks that the "eradication campaign had many characteristics of a religious crusade. . . . The campaign was designed to rid the patient/sinner of his or her individual disease/sin, bypassing politics, society, economics, and culture" (143). He goes on to explain that "The older religious conception of sin and the new scientific conception of disease were mutually resonant; both supported a vision of individual uplift leading to social improvement. That is, for Stiles, Gates, and others like them the germ theory was assimilated to a religious conception of individual sin and redemption suited to a particular style of reform, one that required little institutional or social change and much personal transformation" (143). Kunitz argues that the holistic model was applied in the investigation of pellagra, one of the other chronic diseases that afflicted poor whites and blacks in the South. For more on pellagra and the efforts to rid the South of it, see Etheridge 1972 and Roe 1973.

16. R. N. Whitfield, "Health Catechism: The Fable of the Fly and the Hook-

worm," folder 35, box 2, series 1, RG 4, Rockefeller Foundation Archives, Rockefeller Archives Center, North Tarrytown, New York (hereafter RAC). On moralisms, see Rozin 1997.

17. See Hoy 1995, esp. 129–33, for a provocative discussion of the nationalist compulsions behind the hookworm campaign. As the sociologist Norbert Elias (1939/1978) has asserted, the primary focus for shifts in notions of sanitation and personal hygiene "does not come from rational understanding of the causes of illness, but . . . from changes in the way people live together, in the structure of society" (159). This perspective informs the work of Douglas (1966/1984) and Stallybrass and White (1986) regarding the moral, political, and sociocultural nature of concepts of pollution and purity. On the moral dimensions of disease and behavior, see Brandt and Rozen 1997.

18. Stiles and other scientists believed that dirt eating was an attempt to compensate for the malnutrition and anemia brought on by the disease. In a circular published by the RSC, Stiles authored the following: "Question 41. *Is dirt-eating the cause of hookworm disease?* It is the result of the disease, not the cause. Question 42. *Can dirt-eating be prevented?* Yes, very easily; by preventing soil pollution and thus ground itch and hookworm disease" (1910: 22–23). Stiles was wrong in his predictions. Dirt eating persists as a cultural (and perhaps, as it supplies small quantities of iron, nutritional) practice even though hookworm disease, in the United States, is now rare. See Twyman 1971. For a more recent assessment, see Grigsby et al. 1999.

19. It would be difficult to overestimate the influence of these middle-class taste-making publications. See Ohmann 1996.

20. Countering eugenical science, RSC physicians and campaigners interpreted feeblemindedness not as a genetic trait, but as a consequence of developmental retardation brought on by the hookworm. See Strong 1916.

21. Cash (1941/1991) described the physical attributes of southern poor whites in this way: "The whole pack of them exhibited, in varying measure, a distinctive physical character—a striking lankness of frame and slackness of muscle in association with a shambling gait, a boniness and misshapeliness of head and feature, a peculiar sallow swartness, or alternately a not less peculiar and a not less faded-out colorlessness of skin and hair" (24). The characteristics Cash describes—"the classic stigmata of true degeneracy," as he revealingly terms them—were the precise physical symptoms of the chronic anemia brought on by hookworm infection.

22. As late as 1947, Edgar T. Thompson, a Duke University professor, wrote in a leading sociology journal that hookworm was only symptomatic of the social and economic traditions of poor whites. Their purposelessness resulted from "improvidence, moral degeneracy, lack of ambition, and indifference to profitable labor" (quoted in Flynt 1979: 7).

23. Economic historians attribute a small portion of the decline to the Civil

War, but the debate about how to account for the overall drop in production has yet to be resolved. However, at least one economic historian has argued that the decline in agricultural output and loss of productivity following the Civil War can be largely explained on the basis of an increase in hookworm infection that was precipitated by the substandard living conditions, including widespread malnutrition, brought about by the ravages and destruction of the war itself. See Brinkley 1997.

24. This was compared to a national average of less than 20 percent. The figures here and following are from Woodward 1951/1971: 132–34.

25. In an official congressional report, Stiles (1912) documented the incidence of hookworm infection in cotton-mill towns. Additional reports may be found in Rockefeller Foundation International Health Board 1922.

26. These are, of course, precisely the phenotypical distinctions that have long been used to mark out racial otherness. On this point, see Otter 1999: 1–8. This example casts doubt on any easy assertion that, as subjective modes of social categorization, assigning race and class are always distinct processes. Here, they appear to have merged.

27. *New York Times*, October 29, 1909.

28. Although Page does not identify them, the group he discusses is almost certainly the so-called Forkemites of Virginia. See Rockefeller Sanitary Commission 1914: 121 and Ettling 1981: 5.

29. Ferrell to Rose, April 23, 1910, folder 141, box 8, series 2, RG 4, Rockefeller Foundation Archives, RAC.

30. Stiles, "Confidential Letter," September 30, 1914, folder 76, box 3, series 1, RG 4, Rockefeller Foundation Archives, RAC.

31. On the symbolic and social significance of human excrement, see LaPorte 2000.

32. Stiles to Ferrell, February 3, 1939, folder 33, box 2, series 1, RG 4, Rockefeller Foundation Archives, RAC.

33. As with the "*menace* of the feebleminded" discussed in chapter 3, poor whites were viewed with alarm as threatening agents of corruption. In the winter and spring of 1910, the *New York Times* coverage contained several references to the "hookworm invasion." See, for instance, *New York Times*, January 9, 1910.

34. *New York Times*, January 31, 1910.

35. Both the original letter, from the office of Clarence Shearn in New York City, and Wycliffe's response may be found in folder 67, box 3, series 1, RG 4, Rockefeller Foundation Archives, RAC.

36. In 1935, Stiles raised the ire of NAACP director Walter White when he delivered a public lecture, "Medico-Zoological Aspects of the Race Problem," in which he laid much of the responsibility for both racial unrest and the persistence of hookworm disease on African Americans. Recall, he asserted, that

"the Negro is double the soil polluter that the white man is." In addition to arguing that African Americans were primary vectors of disease into the white population, Stiles went on to argue that southern lynchings were a result of African American men raping white virgins to cure venereal diseases, which were rampant in African American communities. Stiles's speech, White complained in a sharply worded letter to President Roosevelt, was "full of wild, loose, and unsubstantiated statements born of race prejudice, but intended to carry impressions of scientific statements with regard to general conditions." White to Roosevelt, July 17, 1935, folder "New Deal-Black Americans," box 1. Franklin D. Roosevelt Library, Hyde Park, N.Y.

37. According to Marcus (1989), the hookworm campaign "promised that the situation among southerners could be corrected and that the South might become American" (104–5, 114). See also Stiles 1909a, 1909b.

38. In the following decades, Weston was joined by others who sought to increase cotton-mill operative productivity through medicine. See Sydenstricker 1918 and Wiehl and Sydenstricker (1924).

39. See Whites 1988, which quotes Claire De Graffenreid, a progressive journalist who authored a controversial expose of mill conditions, as saying, "This neglect [of poor whites] needs deep pondering, and I, to whom the supremacy of the white race is dear, believe that it should be widely proclaimed and quickly remedied" (477).

40. *New York Times*, October 30, 1909.

41. A week later, Candler's argument was given some northern support by a report of the New York City *Medical Record,* which declared that the RSC, comprised as it was of only one zoologist, two physicians (both nonpracticing), five educators, and a few businessmen and philanthropists, was poised to rely most heavily upon whipping up public outrage in its battle against the worm, rather than relying upon medicine and science as it should. The report was described in the *New York Times*, November 8, 1909.

42. *New York Times*, January 7, 1910.

43. How does one answer these questions? Admittedly, the larger cultural effects of the campaign are difficult to measure, yet even the quantifiable aspects are equivocal at best. While between 1909–15, hookworm infection was completely brought under control in some limited areas, and reinfection rates were sharply reduced in several more, by 1931, the infection rates for the southern states had returned to very high levels. Stiles himself established this in a 1931 survey and he subsequently objected strenuously (1933) to the RSC's claim that it had successfully eradicated hookworm.

44. For further elaboration of this argument by scholars engaged with whiteness studies, see Brattain 1999 and Sallee 2004. For a brief review that touches on these matters, see Wray 2005.

5 Limning the Boundaries of Whiteness

1. To reiterate, I define social closure as a particular kind of boundary work that results in the successful hoarding of and control over social resources and opportunities. As Weber (1968) noted, "This monopolization is directed against competitors who share some positive or negative characteristics; its purpose is always the closure of social and economic opportunities to *outsiders*" (342). Parkin (1979) extended Weber's notion of closure to encompass "other forms of collective action designed to maximize claims to rewards and opportunities" and concluded that "strategies of exclusion are the predominant mode of closure in all stratified systems" (44, 45). For my purposes, social closure represents an important type of the more general category of Gieryn's (1983) *boundary work*. For an empirical study of ethnoracial differentiation and domination that uses the concept of closure, see the work of Almaguer (1994), whose approach shares many features with boundary theory, although he does not explicitly draw from this theoretical tradition, which was less well developed at the time of his writing than it is now.

2. Having said that, there is no question that this book is marked more by my encounter with sociology than with any other discipline. American sociology has long focused on white ethnic groups (for an overview of this literature, see Alba 1990, esp. 27–30) and perhaps, as a result of this self-assuredness, was initially quite slow to embrace whiteness as a category of analysis. An increasing number of sociologists are choosing to explicitly engage whiteness studies in their work. For examples, see Conley 2000, 2001; Bettie 2003; Doane and Bonilla-Silva 2003; Duster 2001; A. Lewis 2004; Perry 2002; Twine 1997; Ware and Back 2002; Wellman 1997; and Winant 2001. For a useful and concise discussion of the political limits and possibilities of whiteness studies, see Klinenberg 2002. McDermott and Sampson 2005 provides a summary review of sociological research on white identity.

3. For further examples of research that critically engages both boundary theory and the new focus on whiteness, see Lamont 1999, 2000; Nagel 2003; and Vallas 2003.

4. I have also sought to show a more subtle and paradoxical effect: how boundary terms like *white trash* indicate transition and liminality, confounding our attempts to delineate clear, consistent, and fixed identities. As a symbolic identity, *white trash* has a subversive potential to upset stable categories. This, I suggest, is one of the most intriguing things about *white trash* and may help to explain its curious durability, its persistent attractiveness, and its weird historical recurrence. For the historical periods discussed in this book, that subversive potential was largely, although not completely, untapped. However, *white trash* in the popular culture of the late twentieth century is an entirely different story. It has been used in parodic, satirical, and

ironic ways to subvert ideas about class, sex, race, and gender identities or as a badge of resistance against assimilation. See Allison 1994, 1995; Huber 1995; Goad 1997; Kipnis and Reeder 1997; Wray and Newitz 1997; Horwitz 1999; and Hartigan 1997, 2005, esp. 109–133. For theories of how defaming language and defiled speech can work to disrupt settled meanings when used strategically, see Butler 1993.

5. For concise overviews of these origins, see Slack 1974; Innes 1987; and Hartigan 2005: 33–57. Linebaugh and Rediker 2000 provides the most authoritative account of transatlantic conceptions of and treatment toward the poor, the dispossessed, and the criminal.

6. For more on the symbolic significance of borderlands and border dwellers, see Saldívar 1997.

7. Indeed, it still resonates strongly in our culture today. For instance, jokes that are told about poor white trash often feature direct or indirect references to incest, sex with cousins, and so on. They do so to an extent not found in humor about other social groups. Why? I attributed it to the successful, but now largely forgotten efforts of eugenics rhetoric in constructing the poor rural white as incestuous and dangerously endogamous. See Wray 2006b.

8. This book foreshadows this slowly rising status, but does not detail any of the important shifts in the 1930s and 1940s that led to a greater—albeit still incomplete—national acceptance of some southern poor whites as "respectable" white Americans. The era falls outside of the historical limits of this study. Part of this development involved poor whites—in this case known derisively as *lintheads*—acting "as a group" (in the sociological sense of acting for themselves and in their own interests) in the textile strikes and labor unrest of the Piedmont region. For scholarship that addresses the important transformations of this era, see Tullos 1989; Foley 1997; Botsch 1993; Brattain 1999; and Sallee 2004. See Cook 1976 for comments on the literary transformation of the poor white during this era. Of course, another important historical moment in which poor whites can be seen acting "as a group" is the era of populism, a moment so complex that it requires separate study. For a wide range of views, see Key 1962; Kousser 1974; Goodwyn 1978; Hahn 1983; Shaw 1984; McNall 1988; McMath and Foner 1993; Kantrowitz 2000a, 2000b; and Feldman 2004.

9. One obvious and compelling reason to do so is to enlarge the terrain on which the struggle against racism and white supremacy can take place. If antiracists can succeed in making the claim that race is the central and most consequential form of social inequality in modern societies, then the importance and value of antiracist efforts also rises. Thus scholars of race and social inequality who are also committed to antiracist principles (and there are few who, in one way or another, are not) may tend to overstate the importance of race relative to other forms of social inequality. We should be aware and be wary of the status effects of this tendency. In Wray and Newitz 1997, I made

strong claims about the antiracist value in studying whiteness. In Brander
Rasmussen et al. 2001, I was more circumspect. In the present book I make
no explicit claims about the antiracist value of studying whiteness, but not
because I think that work is unimportant. Quite the contrary, scholarship
that critiques prejudice and discrimination is both morally, politically, and
intellectually necessary. It is also too valuable to be left behind as intellectual
paradigms change. See Mullings 2005. My overriding concern is that when we
tie our analyses to specific moral and political goals and strategies, we limit
the kinds of questions we can ask as well as the kinds of answers we find acceptable. Intellectual work worthy of the name can guarantee no politics. For
those of us with antiracist commitments, this is a real dilemma. My strategy
is to try to draw ideas from boundary theory that can reinvigorate all forms
of scholarship about social difference, including antiracist scholarship.

10. In other words, *white trash* is an important case for applying some
of these ideas because *white trash* so clearly does not name an externally
bounded group. There is no bounded social collective. Those so labeled do
not form a group in the sociological sense (i.e., having members who interact
with each other, share values and norms, and share a sense of "we-ness" or
collective identity), yet, historically, the attribution of the term has resulted
in different kinds of group effects. One of the effects is to make us think and
act as if there is a group being referred to, when there is in fact a situation
being referred to, an encounter between peoples, *some of whom* may have differing habits, morals, and worldviews. Some of these effects appear to have to
do with generic status differentiation, but at other times, the meaning of the
differences asserted appear to have to do with what we would today think of
as race, ethnicity, class, gender, and sexuality. Most of the time, one or more
of these areas of meaning seem to be competing for our attention, and it is
seldom easy to decide which area of meaning is predominant.

11. For major critiques of prevailing forms of identity analysis in the United
States that have influenced my thinking, see W. Brown 1995; Gilroy 1993,
2000; Rorty 1998; Stoler 1997; and Wacquant 1997.

12. See Ortner and Whitehead 1981; Bederman 1995; Glenn 2001; and Nagel
2003 for leading examples of research on "intersectionality." See Balibar 1991
for a theoretical statement on the intersecting languages of race and class.

13. In other words, systems of classification and categorization require different kinds of "mastery," both technical and practical (Bourdieu 1977 and
1990), and, as Jenkins (1997) has pointed out, in different domains and orders:
the institutional, the interactional, and the individual. The variability at each
level is important and can be captured methodologically. See Washington
2006.

14. In making this case, I am influenced by Goffman 1959; Barth 1969, 1994,
1998; Blumer 1969; and Hughes 1971/1984.

15. Interdisciplinary research on ethnoracial boundaries seems now to be

at a taking-off point. In November 2005, Harvard University hosted a conference titled "Culture Lines: Emerging Research on Ethno-racial Boundaries" that aimed to "shift attention toward the dynamics of boundaries: how they are created, imposed, defended, bridged, subverted, and transformed." Conference themes included: "Properties of boundaries: permeability, permanence, salience, etc.; Boundary processes: exclusion, bridging, imposition, etc.; Historical research on racial and ethnic formations over time; Ethnographic findings on how boundaries are negotiated in everyday life; Boundaries in cultural production and reception: contesting authenticity, dynamics of collaboration and competition, etc.; Imagery of boundaries in cultural artifacts and performance; [and] How boundaries operate in the expression of collective identity, through cultural and linguistic practices" (http://www.wjh.harvard.edu/boundaries/purpose.html, accessed March 15, 2006). In addition, the theme for the 2006 American Sociology Association's annual meeting, "Great Divides: Transgressing Boundaries," explored "the complex processes and institutional underpinnings that create boundaries." The conference featured dozens of panels devoted to ethnoracial boundaries (see, for example, Wray 2006d).

References

Adams, Mark B. 1990. *The Wellborn Science: Eugenics in Germany, France, Brazil, and Russia.* New York: Oxford University Press.

Agee, James, and Walker Evans. 1939/1960. *Let Us Now Praise Famous Men: Three Tenant Families.* Boston: Houghton Mifflin Co.

Alba, Richard. 1990. *Ethnic Identity: The Transformation of White America.* New Haven, Conn.: Yale University Press.

Allen, Garland. 1986. "The Eugenics Record Office at Cold Spring Harbor, 1910–1940: An Essay in Institutional History." *OSIRIS*, 2nd ser., 2: 225–64.

Allen, Harold B. 1958. "Pejorative Terms for Midwest Farmers." *American Speech* 33: 260–65.

Allen, Irving Lewis. 1983. *The Language of Social Conflict: Social Organization and Lexical Culture.* New York: Columbia University Press.

———. 1990. *Unkind Words: Ethnic Labeling from* Redskin *to* WASP. New York: Bergin & Garvey.

———. 1993. *The City in Slang: New York Life and Popular Speech.* New York: Oxford.

Allen, Theodore W. 1994. *Racial Oppression and Social Control.* Vol. 1 of *The Invention of the White Race.* New York: Verso.

———. 1997. *The Origin of Racial Oppression in Anglo-America.* Vol. 2 of *The Invention of the White Race.* New York: Verso.

Allison, Dorothy. 1994. *Skin: Talking about Sex, Class, and Literature.* Ithaca, N.Y.: Firebrand Books.

———. 1995. *Two or Three Things I Know for Sure.* New York: Dutton.

Almaguer, Tómas. 1994. *Racial Fault Lines: The Historical Origins of White Supremacy in California.* Berkeley: University of California Press.

Anderson, Sherwood. 1920/1993. *Poor White.* New York: New Directions.

Anderson, Warwick. 2003. *The Cultivation of Whiteness: Science, Health, and Racial Destiny in Australia.* New York: Basic Books.

Aptheker, Herbert. 1996. "Maroons within the Present Limits of the United States." In *Maroon Societies: Rebel Slave Communities in the Americas*, ed. Richard Price. Baltimore: Johns Hopkins University Press.

Arneson, Eric. 2001. "Whiteness in the Historian's Imagination." *International Labor and Working-Class History* 60: 3–32.

Ash, Stephen V. 1999. *When the Yankees Came: Conflict and Chaos in the Occupied South, 1861–1865.* Chapel Hill: University of North Carolina Press.

Axtell, James. 1988. *After Columbus: Essays in the Ethnohistory of Colonial North America.* New York: Oxford.

Ayers, Edward L. 1992. *The Promise of the New South: Life after Reconstruction.* New York: Oxford University Press.

———. 1996. "What We Talk about When We Talk about the South." In *All Over the Map: Rethinking American Regions,* ed. Edward L. Ayers et al., 62–82. Baltimore: Johns Hopkins University Press.

Bakhtin, Mikhail. 1984. *Rabelais and His World.* Trans. Hélène Iswolsky. Bloomington: Indiana University Press.

Balibar, Etienne. 1991. "Class Racism." In *Race, Class, and Nation,* ed. Etienne Balibar and Immanuel Wallerstein, 204–16. New York: Verso.

Ballagh, James C. 1895. *White Servitude in the Colony of Virginia.* Baltimore: Johns Hopkins University Press.

Barkan, Elazar. 1992. *The Retreat of Scientific Racism: Changing Concepts of Race in Britain and the United States between the World Wars.* Cambridge: Cambridge University Press.

Barnhart, Robert K., ed. 1988. *The Barnhart Dictionary of Etymology.* New York: H. H. Wilson Co.

Barth, Fredrik. 1969/1998. *Ethnic Groups and Boundaries: The Social Organization of Cultural Difference.* Long Grove, Ill.: Waveland Press.

———. 1994. "Enduring and Emerging Issues in the Analysis of Ethnicity." In *The Anthropology of Ethnicity: Beyond "Ethnic Groups and Boundaries,* ed. H. Vermuelen and C. Govers. Amsterdam: Het Spinhuis.

Batteau, Allen W. 1990. *The Invention of Appalachia.* Tucson: University of Arizona Press.

Beale, Calvin L. 1972. "An Overview of the Phenomenon of Mixed Racial Isolates in the United States." *American Anthropologist* 74: 704–10.

Bederman, Gail. 1995. *Manliness and Civilization: A Cultural History of Gender and Race in the United States, 1880–1917.* Chicago: University of Chicago Press.

Beecher, Catherine, and Harriet Beecher Stowe. 1869. *The American Woman's Home; or, Principles of Domestic Science.* New York: J. B. Ford.

Beisel, Nicola. 1997. *Imperiled Innocents: Anthony Comstock and Family Reproduction in Victorian America.* Princeton, N.J.: Princeton University Press.

Ben-David, Joseph. 1971. *The Scientist's Role in Society: A Comparative Study.* Englewood Cliffs, N.J.: Prentice-Hall.

Berkhofer, Robert F. Jr. 1964. "Space, Time, Culture, and the New Frontier." *Agricultural History* 38: 21–30.

————. 1979. *The White Man's Indian: Images of the American Indian from Columbus to the Present*. New York: Vintage.

Berry, Brewton. 1963. *Almost White*. New York: Macmillan Co.

Bertelson, David. 1967. *The Lazy South*. New York: Oxford University Press.

Bettie, Julie. 2003. *Women without Class: Girls, Race, and Identity*. Berkeley: University of California Press.

Beverley, Robert. 1705/1947. *The History and Present State of Virginia*. Chapel Hill: University of North Carolina Press.

Bieder, Robert E. 1986. *Science Encounters the Indian, 1820–1880: The Early Years of American Ethnology*. Norman: University of Oklahoma Press.

Birn, Anne-Emmanuelle, and Natalia Molina. 2005. "In the Name of Public Health." *American Journal of Public Health* 95: 1095–97.

Blair, Walter. 1953. "Traditions in Southern Humor." *American Quarterly* 5 (2): 132–42.

Bledstein, Burton J. 1976. *The Culture of Professionalism: The Middle Class and the Development of Higher Education in America*. New York: W. W. Norton & Co.

Bleser, Carol. 1991. *In Joy and in Sorrow: Women, Family and Marriage in the Victorian South, 1830–1900*. New York: Oxford University Press.

Blumer, Herbert. 1958. "Race Prejudice as a Sense of Group Position." *Pacific Sociological Review* 1: 3–7.

————. 1969. *Symbolic Interactionism: Perspectives and Methods*. Berkeley: University of California Press.

Blumin, Stuart. 1985. "The Hypothesis of Middle-Class Formation in Nineteenth Century America." *American Historical Review* 90 (2): 299–338.

Boccacio, Mary. 1972. "Ground Itch and Dew Poison: The Rockefeller Sanitary Commission, 1909–1914." *Journal of Medicine and Allied Sciences* 27 (1): 30–53.

Bolton, Charles C. 1994. *Poor Whites of the Antebellum South: Tenants and Laborers in Central North Carolina and Northeast Mississippi*. Durham, N.C.: Duke University Press.

Bonilla-Silva, Eduardo. 1997. "Rethinking Racism." *American Sociological Review* 62: 465–80.

Bonnell, Victoria, and Lyn Hunt, eds. 1999. *Beyond the Cultural Turn: New Directions in the Study of Society and Culture*. Berkeley: University of California Press.

Botsch, Robert Emil. 1993. *Organizing the Breathless: Cotton Dust, Southern Politics and the Brown Lung Association*. Lexington: University Press of Kentucky.

Bourdieu, Pierre. 1977. *Outline of a Theory of Practice*. Cambridge: Cambridge University Press.

————. 1984. *Distinction: A Social Critique of the Judgement of Taste*. Trans. Richard Nice. Cambridge, Mass.: Harvard University Press.

———. 1990. *In Other Words: Essays towards a Reflexive Sociology.* Palo Alto, Calif.: Stanford University Press.

———. 1991. *Language and Symbolic Power.* Cambridge, Mass.: Harvard University Press.

Bradford, J. S. 1870. "Crackers." *Lippincott's Magazine of Literature, Science and Education* 6: 457–67.

Brander Rasmussen, Birgit, Eric Klinenberg, Irene Nexica, and Matt Wray, eds. 2001. *The Making and Unmaking of Whiteness.* Durham, N.C.: Duke University Press.

Brandt, Allan, and Paul Rozen, eds. 1997. *Morality and Health.* New York: Routledge.

Braslow, J. T. 1996. "In the Name of Therapeutics: The Practice of Sterilization in a California State Hospital." *Journal of the History of Medicine and Allied Sciences* 51 (1): 29–51.

Brattain, Michelle. 1999. *The Politics of Whiteness: Race, Workers, and Culture in the Modern South.* Athens: University of Georgia Press.

Breedon, James O. 1988. "Disease as a Factor in Southern Distinctiveness." In *Disease and Distinctiveness in the American South*, ed. Todd L. Savitt and James Harvey Young, 1–28. Knoxville: University of Tennessee Press.

Breen, T. H., ed. 1976. *Shaping Southern Society: The Colonial Experience.* New York: Oxford University Press.

Brewer, William. 1930. "Poor Whites and Negroes in the South Since the Civil War." *Journal of Negro History* 15 (January): 26–37.

Briggs, Laura. 2002. *Reproducing Empire: Race, Sex, Science, and U.S. Imperialism in Puerto Rico.* Berkeley: University of California Press.

Brinkley, Garland. 1997. "The Decline in Southern Agricultural Output, 1860–1880." *Journal of Economic History* 57 (1): 116–38.

Broberg, Gunnar, and Nils Roll-Hansen. 1996. *Eugenics and the Welfare State: Sterilization Policy in Denmark, Sweden, Norway, and Finland.* East Lansing: Michigan State University Press.

Brown, E. Richard. 1976. "Public Health in Imperialism: Early Rockefeller Programs at Home and Abroad." *American Journal of Public Health* 66: 897–903.

———. 1979. *Rockefeller Medicine Men: Medicine and Capitalism in America.* Berkeley: University of California Press.

Brown, Kathleen M. 1996. *Good Wives, Nasty Wenches, and Anxious Patriarchs: Gender, Race, and Power in Colonial Virginia.* Chapel Hill: University of North Carolina Press.

Brown, Richard Maxwell. 1963. *The South Carolina Regulators.* Cambridge, Mass.: Harvard University Press.

Brown, Wendy. 1995. *States of Injury: Power and Freedom in Late Modernity.* Princeton, N.J.: Princeton University Press.

Brubacher, John S., and Willis Rudy. 1976. *Higher Education in Transition:*

A History of American Colleges and Universities, 1636–1976. New York: Harper & Row.

Brubaker, Rogers. 2004. *Ethnicity without Groups*. Cambridge, Mass.: Harvard University Press.

Brubaker, Rogers, and Frederick Cooper. 2000. "Beyond 'Identity.'" *Theory and Society* 29: 1–47.

Buck, Paul H. 1925. "The Poor Whites of the Antebellum South." *American Historical Review* 31: 41–54.

———. 1937. *The Road to Reunion, 1865–1900*. Boston: Little, Brown & Co.

Burbank, Luther. 1906. *The Training of the Human Plant*. New York: The Century Co.

Burrow, James G. 1977. *Organized Medicine in the Progressive Era: The Move toward Monopoly*. Baltimore: Johns Hopkins University Press.

Burton, Orville Vernon, and Robert C. McMath Jr. 1982. *Class, Conflict, and Consensus*. Westport, Conn.: Greenwood Press.

Butler, Judith. 1993. *Excitable Speech: A Politics of the Performative*. New York: Routledge.

Bynum, Victoria E. 1992. *Unruly Women: The Politics of Social and Sexual Control in the Old South*. Chapel Hill: University of North Carolina Press.

Byrd, William, II. 1728/1929. *William Byrd's Histories of the Dividing Line betwixt Virginia and North Carolina*. Raleigh: North Carolina Historical Commission.

Caldwell, Erskine. 1933. *God's Little Acre*. New York: Modern Library.

Carlton, David L. 1982. *Mill and Town in South Carolina, 1880–1920*. Baton Rouge: Louisiana State University Press.

Carr, Duane. 1996. *A Question of Class: The Redneck Stereotype in Southern Fiction*. Bowling Green: Bowling Green State University Popular Press.

Carr, Lois Green, and Lorena S. Walsh. 1988. "The Standard of Living in the Colonial Chesapeake." *William and Mary Quarterly* 45: 135–59.

Carson, Barbara G., Ellen Kirven Donald, and Kym S. Rice. 1998. "Household Encounters: Servants, Slaves, and Mistresses in Early Washington." In *The American Home: Material Culture, Domestic Space, and Family Life*, ed. Eleanor McD. Thompson. Hanover: University of New Hampshire Press.

Carter, Marion. 1909. "The Vampire of the South." *McClure's Magazine* 53: 617–31.

Cash, Wilbur J. 1941/1991. *The Mind of the South*. New York: Vintage.

Cashin, Joan E. 1991. *A Family Venture: Men and Women on the Southern Frontier*. Baltimore: Johns Hopkins University Press.

Cassedy, James. 1971. "The 'Germ of Laziness' in the South, 1901–1915: Charles Ward Stiles and the Progressive Paradox." *Bulletin of the History of Medicine* 45: 159–69.

Cecil-Fronsman, Bill. 1992. *Common Whites: Class and Culture in Antebellum North Carolina*. Lexington: University Press of Kentucky.

Chandler, Asa. 1929. *Hookworm Disease: Its Distribution, Biology, Epidemiology, Pathology, Diagnosis, Treatment, and Control*. New York: Macmillan Co.

Chapple, W. A. 1904. *The Fertility of the Unfit*. Melbourne: Whitcombe & Tombs.

Chase, Allan. 1975. "Eugenics vs. Poor White Trash: The Great Pellagra Cover-Up." *Psychology Today*, February.

Chesnutt, Charles W. 1899/1969. *The Conjure Woman*. Reprint. Ann Arbor: University of Michigan Press.

Chesterton, G. K. 1922. *Eugenics and Other Evils*. New York: Cassell.

Ching, Barbara, and Gerald W. Creed, eds. 1997. *Knowing Your Place: Rural Identity and Cultural Hierarchy*. New York: Routledge.

Clinton, Catherine, ed. 2002. *Fanny Kemble's Journals*. Cambridge, Mass.: Harvard University Press.

Cohen, Stanley. 1972/2002. *Folk Devils and Moral Panics*. New York: Routledge.

Coles, Robert. 1971a. *Migrants, Sharecroppers, and Mountaineers*. Vol. 2. Boston: Little, Brown & Co.

———. 1971b. *The South Goes North*. Vol. 3. Boston: Little, Brown & Co.

Conley, Dalton. 2000. *Honky*. Berkeley: University of California Press.

———. 2001. "Universal Freckle, or How I Learned to Be White." In Brander Rasmussen et al. 2001.

Cook, Sylvia Jenkins. 1976. *From Tobacco Road to Route 66: The Southern Poor White in Fiction*. Chapel Hill: University of North Carolina Press.

Coontz, Stephanie. 1988. *The Social Origins of Private Life: A History of American Families, 1600–1900*. New York: Verso.

Cox, Oliver Cromwell. 1948/2000. *Caste, Class, and Race: A Study in Social Dynamics*. New York: Monthly Review.

Cowan, Ruth Schwartz. 1985. *Sir Francis Galton and the Study of Heredity in the Nineteenth Century*. New York: Garland Publishing.

Craigie, William, and James Hulbert, eds. 1940. *Dictionary of American English on Historical Principles*. Chicago: University of Chicago Press.

Crane, Robert Newton, and Eugenics Education Society. 1910. *Marriage Laws and Statutory Experiments in Eugenics in the United States*. London: Eugenics Education Society.

Crane, Verner. 1919. "A Lost Utopia of the First American Frontier." *Sewanee Review Quarterly* 27: 48–61.

Craven, Avery O. 1930. "Poor Whites and Negroes in the Antebellum South." *Journal of Negro History* 15 (1): 14–25.

Craven, Wesley Frank. 1971. *White, Red, and Black: The Seventeenth Century Virginian*. Charlottesville: University Press of Virginia.

Cutler, William G. 1883. *History of the State of Kansas*. Chicago: A. T. Andreas.

Cynkar, R. J. 1981. "Buck v. Bell: 'Felt Necessities' v. Fundamental Values?" *Columbia Law Review* 81: 1418–61.

Daniel, Pete. 1985. *Breaking the Land: The Transformation of Cotton, Tobacco, and Rice Cultures since 1880*. Urbana: University of Illinois Press.

———. 1990. *The Shadow of Slavery: Peonage in the South, 1901–1969*. Urbana: University of Illinois Press.

Danielson, Florence, and Charles B. Davenport. 1912. *The Hill Folk: Report on a Rural Community of Hereditary Defections*. In Rafter 1988a: 81–163.

Darrow, Clarence. 1926. "The Eugenics Cult." *American Mercury* (June): 129–37.

Davenport, Charles B. 1910. *Eugenics, the Science of Human Improvement by Better Breeding*. New York: H. Holt & Co.

———. 1911. *Heredity in Relation to Eugenics*. New York: H. Holt & Co.

———. 1913a. *State Laws Limiting Marriage Selection Examined in the Light of Eugenics*. Cold Spring Harbor, N.Y.: Eugenics Record Office.

———. 1913b. *How to Make a Eugenical Family Study. Eugenics Record Office, Bulletin no. 13*. Cold Spring Harbor, N.Y.: Eugenics Records Office.

Davenport, Charles B., Harry Hamilton Laughlin, David Fairchild Weeks, Edward Ransom Johnstone, and Henry Herbert Goddard. 1911. *The Study of Human Heredity*. Cold Spring Harbor, N.Y.: Eugenic Records Office.

Davis, Allison, Burleigh B. Gardner, and Mary R. Gardner. 1941. *Deep South: A Social Anthropological Study of Caste and Class*. Chicago: University of Chicago Press.

Deaderick, William H., and Lloyd O. Thompson. 1916. *The Endemic Diseases of the Southern States*. Philadelphia, Pa.: Lippincott.

Degler, Carl. 1977. *Place over Time: The Continuity of Southern Distinctiveness*. Baton Rouge: Louisiana State University Press.

———. 1991. *In Search of Human Nature: The Decline and Revival of Darwinism in American Social Thought*. New York: Oxford University Press.

Demarce, V. 1993. "Looking at Legends — Lumbee and Melungeon: Applied Genealogy and the Origins of Tri-Racial Isolate Settlements." *National Genealogical Society Quarterly* (March): 24–45.

Dikötter, Frank. 1998. "Race Culture: Recent Perspectives on the History of Eugenics." *American Historical Review* 103: 467–78.

DiMaggio, Paul. 1997. "Culture and Cognition." *Annual Review of Sociology* 23: 263–87.

Diner, Hasia. 1983. *Erin's Daughters in America: Irish Immigrant Women in the Nineteenth Century*. Baltimore: Johns Hopkins University Press.

Doane, Ashley, and Eduardo Bonilla-Silva, eds. 2003. *White Out: The Continuing Significance of Racism*. New York: Routledge.

Dock, George, and Charles Cassedy Bass. 1910. *Hookworm Disease: Etiology, Pathology, Diagnosis, Prognosis, Prophylaxis, and Treatment*. St. Louis, Mo.: C. V. Mosby Co.

Dollard, John. 1937/1949. *Caste and Class in a Southern Town*. New York: Harper.

Dorrill, George T. 1986. *Black and White Speech in the Southern United States: Evidence from the Linguistic Atlas of the Middle and South Atlantic States*. New York: Peter Lang.

Douglas, Mary. 1966/1984. *Purity and Danger: An Analysis of the Concepts of Pollution and Taboo*. London: ARK Paperbacks.

Douglass, Frederick. 1855/2003. *My Bondage and My Freedom*. New York: Penguin.

Dowbiggin, Ian Robert. 1997. *Keeping America Sane: Psychiatry and Eugenics in the United States and Canada, 1880–1940*. Ithaca, N.Y.: Cornell University Press.

Du Bois, W. E. B. 1935/1962. *Black Reconstruction in America: An Essay toward a History of the Part Which Black Folk Played in the Attempt to Reconstruct Democracy in America, 1860–1880*. New York: Russell & Russell, Inc.

Dubow, Saul. 1995. *Scientific Racism in Modern South Africa*. Cambridge: Cambridge University Press.

Dudden, Faye. 1983. *Serving Women: Household Service in Nineteenth-Century America*. Middletown, Conn.: Wesleyan University Press.

Duffy, John. 1990. *The Sanitarians: A History of American Public Health*. Urbana: University of Illinois Press.

Dugdale, Richard L. 1877/1910. *The Jukes: A Study in Crime, Pauperism, Disease, and Heredity*. 4th ed. New York: Putnam.

Dunlap, A. R., and C. A. Weslager. 1947. "Trends in the Naming of Tri-Racial Mixed-Blood Groups in the Eastern United States." *American Speech* 22: 81–87.

Dunning, Charles. 1882. "In a Florida Cracker's Cabin." *Lippincott's Magazine of Popular Literature and Science* 3 (April): 367–74.

Durkheim, Emile. 1915/1965. *The Elementary Forms of Religious Life*. New York: Free Press.

Duster, Troy. 1990. *Backdoor to Eugenics*. New York: Routledge.

———. 2001. "The 'Morphing' Properties of Whiteness." In Brander Rasmussen et al. 2001.

Eberson, Frederick. 1980. "Eradication of Hookworm Disease in Florida." *Journal of the Florida Medical Association* 67: 736–42.

Ehrenreich, Barbara. 1989. *Fear of Falling: The Inner Life of the Middle Class*. New York: Harpercollins.

Elias, Norbert. 1939/1978. *The History of Manners*. Vol. 1 of *The Civilizing Process*. Oxford: Blackwell.

Eller, Ronald D. 1982. *Miners, Millhands, and Mountaineers: Industrialization of the Appalachian South, 1880–1930*. Knoxville: University of Tennessee Press.

Ellis, Havelock. 1912. *The Task of Social Hygiene*. London: Constable & Co. Ltd.

Ellis, John. 1992. *Yellow Fever and Public Health in the South*. Lexington: University of Kentucky.

Engels, Frederick. 1884/1942. *The Origin of the Family, Private Property and the State*. New York: International Publishers.

Estabrook, Arthur, and Charles B. Davenport. 1912. *The Nam Family: A Study in Cacogenics*. Cold Spring Harbor, N.Y.: Eugenics Record Office.

Estabrook, Arthur, and Ivan McDougle. 1926. *Mongrel Virginians: The Win Tribe*. Baltimore: Williams & Wilkens.

Etheridge, Elizabeth. 1972. *The Butterfly Caste: A Social History of Pellagra in the South*. Westport, Conn.: Greenwood.

Ettling, John. 1981. *The Germ of Laziness: Rockefeller Philanthropy and Public Health in the New South*. Cambridge, Mass.: Harvard University Press.

Farmer, H. Frank. 1986. "Hookworm Eradication Program of Florida in the Early Twentieth Century." *Journal of the Florida Medical Association* 73: 300–304.

Farrall, Lyndsay Andrew. 1985. *The Origins and Growth of the English Eugenics Movement, 1865–1925*. New York: Garland Publishing.

Feldberg, Georgina D. 1995. *Disease and Class: Tuberculosis and the Shaping of Modern North American Society*. New Brunswick, N.J.: Rutgers University Press.

Feldman, Glenn. 2004. *Disfranchisement Myth: Poor Whites and Suffrage Restriction in Alabama*. Athens: University of Georgia Press.

Fields, Barbara Jeanes. 1985. *Slavery and Freedom on the Middle Ground: Maryland during the Nineteenth Century*. New Haven, Conn: Yale University Press.

———. 2001. "Whiteness, Racism, and Identity." *International Labor and Working-Class History* 60 (Fall): 3–32.

Fine, Gary Alan. 1993. "The Sad Demise, Mysterious Disappearance, and Glorious Triumph of Symbolic Interactionism." *Annual Review of Sociology* 19: 61–87.

Fischer, Kirsten. 2002. *Suspect Relations: Sex, Race, and Resistance in Colonial North Carolina*. Ithaca, N.Y.: Cornell University Press.

Fitzhugh, George. 1854. *Sociology for the South, or the Failure of Free Society*. Richmond, Va.: A. Morris.

Fitzhugh, George. 1856/1960. *Cannibals All! Or Slaves without Masters*. Cambridge, Mass.: Belknap.

Flexner, Stuart. 1976. *I Hear America Talking*. New York: Van Nostrand.

Flynt, J. Wayne. 1979. *Dixie's Forgotten People: The South's Poor Whites*. Bloomington: Indiana University Press.

———. 1989. *Poor but Proud: Alabama's Poor Whites*. Tuscaloosa: University of Alabama Press.

Flynt, J. Wayne, and Dorothy S. Flynt. 1981. *Southern Poor Whites: A Selected Annotated Bibliography of Published Sources*. New York: Garland Publishing.

Foley, Douglas. 1994. *Learning Capitalist Culture: Deep in the Heart of Tejas*. Philadelphia: University of Pennsylvania Press.

Foley, Neil. 1997. *The White Scourge: Mexicans, Blacks, and Poor Whites in Texas Cotton Culture*. Berkeley: University of California Press.

Foner, Eric. 2001. "Response to Eric Arneson." *International Labor and Working-Class History* 60 (Fall): 57–60.

Forret, Jeff. 2004. "Slaves, Poor Whites, and the Underground Economy of the Rural Carolinas." *Journal of Southern History* 70: 783–824.

Fox, Aaron. 2004. *Real Country: Music and Language in Working-Class Culture*. Durham: Duke University Press.

Frankenberg, Ruth. 1993. *White Women, Race Matters: The Social Construction of Whiteness*. Minneapolis: University of Minnesota Press.

———, ed. 1997. *Displacing Whiteness: Essays in Social and Cultural Criticism*. Durham, N.C.: Duke University Press.

Fredrickson, George. 1981. *White Supremacy: A Comparative Study in American and South African History*. Oxford: Oxford University Press.

Friedson, Eliot. 1970. *Professional Dominance: The Social Structure of Medical Care*. Chicago: Aldine.

Frykman, Jonas, and Orvar Löfgren. 1987. *Culture Builders: A Historical Anthropology of Middle Class Life*. Trans. Alan Crozier. New Brunswick, N.J.: Rutgers University Press.

Funk, Isaac, ed. 1895. *Funk and Wagnall's Standard Dictionary of the English Language*. New York: Funk and Wagnall's Co.

Galenson, David W. 1981. *White Servitude in Colonial America: An Economic Analysis*. Cambridge: Cambridge University Press.

Galton, Francis. 1871. *Hereditary Genius: An Inquiry into Its Laws and Consequences*. New York: D. Appleton.

———. 1909. *Essays in Eugenics*. London: Eugenics Education Society.

García, Juan C. 1981. "The Laziness Disease." *History and Philosophy of the Life Sciences* 3: 31–59.

Gardella, J. E. 1995. "Eugenic Sterilization in America and North Carolina." *North Carolina Medical Journal* 56 (2): 106–10.

Gaston, Paul M. 1970. *The New South Creed: A Study in Southern Mythmaking*. New York: Knopf.

Genovese, Eugene D. 1967. *The Political Economy of Slavery: Studies in the Economy and Society of the Slave South*. New York: Vintage.

———. 1975. *Roll, Jordan, Roll: The World the Slaves Made*. New York: Vintage.

———. 1977. " 'Rather Be a Nigger Than a Poor White Man': Slave Perceptions of Southern Yeomen and Poor Whites." In *Toward a New View of America: Essays in Honor of Arthur C. Cole*, ed. Hans L. Trefousse. New York: Burt Franklin Publishers.

Gieryn, Thomas. 1983. "Boundary-work and the Demarcation of Science from Non-science: Strains and Interests in Professional Ideologies of Scientists." *American Sociological Review* 48: 781–95.

Gilbert, W. H., Jr. 1946. "Memorandum Concerning the Characteristics of the Larger Mixed-Blood Racial Islands of the Eastern United States." *Social Forces* 24: 438–47.

Gilman, Sander L. 1985. *Difference and Pathology: Stereotypes of Sexuality, Race, and Madness*. Ithaca, N.Y.: Cornell University Press.

Gilroy, Paul. 1991. *"There Ain't No Black in the Union Jack": The Cultural Politics of Race and Nation*. Chicago: University of Chicago Press.

———. 1993. *The Black Atlantic: Modernity and Double Consciousness*. Cambridge, Mass.: Harvard University Press.

———. 2000. *Against Race: Imagining Political Culture beyond the Color Line*. Cambridge, Mass.: Harvard University Press.

Gitlin, Todd, and Nanci Hollander. 1970. *Uptown: Poor Whites in Chicago*. New York: Harper & Row.

Glenn, Evelyn Nakano. 2001. *Unequal Freedom: How Race and Gender Shaped American Citizenship and Labor*. Cambridge, MA: Harvard University Press.

Goad, Jim. 1997. *The Redneck Manifesto. America's Scapegoats: How We Got That Way and Why We're Not Going to Take It Anymore*. New York: Simon & Schuster.

Godbeer, Richard. 1998. "William Byrd's 'Flourish': The Sexual Cosmos of a Southern Planter." In *Sex and Sexuality in Early America*, ed. Merril D. Smith. New York: New York University Press.

Goddard, Henry H. 1912. *The Kallikaks: A Study in Hereditary Feeblemindedness*. New York: Macmillan.

Goffman, Erving. 1959. *The Presentation of Self in Everyday Life*. New York: Anchor.

———. 1961. *Asylums*. Garden City, N.Y.: Anchor.

———. 1963. *Stigma: Notes on the Management of Spoiled Identity*. New York: Touchstone.

———. 1981. *Forms of Talk*. Philadelphia: University of Pennsylvania Press.

Goldberg, David Theo. 1993. *Racist Culture: Philosophy and the Politics of Meaning*. Oxford: Blackwell.

Goldfield, David R. 1976. "The Business of Health Planning: Disease Prevention in the Old South." *Journal of Southern History* 62: 557–70.

Goode, Erich, and Nachman Ben-Yehuda. 1994. *Moral Panics*. Oxford: Blackwell.

Goodwin, Jeff, James M. Jasper, and Francesca Polletta, eds. 2001. *Passionate Politics: Emotions and Social Movements.* Chicago: University of Chicago Press.

Goodwyn, Lawrence. 1978. *The Populist Moment: A Short History of the Agrarian Revolt in America.* Oxford: Oxford University Press.

Gordon, Linda, ed. 1990. *Women, the State, and Welfare.* Madison: University of Wisconsin Press.

————. 1994. *Pitied but Not Entitled: Single Mothers and the History of Welfare 1890–1935.* New York: Free Press.

Gosney, Ezra S. 1929. *Sterilization for Human Betterment.* New York: Macmillan Co.

Gossett, Thomas. 1977. *Race: The History of an Idea in America.* New York: Oxford University Press.

Gouldner, Alvin W. 1979. *The Future of Intellectuals and the Rise of the New Class: A Frame of Reference, Theses, Conjectures, Arguments, and an Historical Perspective on the Role of Intellectuals and Intelligentsia in the International Class Contest of the Modern Era.* New York: Seabury.

Grant, Madison. 1916. *The Passing of the Great Race; or, The Racial Basis of European History.* New York: Scribner's Sons.

Greenblatt, Stephen. 1988. "Martial Law in the Land of Cockaigne." In *Shakespearean Negotiations: The Circulation of Social Energy in Renaissance England.* Berkeley: University of California Press.

Greeson, Jennifer Rae. 1999. "The Figure of the South and the Nationalizing Imperatives of Early United States Literature." *Yale Journal of Criticism* 12: 209–48.

Grigsby, R. K., et al. 1999. "Chalk Eating in Middle Georgia: A Culture-bound Syndrome of Pica?" *Southern Medical Journal* 92: 190–92.

Grubb, Farley. 1994. "The End of European Immigrant Servitude in the United States: An Economic Analysis of Market Collapse, 1772–1835." *Journal of Economic History* 54: 794–824.

Gusfield, Joseph R. 1963/1986. *Symbolic Crusade: Status Politics and the American Temperance Movement.* Urbana: University of Illinois Press.

Guterl, Matthew Pratt. 2001. *The Color of Race in America, 1900–1940.* Cambridge, Mass.: Harvard University Press.

Hacking, Ian. 1999. *The Social Construction of What?* Cambridge, Mass.: Harvard University Press.

Hahn, Steven. 1978. "The Yeomanry of the Nonplantation South: Upper Piedmont Georgia, 1850–1860." In Burton and McMath 1982.

————. 1983. *The Roots of Southern Populism: Yeoman Farmers and the Transformation of the Georgia Upcountry, 1850–1890.* New York: Oxford University Press.

Hahn, Steven, and Jonathan Prude, eds. 1985. *The Countryside in the Age of*

Capitalist Transformation: Essays in the Social History of Rural America. Chapel Hill: University of North Carolina Press.

Hale, Grace Elizabeth. 1998. *Making Whiteness: The Culture of Segregation in the South, 1890–1940*. New York: Pantheon Books.

Hall, Stuart, et al. 1978. *Policing the Crisis: Mugging, the State, and Law and Order*. London: Macmillan Education, Ltd.

Haller, Mark H. 1963. *Eugenics: Hereditarian Attitudes in American Thought*. New Brunswick, N.J.: Rutgers University Press.

Haney López, Ian F. 1996. *White by Law: The Legal Construction of Race*. New York: New York University Press.

Harkins, Anthony. 2004. *Hillbilly: A Cultural History of an American Icon*. New York: Oxford University Press.

Harris, Cheryl. 1993. "Whiteness as Property." *Harvard Law Review* 106 (1707): 1709–91.

Hartigan, John, Jr. 1997. "Name Calling: Objectifying 'Poor Whites' and 'White Trash' in Detroit." In Wray and Newitz 1997.

———. 1999. *Racial Situations: Class Predicaments of Whiteness in Detroit*. Princeton, N.J.: Princeton University Press.

———. 2005. *Odd Tribes: Toward a Cultural Analysis of White People*. Durham, N.C.: Duke University Press.

Hasian, Marouf Arif. 1996. *The Rhetoric of Eugenics in Anglo-American Thought*. Athens: University of Georgia Press.

Haskell, Thomas. 1977. *The Emergence of Professional Social Science: The American Social Science Association and the Nineteenth Century Crisis of Authority*. Urbana: University of Illinois.

Haveman, Heather. 2004. "Antebellum Literary Culture and the Evolution of American Magazines." *Poetics* 32: 5–28.

Henige, David, and Darleen Wilson. 1998. "Exchange." *Appalachian Journal* 25 (3): 1–6.

Herrick, Cheesman A. 1926. *White Servitude in Pennsylvania: Indentured and Redemption Labor in Colony and Commonwealth*. New York: Negro Universities Press.

Higham, John. 1988. *Strangers in the Land: Patterns of American Nativism, 1860–1925*. 2nd ed. New Brunswick, N.J.: Rutgers University Press.

Hill, Mike, ed. 1997. *Whiteness: A Critical Reader*. New York: New York University Press.

———. 2004. *After Whiteness: Unmaking an American Majority*. New York: New York University Press.

Hirsch, Nathaniel. 1928. *An Experimental Study of the East Kentucky Mountaineers: A Study in Heredity and Environment, from the Psychological Laboratories of Harvard University and Duke University*. Worcester, Mass.: Clark University.

Hobsbawm, E. J. 1959. *Primitive Rebels: Studies in Archaic Forms of Social Movement in the Nineteenth and Twentieth Centuries*. New York: W. W. Norton & Co.

Hollander, A. J. N. Den. 1934. "The Tradition of 'Poor-Whites,'" in W. T. Couch, ed. 1934. *Culture in the South*. Chapel Hill: University of North Carolina Press.

Holton, Woody. 1999. *Forced Founders: Indians, Debtors, Slaves, and the Making of the American Revolution in Virginia*. Chapel Hill: University of North Carolina Press.

Horsman, Reginald. 1981. *Race and Manifest Destiny: The Origins of American Racial Anglo-Saxonism*. Cambridge, Mass.: Harvard University Press.

Horwitz, Tony. 1999. *Confederates in the Attic: Dispatches from the Unfinished Civil War*. New York: Random House.

House, Robert V. 1982. "A Brief History of Hookworm Disease in North Carolina." *North Carolina Medical Journal* 43: 765–68.

Howell, Joseph T. 1973. *Hard Living on Clay Street: Portraits of Blue Collar Families*. New York: Anchor.

Hoy, Suellen. 1995. *Chasing Dirt: The American Pursuit of Cleanliness*. New York: Oxford University Press.

Huber, Patrick. 1995. "A Short History of 'Redneck': The Fashioning of a Southern White Masculine Identity." *Southern Cultures* 1 (2): 144–66.

Hudson, C., ed. 1971. *Red, White, and Black: Symposium on Indians in the Old South*. Athens: University of Georgia Press.

Hughes, Everett C. 1971/1984. *The Sociological Eye: Selected Papers on Work, Self, and Society*. New Brunswick, N.J.: Transaction.

Hughes, Everett C., and Helen MacGill Hughes. 1953. *Where Peoples Meet*. Glencoe: Free Press.

Humphreys, Margaret. 1992. *Yellow Fever and the South*. Baltimore: Johns Hopkins University Press.

Hundley, Daniel R. 1860/1979. *Social Relations in Our Southern States*. Baton Rouge: Louisiana State University Press.

Hurley, Rodger. 1969. *Poverty and Mental Retardation: A Causal Relationship*. New York: Random House.

Inge, M. Thomas and Edward J. Piacentino, eds. 2001. *The Humor of the Old South*. Lexington: University of Kentucky Press.

Innes, Joanna. 1987. "Prisons for the Poor: English Bridewells, 1555–1800." In *Labour, Law, and Crime: A Historical Perspective*, ed. Francis Snyder and Douglas Hay. London: Tavistock.

Jacobs, Mark D., and Lyn Spillman. 2005. "Cultural Sociology at the Crossroads of the Discipline." *Poetics* 33 (1): 1–14.

Jacobson, Matthew Frye. 1998. *Whiteness of a Different Color: European Immigrants and the Alchemy of Race*. Cambridge, Mass.: Harvard University Press.

Jenkins, Richard. 1997. *Rethinking Ethnicity: Arguments and Explorations*. London: Sage.

Jones, Hugh. 1724/1956. *The Present State of Virginia, From Whence is Inferred a Short View of Maryland and North Carolina*, ed. Richard Morton. Chapel Hill: University of North Carolina Press.

Jones, Jacqueline. 1986. *Labor of Love, Labor of Sorrow: Black Women, Work, and the Family, From Slavery to the Present*. New York: Vintage.

Jonson, Ben. 1614/1960. *Bartholomew's Fair*. Edited by E. A. Horsman. Cambridge, Mass.: Harvard University Press.

Jordan, David Starr. 1915. *War and the Breed: The Relation of War to the Downfall of Nations*. Boston: Beacon.

Jordan, Winthrop D. 1968/1977. *White over Black: American Attitudes toward the Negro, 1550–1812*. New York: W. W. Norton & Co.

Kahana, Jeffrey. 2000. "Master and Servant in the Early Republic, 1780–1830." *Journal of the Early Republic* 20 (1): 27–57.

Kane, Anne. 2000. "Reconstructing Culture in Historical Explanation: Narratives as Cultural Structure and Practice." *History and Theory* 29: 311–30.

Kantrowitz, Stephen. 2000a. "Ben Tillman and Hendrix McLane, Agrarian Rebels: White Manhood, 'The Farmers,' and the Limits of Southern Populism." *Journal of Southern History* 56: 497–524.

———. 2000b. *Ben Tillman and the Reconstruction of White Supremacy*. Chapel Hill: University of North Carolina Press.

Kars, Marjoleine. 2002. *Breaking Loose Together: The Regulator Rebellion in Pre-Revolutionary North Carolina*. Chapel Hill: University of North Carolina Press.

Katz, Jack. 1988. *Seductions of Crime: Moral and Sensual Attractions in Doing Evil*. New York: Basic Books.

———. 1999. *How Emotions Work*. Chicago: University of Chicago Press.

Katz, Michael B. 2001. *The Price of Citizenship: Redefining the American Welfare State*. New York: Henry Holt.

Kefalas, Maria. 2003. *Working-Class Heroes: Protecting Home, Community, and Nation in a Chicago Neighborhood*. Berkeley: University of California Press.

Kemble, Fanny. 1835. *Journal of a Residence in America*. Paris: Galignani & Co.

———. 1863. *Journal of a Residence on a Georgia Plantation, in 1838–1839*. New York: N.p.

Kennedy, John Pendleton. 1835/1866. *Horse-shoe Robinson: A Tale of Tory Ascendancy*. Reprint. New York: Hurd and Houghton.

Kennedy, Randall. 2002. *Nigger: The Strange Career of a Troublesome Word*. New York: Vintage.

Kevles, Daniel J. 1986/1995. *In the Name of Eugenics: Genetics and the Uses of Human Heredity*. Cambridge, Mass.: Harvard University Press.

Key, V. O. 1962. *Southern Politics in State and Nation*. New York: Vintage Books.

Kipnis, Laura, and Jennifer Reeder. 1997. "White Trash Girl: The Interview." In Wray and Newitz 1997.

Kirwan, Albert D. 1951. *Revolt of the Rednecks: Mississippi Politics, 1876–1925*. Lexington: University of Kentucky Press.

Klein, Rachel N. 1981. "Ordering the Backcountry: the South Carolina Regulation." *William and Mary Quarterly* 38: 661–80.

Klinenberg, Eric. 2002. "The Political Economy of Whiteness Studies." *Souls* 4: 52–55.

Kolchin, Peter. 2002. "Whiteness Studies: The New History of Race in America." *Journal of American History* 89: 154–174.

Kousser, J. Morgan. 1974. *The Shaping of Southern Politics: Suffrage Restriction and the Establishment of the One-Party South, 1880–1910*. New Haven, Conn.: Yale University Press.

Kraut, Alan. 1994. *Silent Travelers: Germs, Genes, and the "Immigrant Menace."* Baltimore: Johns Hopkins University Press.

Kretzschmar, William A., Jr., et al. 1976. *Handbook of the Linguistic Atlas of the Middle and South Atlantic States*. Chicago: University of Chicago Press.

Kühl, Stefan. 1994. *The Nazi Connection: Eugenics, American Racism, and German National Socialism*. New York: Oxford University Press.

Kulikoff, Alan. 2000. *From British Peasants to Colonial Farmers*. Chapel Hill: University of North Carolina Press.

Kunitz, Stephen J. 1988. "Hookworm and Pellagra: Exemplary Diseases in the New South." *Journal of Health and Social Behavior* 29 (June): 139–48.

Lamont, Michèle, ed. 1999. *The Cultural Territories of Race: Black and White Boundaries*. New York: Russell Sage.

———. 2000. *The Dignity of Working Men: Morality and the Boundaries of Race, Class, and Imagination*. New York: Russell Sage.

Lamont, Michèle, and Marcel Fournier, eds. 1992. *Cultivating Differences: Symbolic Boundaries and the Making of Inequality*. Chicago: University of Chicago Press.

Lamont, Michèle, and Virág Molnar. 2002. "The Study of Boundaries in the Social Sciences." *Annual Review of Sociology* 28: 167–95.

Landry, Bart. 1987. *The New Black Middle Class*. Berkeley: University of California Press.

LaPorte, Dominique. 2000. *History of Shit*. Cambridge, Mass.: MIT Press.

Larson, Edward J. 1995. *Sex, Race, and Science: Eugenics in the Deep South*. Baltimore: Johns Hopkins University Press.

Laslett, Barbara, and Joanna Brenner. 1989. "Gender and Social Reproduction: Historical Perspectives." *Annual Review of Sociology* 15: 381–404.

Laughlin, Harry H., and United States Congress House Committee on Immigration and Naturalization. 1921. *Biological Aspects of Immigration. Hear-*

ings, Sixty-Sixth Congress, Second Session. April 16–17, 1920. Washington, D.C.: Government Printing Office.

————. 1926. *Eugenical Sterilization: 1926; Historical, Legal, and Statistical Review of Eugenical Sterilization in the United States.* New Haven, Conn.: The American Eugenics Society.

Laughlin, Harry H., and Chicago (Ill.) Municipal Court. 1929. *Eugenical Sterilization in the United States.* Chicago: Psychopathic Laboratory of the Municipal Court of Chicago.

Lévi-Strauss, Claude. 1966. *The Savage Mind.* Chicago: University of Chicago Press.

Lewis, Amanda E. 2004. " 'What Group?' Studying Whites and Whiteness in the Era of 'Color-Blindness.' " *Sociological Theory* 22: 623–46.

Lewis, Edwin H. 1909. "The Prevalence of Uncinariasis in America." *American Medicine* 15: 497–98.

Lewis, Helen, L. Johnson, and D. Askins, eds. 1978. *Colonialism in Modern America: The Appalachian Case.* Boone, N.C.: Appalachian Consortium.

Linden, Fabian. 1946. "Economic Democracy in the Slave South: An Appraisal of Some Recent Views." *Journal of Negro History* 31: 140–89.

Linebaugh, Peter, and Marcus Rediker. 2000. *The Many-Headed Hydra: The Hidden History of the Revolutionary Atlantic.* Boston: Beacon.

Link, William A. 1990. " 'The Harvest is Ripe, but the Laborers are Few': The Hookworm Crusade in North Carolina, 1909–1915." *North Carolina Historical Review* 67: 1–27.

————. 1992. *The Paradox of Southern Progressivism, 1880–1930.* Chapel Hill: University of North Carolina Press.

Lockley, Timothy J. 1997. "Partners in Crime: African Americans and Non-slaveholding Whites in Antebellum Georgia." In Wray and Newitz 1997.

————. 2001. *Lines in the Sand: Race and Class in Lowcountry Georgia, 1750–1860.* Athens: University of Georgia Press.

Lockridge, Kenneth A. 1987. *The Diary, and Life, of William Byrd II of Virginia, 1674–1744.* New York: W. W. Norton & Co.

————. 1992. *On the Sources of Patriarchal Rage: The Commonplace Books of William Byrd and Thomas Jefferson and the Gendering of Power in the Eighteenth Century.* New York: New York University Press.

Longstreet, Augustus Baldwin. 1835/1992. *Georgia Scenes.* Nashville, Tenn.: J. S. Sanders.

Lott, Eric. 1995. *Love and Theft: Blackface Minstrelsy and the American Working Class.* New York: Oxford University Press.

Loveman, Mara. 1999. "Is 'Race' Essential?" *American Sociological Review* 64: 891–98.

Ludmerer, Kenneth M. 1972. *Genetics and American Society: A Historical Appraisal.* Baltimore: Johns Hopkins University Press.

Lynn, Kenneth. 1959. *Mark Twain and Southwestern Humor*. Boston: Little, Brown, & Co.

Manne, Jack. 1936. "Mental Deficiency in a Closely Inbred Mountain Clan." *Mental Hygiene* 20: 269–79.

Marcus, Alan I. 1988. "Hookworm and Southern Distinctiveness." In *Disease and Distinctiveness in the American South*, ed. Todd L. Savitt and James H. Young, 79–99. Knoxville: University of Tennessee Press.

———. 1989. "Physicians Open a Can of Worms: American Nationality and Hookworm in the United States, 1893–1909." *American Studies* 30 (2): 103–21.

Mark, Noah. 1998. "Beyond Individual Differences: Social Differentiation from First Principles." *American Sociological Review* 69: 309–330.

Martineau, Harriet. 1838/1989. *How to Observe Morals and Manners*. New Brunswick: Transaction Publishers.

Marx, Karl. 1852/1963. *The Eighteenth Brumaire of Louis Bonaparte*. New York: International Publishers.

———. 1848/1998. *The Communist Manifesto*. New York: Verso.

Marx, Leo. 1964. *The Machine in the Garden: Technology and the Pastoral Ideal in America*. New York: Oxford University Press.

Mason, Julian. 1960. "The Etymology of Buckaroo." *American Speech* 35: 51–55.

Masterson, James R. 1937. "William Byrd in Lubberland." *American Literature: A Journal of Literary History, Criticism, and Bibliography* 9: 153–70.

Mathews, Mitford M. 1959. "Of Matters Lexicographical." *American Speech* 34: 126–30.

———, ed. 1951. *Dictionary of Americanisms*. Chicago: University of Chicago Press.

Mazumdar, Pauline M. H. 1992. *Eugenics, Human Genetics, and Human Failings: The Eugenics Society, Its Sources and Its Critics in Britain*. New York: Routledge.

McClintock, Anne. 1995. *Imperial Leather: Race, Gender, and Sexuality in the Colonial Contest*. New York: Routledge.

McCormac, Eugene Irving. 1904. *White Servitude in Maryland, 1634–1824*. Baltimore: Johns Hopkins University Press.

McCullough, David. 2001. *John Adams*. New York: Simon & Schuster.

McCurry, Stephanie. 1995. *Masters of Small Worlds: Yeoman Households, Gender Relations, and the Political Culture of the Antebellum South Carolina Low Country*. New York: Oxford University Press.

McDavid, Raven I., Jr., and Virginia McDavid. 1973. "Cracker and Hoosier." *Journal of the American Name Society* 21 (3): 161–67.

McDavid, Raven I., Jr., and Raymond O'Cain. 1980. *Linguistic Atlas of the South and Mid-Atlantic States*. Chicago: University of Chicago Press.

McDermott, Monica, and Frank L. Sampson. 2005. "White Racial and Ethnic Identity in the United States." *Annual Review of Sociology* 31: 245–61.

McDougall, William. 1921a. *Is America Safe for Democracy?* New York: Scribner's.

———. 1921b. *National Welfare and National Decay.* London: Methuen & Co. Ltd.

McIlwaine, Shields. 1939. *The Southern Poor-White from Lubberland to Tobacco Road.* Norman: University of Oklahoma Press.

McLaren, Angus. 1990. *Our Own Master Race: The Eugenic Crusade in Canada.* Toronto: McClelland & Stewart.

MacLeod, Jay. 1987/2004. *Ain't No Makin' It: Leveled Aspirations in a Low-Income Neighborhood.* Reissue. Boulder: Westview.

McMath, Robert C., and Eric Foner. 1993. *American Populism: A Social History, 1877–1898.* New York: Hill & Wang.

McNall, Scott G. 1988. *The Road to Rebellion: Class Formation and Kansas Populism, 1865–1900.* Chicago: University of Chicago Press.

McWhiney, Grady. 1988. *Cracker Culture: Celtic Ways in the Old South.* Tuscaloosa: University of Alabama Press.

Mell, Mildred Rutherford. 1938. "Poor Whites of the South." *Social Forces* 17 (2): 153–67.

Mellon, Knox, Jr. 1960. "Christian Priber and the Jesuit Myth." *South Carolina Historical Magazine* 51: 75–81.

———. 1973. "Christian Priber's Cherokee 'Kingdom of Paradise.'" *Georgia Historical Quarterly* 53 (3): 319–31.

Michaels, Walter Benn. 1998. "Autobiography of an Ex-White Man: Why Race is Not a Social Construction." *Transition* 7 (1): 122–43.

Miller, Marvin D. 1996. *Terminating the "Socially Inadequate": The American Eugenicists and the German Race Hygienists, California to Cold Spring Harbor, Long Island to Germany.* Commack, N.Y.: Malamud-Rose.

Miller, William Ian. 1997. *The Anatomy of Disgust.* Cambridge, Mass.: Harvard University Press.

Mink, Gwendolyn. 1990. "The Lady and the Tramp: Gender, Race, and the Origins of the American Welfare State." In *Women, the State, and Welfare,* ed. Linda Gordon. Madison: University of Wisconsin Press.

Morgan, Edmund S. 1975. *American Slavery American Freedom: The Ordeal of Colonial Virginia.* New York: W. W. Norton & Co.

Morgan, Kenneth. 2001. *Slavery and Servitude in Colonial North America.* New York: New York University Press.

Morgan, Philip. 2004. "Slaves and Poverty." In *Down and Out in Early America,* ed. Billy G. Smith. University Park: Pennsylvania State University Press.

Morrison, Toni. 1992. *Playing in the Dark: Whiteness and the Literary Imagination.* Cambridge, Mass.: Harvard University Press.

Moss, Kirby. 2003. *The Color of Class: Poor Whites and the Paradox of Privilege*. Philadelphia: University of Pennsylvania Press.

Mott, F. L. 1930. *A History of American Magazines, 1741–1850*. Cambridge, Mass.: Harvard University Press.

———. 1938a. *A History of American Magazines, 1850–1865*. Cambridge, Mass.: Harvard University Press.

———. 1938b. *A History of American Magazines, 1865–1885*. Cambridge, Mass.: Harvard University Press.

Mullings, Leith. 2005. "Interrogating Racism: Toward an Antiracist Anthropology." *Annual Review of Anthropology* 34: 667–93.

Nagel, Joane. 2003. *Race, Ethnicity, and Sexuality: Intimate Intersections, Forbidden Frontiers*. New York: Oxford University Press.

Nash, Gary B. 1974. *Red, White, and Black: The Peoples of Early America*. Englewood Cliffs, N.J.: Prentice-Hall.

Navarro, Vincente. 1976. *Medicine under Capitalism*. New York: Prodist.

Newby, I. A. 1989. *Plain Folk in the New South: Social Change and Cultural Persistence 1880–1915*. Baton Rouge: Louisiana State University Press.

Newitz, Annalee. 1997. "White Savagery and Humiliation, or a New Racial Consciousness in the Media." In Wray and Newitz 1997.

Newitz, Annalee, and Matt Wray. 1997. "What Is 'White Trash'? Stereotypes and Economic Conditions of Poor Whites in the United States." In Hill 1997.

Nietzsche, Friedrich. 1887/1968. *On the Genealogy of Morals*. New York: Vintage.

Noble, David W. 1953. "The Paradox of Progressive Thought." *American Quarterly* 5: 201–12.

Nobles, Gregory. 1997. *American Frontiers: Cultural Encounters and Continental Conquest*. New York: Hill & Wang.

Noll, Steven. 1995. *Feeble-Minded in Our Midst: Institutions for the Mentally Retarded in the South, 1900–1940*. Chapel Hill: University of North Carolina Press.

Nunnally, Thomas. 2001. "Glossing the Folk: A Review of Selected Lexical Research into American Slang and Americanisms." *American Speech* 76: 158–76.

Nussbaum, Martha. 2004. *Hiding from Humanity: Disgust, Shame, and the Law*. Princeton, N.J.: Princeton University Press.

O'Brien, Michael. 1979. *The Idea of the American South: 1920–1941*. Baltimore: Johns Hopkins University Press.

———. 1988. *Rethinking the South: Essays in Intellectual History*. Baltimore: Johns Hopkins University Press.

———. 2004. *Conjectures of Order: Intellectual Life in the American South: 1810–1860*. Vol. 1. Chapel Hill: University of North Carolina Press.

Ohmann, Richard. 1996. *Selling Culture: Magazines, Markets, and Class at the Turn of the Century*. New York: Verso.

O'Leary, Elizabeth. 1996. *At Beck and Call: The Representation of domestic Servants in Nineteenth-Century American Painting*. Washington, D.C.: Smithsonian Institution Press.

Omi, Michael, and Howard Winant. 1994. *Racial Formation in the United States: From the 1960s to the 1990s*. New York: Routledge.

Ordover, Nancy. 2003. *American Eugenics: Race, Queer Anatomy, and the Science of Nationalism*. Minneapolis: University of Minnesota Press.

Ortner, Sherry, and Harriet Whitehead, eds. 1981. *Sexual Meanings: The Cultural Construction of Gender and Sexuality*. New York: Cambridge University Press.

Ott, Katherine. 1996. *Fevered Lives: Tuberculosis in American Culture since 1870*. Cambridge, Mass.: Harvard University Press.

Otter, Samuel. 1999. *Melville's Anatomies*. Berkeley: University of California Press.

Otto, John Soloman, and Augustus Marion Burns III. 1983. "Black Folks and Poor Buckras: Archeological Evidence of Slave and Overseer Living Conditions on an Antebellum Plantation." *Journal of Black Studies* 14: 185–200.

Owsley, Frank L. 1949. *Plain Folk of the Old South*. Chicago: Quadrangle Books.

Owsley, Frank L., and Harriet C. Owsley. 1940. "The Economic Basis of Society in the Late Antebellum South." *Journal of Southern History* 6: 25–45.

Page, Walter Hines. 1912. "The Hookworm and Civilization." *World's Work* 54 (September): 504–18.

Parkin, Frank. 1979. *Marxism and Class Theory: A Bourgeois Critique*. New York: Columbia University Press.

Pascoe, Peggy. 1996. "Miscegenation Law, Court Cases, and Ideologies of 'Race' in Twentieth-Century America." *Journal of American History* 83: 44–69.

Patillo-McCoy, Mary. *Black Picket Fences: Privilege and Peril Among the Black Middle Class*. Chicago: University of Chicago Press.

Patterson, K. David. 1989. "Disease Environments of the Antebellum South." In *Science and Medicine in the Old South*, ed. Ronald L. Numbers and Todd Savitt. Baton Rouge: Louisiana State University Press.

Paul, Diane B. 1998. *Controlling Human Heredity: 1865 to the Present*. Amherst, N.Y.: Humanity Books.

Pauly, Philip J. 1993. "Essay Review: The Eugenics Industry—Growth or Restructuring?" *Journal of the History of Biology* 26 (1): 131–46.

Pederson, Lee, et al. 1981. *Linguistic Atlas of the Gulf States*. Ann Arbor: University Microfilms International.

Perry, Pamela. 2002. *Shades of White: White Kids and Racial Identities in High School*. Durham, N.C.: Duke University Press.

Philliber, William W. 1981. *Appalachian Migrants in Urban America: Cultural Conflict or Ethnic Group Formation?* New York: Praeger.

Phillips, Ulrich Bonnell. 1929. *Life and Labor in the Old South.* Boston: Little, Brown, & Co.

Pickens, Donald K. 1968. *Eugenics and the Progressives.* Nashville, Tenn.: Vanderbilt University Press.

Pleij, Herman. 2000. *Dreaming of Cockaigne: Medieval Fantasies of the Perfect Life.* Trans. Diane Webb. New York: Columbia University Press.

Popenoe, Paul Bowman, and Roswell Hill Johnson. 1918. *Applied Eugenics.* New York: The Macmillan Co.

Presley, Delma. 1976. "The Crackers of Georgia." *Georgia Historical Quarterly* 60 (2): 102–16.

Price, Richard, ed. 1973/1996. *Maroon Societies: Rebel Slave Communities in the Americas.* 3rd ed. Baltimore: Johns Hopkins University Press.

Prude, Jonathan. 1985. "Town and Country Conflicts in Antebellum Rural Massachusetts." In Hahn and Prude 1985.

Pudup, Mary Beth, Dwight B. Billings, Altina L. Waller, eds. 1995. *Appalachia in the Making: The Mountain South in the Nineteenth Century.* Chapel Hill: University of North Carolina Press.

Rafter, Nicole Hahn. 1988a. "White Trash: Eugenics as Social Ideology." *Society* 26 (1): 43–49.

———, ed. 1988b. *White Trash: The Eugenic Family Studies, 1877–1919.* Boston: Northeastern University Press.

———. 1997. *Creating Born Criminals.* Urbana: University of Illinois Press.

Reed, John Shelton. 1972. *The Enduring South: Subcultural Persistence in Mass Society.* Chapel Hill: University of North Carolina Press.

———. 1986. *Southern Folk Plain and Fancy: Native White Social Types.* Athens: University of Georgia Press.

Reilly, Philip. 1987. "Involuntary Sterilization in the United States: A Surgical Solution." *Quarterly Review of Biology* 62: 153–70.

———. 1991. *The Surgical Solution: A History of Involuntary Sterilization in the United States.* Baltimore: Johns Hopkins University Press.

Reisman, David. 1903. "The American Hookworm in Chimpanzees." *American Medicine* 6: 611–23.

Rhode, Deborah, 1993–94. "Adolescent Pregnancy and Public Policy." *Political Science Quarterly* 103: 635–70.

Roberts, Dorothy. 1997. *Killing the Black Body: Race, Reproduction, and the Meaning of Liberty.* New York: Vintage.

Rockefeller Foundation International Health Board. 1922. *Bibliography of Hookworm Disease.* New York: Rockefeller Foundation International Health Board.

Rockefeller Sanitary Commission. 1914. *Annual Reports, 1910–1914.* Washing-

ton, D.C.: Rockefeller Sanitary Commission for the Eradication of Hookworm Diseases.

Rockefeller Sanitary Commission. 1911. *Hookworm Infection in Foreign Countries*. Washington, D.C.: Offices of the Commission.

Roe, Daphne. 1973. *A Plague of Corn: The Social History of Pellagra*. Ithaca,
N.Y.: Cornell University Press.

Roebuck, Julian, and Mark Hickson. 1982. *The Southern Redneck: A Phe-
nomenological Class Study*. New York: Praeger.

Roediger, David R. 1991. *The Wages of Whiteness: Race and the Making of the
American Working Class*. New York: Verso.

————. 1994. *Toward the Abolition of Whiteness: Essays on Race, Politics, and
Working Class History*. New York: Verso.

————. 2005. *Working toward Whiteness: How America's Immigrants Become
White. The Strange Journey from Ellis Island to the Suburbs*. New York:
Basic.

Rogers, Naomi. 1989. "Germs with Legs: Flies, Disease, and the New Public
Health." *Bulletin of the History of Medicine* 63: 599–617.

Rogin, Michael. 1975. *Fathers and Children: Andrew Jackson and the Subjuga-
tion of the American Indian*. New York: Knopf.

————. 1996. *Blackface, White Noise: Jewish Immigrants in the Hollywood
Melting Pot*. Berkeley: University of California Press.

Rorty, Richard. 1998. *Achieving Our Country: Leftist Thought in Twentieth-
Century America*. Cambridge, Mass.: Harvard University Press.

Rosen, George. 1958. *A History of Public Health*. New York: MD Publications,
Inc.

Rosenberg, Charles. 1962. *The Cholera Years: The United States in 1832, 1848,
and 1866*. Chicago: University of Chicago Press.

Rossiter, Margaret W. 1982. *Women Scientists in America: Struggles and Strategies to 1940*. Baltimore: Johns Hopkins University Press.

Rothman, David. 1971. *The Discovery of the Asylum: Social Order and Disorder
in the New Republic*. Boston: Little, Brown.

Rothman, David. 1980. *Conscience and Convenience: The Asylum and Its Alter-
natives in Progressive America*. Boston: Little, Brown.

Rozen, Paul, 1997. "Morality." In Brandt and Rozin 1997. *Cradle of the Middle
Class: The Family in Oneida County, New York: 1790–1865*. New York: Cambridge University Press.

Saldívar, José David. 1997. *Border Matters: Remapping American Cultural
Studies*. Berkeley: University of California Press.

Sallee, Shelley. 2004. *The Whiteness of Child Labor Reform in the New South*.
Athens: University of Georgia Press.

Savitt, Todd L. 1978. *Medicine and Slavery: The Diseases and Health Care of
Blacks in Antebellum Virginia*. Urbana: University of Illinois Press.

Savitt, Todd L., and James Harvey Young, eds. 1988. *Disease and Distinctiveness in the American South*. Knoxville: University of Tennessee Press.

Sawyer, Claire Marie. 1961. *Some Aspects of the Fertility of a Tri-Racial Isolate*. Washington: Catholic University of America.

Saxton, Alexander. 1990. *The Rise and Fall of the White Republic: Class Politics and Mass Culture in Nineteenth-Century America*. New York: Verso.

Schauer, Frederick. 2003. *Profiles, Probabilities, and Stereotypes*. Cambridge, Mass.: Belknap.

Schneider, William. 1990. *Quality and Quantity: The Quest for Biological Regeneration in Twentieth Century France*. Cambridge: Cambridge University Press.

Schussler, T. 1989. "Buck v. Bell." *New York State Journal of Medicine* 89: 536.

Sedgwick, Catherine M. 1835. *Home*. Boston: James Munroe.

Selden, Steven. 1999. *Inheriting Shame: The Story of Eugenics in America*. New York: Teachers' College Press.

Sellers, Charles. 1991. *The Market Revolution: Jacksonian America, 1815–1846*. New York: Oxford University Press.

Selzer, Michael, ed. 1972. *Kike! A Documentary History of Anti-Semitism in America*. New York: Meridian.

Shapiro, Henry D. 1978. *Appalachia on Our Mind: The Southern Mountains and Mountaineers in the American Consciousness, 1870–1920*. Chapel Hill: University of North Carolina Press.

Shapiro, Thomas M. 1985. *Population Control Politics: Women, Sterilization, and Reproductive Choice*. Philadelphia: Temple University Press.

Shaw, Barton C. 1984. *The Wool-Hat Boys: Georgia's Populist Party*. Baton Rouge: Louisiana State University Press.

Sherman, Mandel, and Thomas Robert Henry. 1933. *Hollow Folk*. New York: Thomas Y. Crowell Co.

Sherman, Richard B. 1988. " 'The Last Stand': The Fight for Racial Integrity in Virginia in the 1920s." *Journal of Southern History* 54: 69–92.

Shortt, S. E. D. 1983. "Physicians, Science, and Status: Issues in the Professionalization of Anglo-American Medicine in the Nineteenth Century." *Medical History* 27: 51–68.

Shuffelton, Frank. 1993. *A Mixed Race: Ethnicity in Early America*. New York: Oxford University Press.

Shugg, Roger. 1939. *Origins of Class Struggle in Louisiana: A Social History of White Farmers and Laborers during Slavery and After, 1840–1875*. Baton Rouge: Louisiana State University Press.

Simms, William Gilmore. 1856/1882. *Eutaw*. Reprint. New York: A. C. Armstrong & Son.

Simpson, J. A., and E. S. C. Weiner, eds. 1989. *Oxford English Dictionary*. Oxford: Oxford University Press.

Skaggs, Merrill Maguire. 1972. *The Folk of Southern Fiction*. Athens: University of Georgia Press.

Slack, Paul. 1974. "Vagrants and Vagrancy in England, 1598–1644." *English Historical Review* 27: 360–79.

Smith, Abbot Emerson. 1947. *Colonists in Bondage: White Servitude and Convict Labor in America, 1607–1776*. Chapel Hill: University of North Carolina Press.

Smith, Henry Nash. 1950. *Virgin Land: The American West as Symbol and Myth*. Cambridge, Mass.: Harvard University Press.

Smith, J. David, and K. Ray Nelson. 1989. *The Sterilization of Carrie Buck*. Far Hills, N.J.: New Horizon Press.

Smith, Stephanie. 2006. *Household Words: Bloomers, Sucker, Bombshell, Scab, Nigger, Cyber*. Minneapolis: University of Minnesota Press.

Somers, Margaret. 1994. "The Narrative Constitution of Identity: A Relational and Network Approach. *Theory and Society* 23: 605–49.

Soskin, R. M. 1983. "Sterilization of the Mentally Retarded: The Rules Change but the Results Remain the Same." *Medicine and the Law* 2: 267–76.

Stallybrass, Peter, and Allon White. 1986. *The Politics and Poetics of Transgression*. Ithaca, N.Y.: Cornell University Press.

Stangor, Charles, and James E. Lange. 1994. "Mental Representations of Social Groups: Advances in Understanding Stereotypes and Stereotyping." *Advances in Experimental Social Psychology* 26: 357–416.

Starr, Paul. 1982. *The Social Transformation of American Medicine: The Rise of a Sovereign Profession and the Making of a Vast Industry*. New York: Basic Books.

Stepan, Nancy Leys. 1991. *"The Hour of Eugenics": Race, Gender, and Nation in Latin America*. Ithaca, N.Y.: Cornell University Press.

Stewart, Kathleen. 1996. *A Space on the Side of the Road: Cultural Poetics in an "Other" America*. Princeton, N.J.: Princeton University Press.

Steyn, Melissa. 2001. *Whiteness Just Isn't What It Used to Be: White Identity in a Changing South Africa*. Albany: SUNY Press.

Stiles, Charles W. 1903. *Report upon the Prevalence and Geographic Distribution of Hookworm Disease (Uncinariasis or Anchylostomiasis) in the United States*. Washington: Government Printing Office.

———. 1909a. *Hookworm Disease and Its Relation to the Negro*. Washington, D.C.: Government Printing Office.

———. 1909b. "The Medical Influence of the Negro in Connection with Anemia in the White." *Twelfth Biennial Report of the North Carolina Board of Health, 1907–1908*. Raleigh: North Carolina Board of Health.

———. 1910. *Soil Pollution as Cause of Ground-Itch, Hookworm Disease (Ground-Itch Anemia), and Dirt Eating*. Washington, D.C.: Rockefeller Sanitary Commission.

———. 1912. *Hookworm Disease among Cotton Mill Operatives.* Vol. 61st Congress, 2nd Session, Document 645, Washington, D.C.: Government Printing Office.

———. 1933. "Is It Fair to Say That Hookworm Has Almost Disappeared from the U.S.?" *Science* 77: 237–39.

———. 1939. "Early History, in Part Esoteric, of the Hookworm (Uncinariasis) Campaign in Our Southern States." *Journal of Parasitology* 25: 283–308.

Stock, Catherine McNicol. 1996. *Rural Radicals: From Bacon's Rebellion to the Oklahoma City Bombing.* New York: Penguin Books.

Stocking, George W. Jr. 1993. "The Turn-of-the-Century Concept of Race." *MODERNISM/modernity* 1: 4–16.

Stoddard, Lathrop. 1920. *The Rising Tide of Color against White World-Supremacy.* New York: Scribner's Sons.

Stoler, Ann Laura. 1989. "Rethinking Colonial Categories: European Communities and the Boundaries of Rule." *Society for Comparative Study of Society and History* 13 (1): 134–61.

———. 1997. "Racial Histories and Their Regimes of Truth." *Political Power and Social Theory* 11: 183–225.

Stowe, Harriet Beecher. 1854. *The Key to Uncle Tom's Cabin; Presenting the Original Facts and Documents upon which the Story is Founded Together with Collaborative Statements Verifying the Truth of the Work.* London: Clarke, Beeton, & Co.

———. 1856. *Dred: A Tale of the Great Dismal Swamp.* Boston: Phillips, Sampson and Co.

Strong, Edward K. 1916. *Effects of Hookworm Disease on the Mental and Physical Development of Children.* New York: Rockefeller Foundation.

Sutherland, Daniel. 1981. *Americans and Their Servants.* Baton Rouge: University of Louisiana Press.

Swidler, Ann. 1986. "Culture in Action: Symbols and Strategies." *American Sociological Review* 51: 273–86.

Sydenstricker, Edgar, et al. 1918. "Disabling Sickness among the Population of Seven Cotton Mill Villages of South Carolina in Relation to Family Income." *Public Health Reports* 33: 2038–51.

Takaki, Ronald. 1992. "The Tempest in the Wilderness: The Racialization of Slavery." *Journal of American History* 79: 892–912.

Thompson, E. P. 1975. *Whigs and Hunters: The Origin of the Black Act.* New York: Pantheon.

Thomson, Mathew. 1997. *The Problem of Mental Deficiency: Eugenics, Democracy, and Social Policy in Britain c. 1870–1959.* Oxford: Oxford University Press.

Thornton, Richard H. 1912. *An American Glossary.* Philadelphia: Lippincott.

Tillson, Albert H. 1991. *Gentry and Common Folk: Political Culture on a Virginia Frontier, 1740–1789.* Lexington: University Press of Kentucky.

Tilly, Charles. 2004. "Social Boundary Mechanisms." *Philosophy of the Social Sciences* 34: 211–36.

Timberg, Craig. 2001. "Va. House Voices Regret for Eugenics." *Washington Post*, February 3.

Tindall, George B. 1964. "Mythology: A New Frontier in Southern History." In *The Idea of the South: Pursuit of a Central Theme*, ed. Frank E. Vandiver. Chicago: University of Chicago Press.

————. 1967. *The Emergence of the New South, 1913–1946.* Baton Rouge: Louisiana State University Press.

Tocqueville, Alexis de. 1840/1994. *Democracy in America.* New York: Knopf.

Tomes, Nancy. 1990. "The Private Side of Public Health: Sanitary Science, Domestic Hygiene, and the Germ Theory, 1870–1900." *Bulletin of the History of Medicine* 64: 509–39.

Tracy, Susan J. 1995. *In the Master's Eye: Representations of Women, Blacks, and Poor Whites in Antebellum Southern Literature.* Amherst: University of Massachusetts Press.

Trent, James W., Jr. 1994. *Inventing the Feeble Mind: A History of Mental Retardation in the United States.* Berkeley: University of California Press.

Trombley, Stephen. 1988. *The Right to Reproduce: A History of Coercive Sterilization.* London: Weidenfeld & Nicolson.

Tullos, Allen. 1978. "The Great Hookworm Crusade." *Southern Exposure* 6 (2): 40–49.

————. 1989. *Habits of Industry: White Culture and the Transformation of the Carolina Piedmont.* Chapel Hill: University of North Carolina Press.

Turner, Frederick Jackson. 1894. "The Significance of the Frontier in American History." In *Annual Report of the American Historical Association for the Year 1893*. Washington, D.C.: Government Printing Office.

Twine, France Winddance. 1997. "Brown-Skinned White Girls: Class, Culture, and the Construction of White Identity in Suburban Communities." In Frankenberg 1997.

Twyman, Robert. 1971. "The Clay Eater: A New Look at an Old Southern Enigma." *Journal of Southern History* 37: 439–48.

Vallas, Steven P. 2003. "Rediscovering the Color Line within Work Organizations: The 'Knitting of Racial Groups' Revisited." *Work and Occupations* 30: 379–400.

Wacquant, Löic. 1997. "For an Analytic of Racial Domination." *Political Power and Social Theory* 11: 221–34.

Walker, Alexander. 1872. *Intermarriage: Or the Mode in Which, and the Causes Why, Beauty, Health and Intellect Result from Certain Unions, and Deformity, Disease and Insanity from Others.* Philadelphia: Lindsay & Blakiston.

Walkowitz, Daniel J. 1999. *Social Workers and the Politics of Middle-Class Identity*. Chapel Hill: University of North Carolina Press.

Ware, Vron, ed. 2004. *Branquidade: Identidade branca e multicultaralismo*. Rio de Janeiro: Garamond.

Ware, Vron, and Les Back. 2002. *Out of Whiteness: Color, Politics, and Culture*. Chicago: University of Chicago Press.

Warner, John Harley. 1985. "The Idea of Southern Medical Distinctiveness: Medical Knowledge and Practice in the Old South." In *Sickness and Health in America*, ed. Judith Walzer Leavitt and Ronald Numbers. Madison: University of Wisconsin Press.

Washington, Scott Leon. 2006. "Principles of Racial Taxonomy." *American Journal of Sociology*.

Weber, Max. 1958. *The Protestant Ethic and the Spirit of Capitalism*. Trans. Talcott Parson. New York: Scribner's.

———. 1968. *Economy and Society*. Ed. Guenther Roth and Claus Wittich. Berkeley: University of California Press.

Weiss, Sheila Faith. 1987. *Race Hygiene and National Efficiency: The Eugenics of Wilhelm Schallmayer*. Berkeley: University of California Press.

Wellman, David. 1997. "Minstrel Shows, Affirmative Action Talk, and Angry White Men: Marking Racial Otherness in the 1990s." In Frankenberg 1997.

Weston, George Melville. 1856. *The Poor Whites of the South*. Washington, D.C.: Buell & Blanchard Printers.

Weston, William. 1908. "Uncinariasis." *Journal of the South Carolina Medical Association* 4: 124–36.

Whisnant, David E. 1980. *Modernizing the Mountaineer: People, Power, Planning in Appalachia*. New York: B. Franklin.

White, Ed. 2005. *The Backcountry and City: Colonization and Conflict in Early America*. Minneapolis: University of Minnesota Press.

Whites, Lee Ann. 1988. "The De Graffenreid Controversy: Class, Race, and Gender in the New South." *Journal of Southern History* 54: 449–478.

Whittenburg, James P. 1977. "Planters, Merchants, and Lawyers: Social Change and the Origins of the North Carolina Regulation." *William and Mary Quarterly* 34: 215–38.

Wiehl. Dorothy and Edgar Sydenstricker. 1924. "Disabling Sickness in Cotton Mill Communities of South Carolina, 1917," *Public Health Reports* 39: 1417–21.

Wiggam, Albert Edward. 1924. *The Fruit of the Family Tree*. Indianapolis: Bobbs-Merrill.

Williams, Raymond. 1973. *The Country and the City*. New York: Oxford University Press.

———. 1985. *Keywords: A Vocabulary of Culture and Society*. Rev. ed. New York: Oxford University Press.

Williamson, J. W. 1995. *Hillbillyland: What the Movies Did to the Mountains and What the Mountains Did to the Movies.* Chapel Hill: University of North Carolina Press.

Winant, Howard. 1994. *Racial Conditions: Politics, Theory, Comparisons.* Minneapolis: University of Minnesota Press.

———. 2001. "White Racial Projects." In Brander Rasmussen et al. 2001.

Woodmason, Charles. 1766/1953. *The Carolina Backcountry on the Eve of Revolution.* Chapel Hill: University of North Carolina Press.

Woodside, Moya. 1950. *Sterilization in North Carolina: A Sociological and Psychological Study.* Chapel Hill: University of North Carolina Press.

Woodward, C. Vann. 1951/1971. *Origins of the New South, 1877–1913.* Baton Rouge: Louisiana State University Press.

Woody, J. D. 1992. "The Hookworm Campaign in North Carolina." *North Carolina Medical Journal* 53 (2): 106–9.

Wray, Matt. 1997. "White Trash Religion." In *White Trash: Race and Class in America,* ed. Matt Wray and Annalee Newitz, 193–210. New York: Routledge.

———. 2004. "Left Conservatism." In Megan Prelinger and Joel Schalit, eds. *Collective Action: A Bad Subjects Anthology.* London: Pluto Press.

———. 2005. "Review of *The Whiteness of Child Labor Reform in the New South* by Shelley Sallee." *Journal of Interdisciplinary History* 36: 111–12.

———. 2006a. "Eugenics Programs." 2006. In Rudy Abramson and Jean Haskell, eds. *The Encyclopedia of Appalachia.* Johnson City: East Tennessee State University Press, 2006.

———. 2006b. "Incest." In Rudy Abramson and Jean Haskell, eds. *The Encyclopedia of Appalachia.* Johnson City: East Tennessee State University Press,

———. 2006c. "Reframing the Picture(s): The Shelby Lee Adams Controversy and the Paranoid Style in Appalachian Studies." *Journal of Appalachian Studies.*

———. 2006d. "Group Boundaries Without Groups: The Case of *Poor White Trash.*" Paper delivered at the American Sociological Association, Washington, D.C. August.

Wray, Matt, and Annalee Newitz, eds. 1997. *White Trash: Race and Class in America.* New York: Routledge.

Wright, Gavin. 1986. *Old South, New South: Revolutions in the Southern Economy since the Civil War.* New York: Basic Books.

Wright, Louis B. 1940. *The First Gentlemen of Virginia.* San Marino, Calif.: Huntington Library.

Wu, Cheng-Tsu, ed. 1972. *Chink! Anti-Chinese Prejudice in America.* New York: Meridian.

Wuthnow, Robert. 1987. *Meaning and Moral Order: Explorations in Cultural Analysis.* Berkeley: University of California Press.

Wuthnow, Robert, and Marsha Witten. 1988. "New Directions in the Study of Culture." *Annual Review of Sociology* 14: 49–67.

Zerubavel, Eviatar. 1991. *The Fine Line: Making Distinctions in Everyday Life.* Chicago: University of Chicago Press.

Zhao, Wei. 2005. "Understanding Classifications: Empirical Evidence from the American and French Wine Industries." *Poetics* 33: 157–252.

Index

Matt Wray

is an assistant professor of sociology at the
University of Nevada, Las Vegas, and a 2006–2008
Robert Wood Johnson Health and Society Scholar
at Harvard University. He is the coeditor of *The
Making and Unmaking of Whiteness* and *White
Trash: Race and Class in America.*

Library of Congress Cataloging-in-Publication Data
Wray, Matt, 1964–
Not quite white : white trash and the boundaries
of whiteness / Matt Wray.
p. cm.
Includes bibliographical references and index.
ISBN-13: 978-0-8223-3882-6 (cloth : alk. paper)
ISBN-10: 0-8223-3882-3 (cloth : alk. paper)
ISBN-13: 978-0-8223-3873-4 (pbk. : alk. paper)
ISBN-10: 0-8223-3873-4 (pbk. : alk. paper)
1. Whites — Race identity — United States.
2. Whites — United States — Public opinion.
3. Rural poor — United States — Public opinion.
4. Stereotype (Psychology) — United States.
5. Difference (Psychology) 6. Social
stratification — United States. 7. Social classes —
United States. 8. United States — Social conditions.
9. United States — Race relations. 10. Public
opinion — United States. I. Title.
E184.A1W83 2006
305.5′6908909 — dc22
2006013300